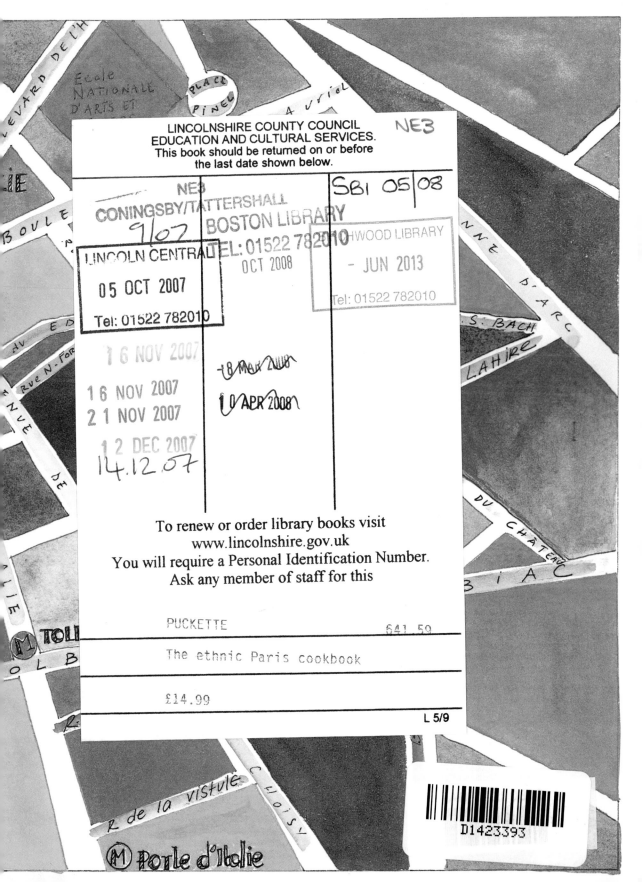

THE ETHNIC
PARIS COOKBOOK

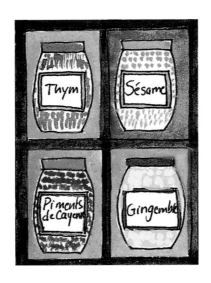

THE ETHNIC PARIS COOKBOOK

BY
CHARLOTTE PUCKETTE
AND OLIVIA KIANG-SNAIJE

DK PUBLISHING

**LONDON, NEW YORK, MUNICH,
MELBOURNE, AND DELHI**

senior editor ANJA SCHMIDT

designer JESSICA PARK

managing art editor MICHELLE BAXTER

art director DIRK KAUFMAN

dtp coordinator KATHY FARIAS

production manager IVOR PARKER

executive managing editor SHARON LUCAS

publisher CARL RAYMOND

Published by DK Publishing
375 Hudson Street, New York, New York 10014

07 08 09 10 10 9 8 7 6 5 4 3 2 1

DK Books are available at special discounts for bulk purchases for sales promotions,
premiums, fund-raising, or educational use. For details contact DK Publishing Special
Markets, 375 Hudson Street, New York, New York 10014 or SpecialSales@dk.com.

A catalog record for this book is available from the Library of Congress.

ISBN 978-0-7566-2645-7
Color reproduction by Colourscan, Singapore
Printed and bound in Singapore by Star Standard (Pte.) Ltd.

Discover more at www.dk.com

CONTENTS

A CULINARY JOURNEY

Tahar Ben Jelloun, the renowned Moroccan writer and Paris resident of 37 years, once wrote, "We cannot take our house, our olive tree, our well water with us. Cooking has an almost therapeutic effect on our nostalgia." Like Tahar Ben Jelloun, a multitude of immigrants from French ex-colonies and protectorates live in Paris. They have arrived in successive waves over the last 60 years: Senegalese, Cameroonians, Algerians, Tunisians, Moroccans, Vietnamese, Cambodians, Laotians, and Lebanese, to name a few. Most of them go to extraordinary lengths to reproduce the food from their countries, retaining their culture through their cuisine. As a result, eating in Paris no longer means just French food.

These days in Paris, it's easy to make a culinary journey through the city, experiencing the best dishes from France's former colonies. We felt that a book that paid tribute to these diverse and sumptuous cuisines was long overdue. When we arrived in Paris years ago, cilantro, star anise, orange blossom water, or preserved lemons were hard to come by. Nowadays it is likely that most Paris residents have a Tunisian greengrocer around the corner who carries most of the necessary ingredients for making a tangy North African carrot and cumin appetizer, or a Lebanese mezzé.

Both transplanted from elsewhere, but long-time residents of Paris, we met while dropping off our children at school. The idea for writing this book came about after we realized our conversations consistently turned to ethnic cuisine in Paris and which new place we had discovered in what neighborhood. Charlotte is a graduate of the Cordon Bleu cooking school and has been running a catering company for several years. She had drifted away from traditional French cuisine, following the lead from her clients who didn't want shrimp hors d'oeuvres with a French sauce anymore. They wanted peanut, ginger, and lime dressing. They weren't interested in pâté en croûte; they wanted an assortment of Moroccan salads.

Olivia is a journalist, freelancing for a variety of newspapers and magazines, mainly covering the foreign communities in Paris. In interviews with exiled writers, filmmakers, and artists, her subjects often talked about food. Discussing, preparing, and eating food from the countries they had left behind was essential—it was a soothing and even healing ritual. It was a poetic way of remembering the good things about their countries.

We realized we had many resources at our fingertips: from the Japanese hairdresser who had been speaking passionately and almost exclusively about food upon each visit, to an anesthesiologist friend with family from Hong Kong—his grandmother's Chinese restaurant turned out to be the first of its kind in the now famously Asian 13th *arrondissement*. Thérèse, the Cameroonian woman who opened the fair trade shop we loved to go to, impressed us by being a first-class cook. Everyone had suggestions and connections.

"THE MERE SMELL OF COOKING CAN EVOKE A WHOLE CIVILIZATION." —Fernand Braudel

Our book includes recipes we sought from chefs, ranging from internationally renowned Fatema Hal, of the Mansouria restaurant (whose line of Moroccan food products are sold around the world), to chefs from tiny neighborhood restaurants. The recipes come from people from former French colonies and protectorates, because the largest ethnic groups in Paris are from these countries. With London right next door, we can't claim Paris is the best place for an Indian dinner, but we can say with confidence that it is for a Vietnamese or Moroccan meal. (We made one exception and included Japan in the book, because of the privileged relationship the French and Japanese have in terms of an intense and mutual admiration for each other's cuisines.)

Most of the people we met were incredibly warm and generous, showing us their kitchens, cooking with us, and patiently answering questions about sahlab or African djansan seeds. Sometimes people were so enthusiastic about feeding us that they

forgot about giving us recipes. We kept returning to Feyrouz, a Lebanese restaurant, where the owner Adel Raad had promised to give us some recipes. He clucked over us and had us eating copious meals on an almost regular basis until we finally extracted the recipes from him.

Other people had heartwarming success stories to tell, such as Ouendeno Moriba, a tall, elegant Malian, who now owns a company that produces natural African fruit juices, teas, spices, and vacuum-packed

"THE SORT OF MEAL ONE CAN HAVE IN PARIS IS A COSMOPOLITAN TOTALITY WITH EVERY PART OF THE WORLD REPRESENTED BY ITS PRODUCTS." —Jean Anthelme Brillat-Savarin

prepared African dishes. As one of the only African students in his field of study in a university in northeastern France, he vowed one day to introduce the French to African cooking. Moriba, Les Saveurs d'Afrique now sells all over Europe and to Fairway in the United States.

As we went along, we asked another mother from school, long-time Paris resident and Lebanese illustrator, Dinah Diwan, to join in on the enterprise. We felt that her evocative and colorful work would perfectly complement the flavors of our cookbook. Needless to say, Dinah is also an excellent cook.

In the end, we don't claim in any way to be experts on any particular type of cuisine. We simply wanted to show this vibrant side of Paris that we felt needed to be celebrated. Our task was to go out and get people from a broad ethnic swath to give us delicious recipes that they cooked here in Paris, even if they had invented them or if they weren't exactly traditional. We adapted their recipes to Western kitchens, and when there was a good story to go along with the recipe, we included it as well.

—Paris, August 2006

ALGERIE
MAROC
TUNISIE

CUMIN
RAS EL HANOUT
POIVRE NOIR
SÉSAME
SAFRAN
THYM

Harissa

HUILE D'OLIVE

BELLEVILLE
BOULEVARD DE BELLEVILLE
BOULEVARD DE BELLEVILLE
RUE RAMPONEAU
RUE J.P. TIMBAUD

Makrout
d'Oran

Kaak
de Tunis

Briouat
de Marrakech

COUSCOUS IN THE CAFETERIA
The Maghreb: Morocco, Algeria, and Tunisia

"She had already placed before us pale girdle-cakes soaked in sugared butter and sprinkled with almonds; pigeons bathed in succulent juice with green olives; chickpeas melting in flour, sweet onions; chickens buried under fresh beans with wrinkled skins; and lemon cooked and recooked and reduced to a savory puree..."
—A Moroccan luncheon by Colette (1873–1954)

WHERE THE SUN SETS

The word *maghreb* in Arabic literally means "where the sun sets," or "the west." It is used to designate the northwest African countries of Morocco, Algeria, and Tunisia, which were under French colonial influence in varying degrees during the 19th and first half of the 20th century. Having gained their independence between 1956 and 1962, the three countries have an ongoing, if complicated, relationship with their former colonial power. Since the 1940s, the most significant group of immigrants to France has been from the Maghreb. Recent statistics show there are 43,000 Algerians, 27,000 Moroccans, and 26,000 Tunisians living within the Paris city limits. This figure does not include the number of North Africans already naturalized as French citizens.

The cultural impact has been far-reaching. Today, the names of writer Tahar Ben Jelloun, soccer player Zinedine Zidane, and actress Isabelle Adjani are synonymous with the word France. North African musicians, actors, stand-up comedians, writers, and film directors are at the forefront of what's hot in Paris. Last year Algerian writer Assia Djebar was inducted into the hallowed Académie Française, and on the political front, in 2005, Azouz Begag, of Algerian origin, was appointed Minister for Equal Opportunities. And, French-born but all raised in Algeria, the writer Albert Camus, the philosopher Jacques Derrida, and the designer Yves St. Laurent definitively altered the cultural horizon in France.

Historically, the Goutte d'Or ("Drop of Gold"), a working-class neighborhood in the 18th *arrondissement* not far from Montmartre, is where the first North Africans settled in Paris. The neighborhood later stretched to the Boulevard Barbès area as well. The Saturday market on Boulevard Barbès under the elevated number 2 metro line is the perfect place to step into this other world. Mounds of spices, olives, and dates, flanked by bottles of orange and rose blossom essences, are piled high in stalls, and sheep's heads replace chickens in rotisseries.

The Belleville neighborhood in the 20th *arrondissement* is also home to a large North African population, mainly Tunisians, both Jewish and Muslim. *Hammams* (steam baths), travel agencies, bookstores selling the Koran, pastry shops, and kosher butchers are lined up side by side. On the Boulevard de Belleville, kosher Tunisian restaurants abound, with customers nostalgic for the grilled fish they ate in the Tunisian port town of La Goulette. The shopkeepers at greengrocers in Paris are very often Tunisians from the island of Djerba. Many sell a homemade variety of harissa, the hot sauce, which is spicier in Tunisia than in Algeria and Morocco.

FRENCH NATIONAL DISH

Just as French cooking influenced the presentation of food in the Maghreb during colonial times, North African dishes have changed the way the French eat. Workers from Algeria brought couscous to France during the First World War, and at the time of independence, with the massive influx of French Algerians, Parisians became acquainted with small family-style restaurants that served Algerian dishes. It didn't take long for couscous to become unofficially French—polls consistently show that couscous is the favorite French national dish, much as curry is in England. Children happily eat couscous served with *merguez*, a spicy lamb sausage, in school cafeterias. No barbecue or village festival in France would feel authentic without these fiery sausages.

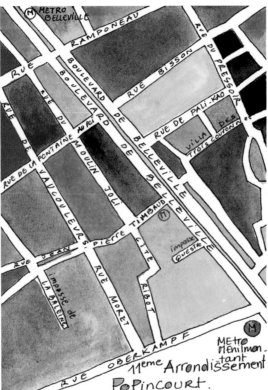

More recently, over the past 20 years, a high-end cuisine has developed, although "we really had to elbow our way in," says Fatema Hal, "the queen of Moroccan cooking" in Paris. In addition to her line of food products sold at Lafayette Gourmet and Le Bon Marché, she has published four cookbooks on Moroccan food. Hal and others have contributed to educating Parisians about North African dishes other than couscous: tagines and *pastillas,* as well as a variety of pastries from Algiers are now common in the Parisian culinary vocabulary. Maghrebian cooking, says Franco-Algerian chef Ghenima Agaoua, "is a symbiosis of many cultures. There are as many specialties as there are women's hands." Cooking techniques range in the Maghreb from steaming, as for certain meat dishes, to stewing, as for tagines.

SAVORY MOROCCAN

Moroccan cooking is one of the most savory and refined cuisines of the world. Berber, Bedouin, and Sephardic Jewish influences all contribute to fragrant dishes in which cumin, ginger, cinnamon, saffron, honey, dried fruit, and/or pepper are deftly blended into lamb stews with melting vegetables or crisp *pastillas* stuffed with pigeon and almonds. The marriage of sweet and salty is

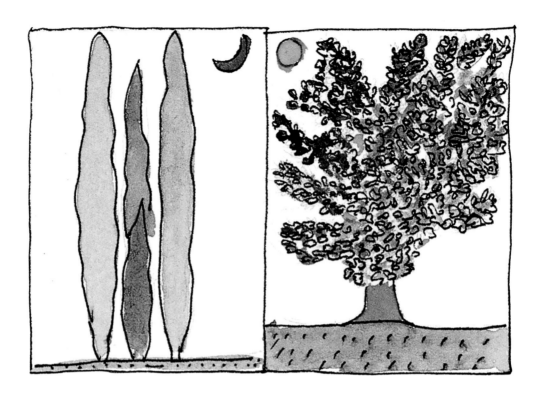

a delicately balance in most dishes. Essential condiments in Moroccan cuisine include preserved lemons; *ras el hanout*, the famous 35-spice mixture blended differently in each household; *harissa*, made from roasted chilies, cumin, and garlic; and the renowned argan oil, believed to have aphrodisiac qualities. Meals traditionally end with a "Moroccan whiskey," mint tea.

DESERT FARE

Algeria was France's first colony in the Maghreb and the last to gain its independence. It is five times as large as France but the Sahara Desert accounts for 85 percent of the country. The arid land means that traditional cooking is often simple and less aromatic than Moroccan cuisine, although the variety of dishes made with couscous is immense. This regional staple, which, like pasta, is made from durum wheat, can be extremely fine grained, as in the city of Sétif; prepared dry with steamed vegetables (*amakfoul*) in the mountainous Kabylia region; or sweetened with dates, milk, and cinnamon. Lamb is the meat eaten most often in Algeria, because sheep are able to thrive in semiarid conditions.

SPICIEST CUISINE

Tunisia, on the other hand, has a fertile Mediterranean climate, similar to southern Italy's, and olives, figs, grapes, pomegranates, and citrus fruits flourish there. Indeed, the Italian presence in Tunisia was constant, and the country was coveted by Italy as a potential colony, but France prevailed and Tunisia became a French protectorate. Tunisian cuisine absorbed influences from both European countries as well as from the cooking of Sephardic Jews, an important population that settled in Tunisia and the rest of the Maghreb following its expulsion from Spain in the 15th century. Of the three countries, Tunisia has the spiciest cuisine—a passion for chili is encapsulated in the condiment harissa.

While the road to integration for North African immigrants in France has not been easy, their cooking, whether simple *plats du jour* or elaborate savory dishes, has been completely integrated into the French diet. For North Africans, whether Muslim, Jewish, or *pieds noirs* (French from Algeria), remaining faithful to their cuisine is the cherished link to their past.

APPETIZERS

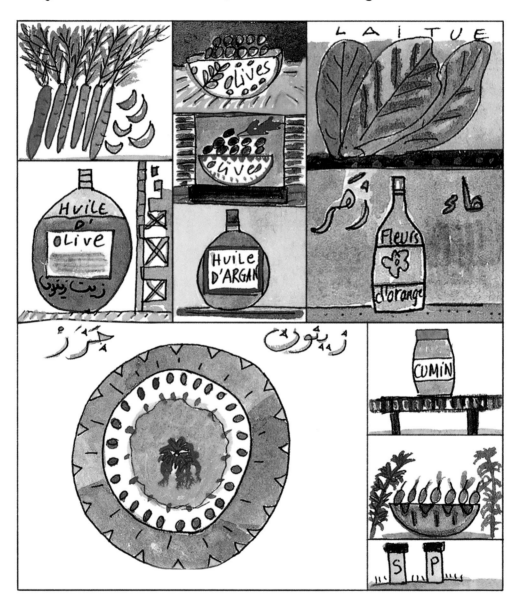

THREE FRESH SALADS

Salads and cold vegetable dishes are a part of every meal in Morocco, and the abundance of natural ingredients is reflected in the wealth of recipes for them. In Fatema Hal's cookbook "Le Grand Livre de la Cuisine Marocaine," there are recipes for almost 50 salads. Her combination of flavors might be surprising for anyone unfamiliar with the subtle seasonings of Moroccan cuisine, but all of the ingredients are quite common and easily found in your local supermarket. The following three recipes, which make use of raw vegetables, are adaptations of some of the salads served at Hal's restaurant, the Mansouria in the 11th arrondissement.

CARROT SALAD WITH FRESH ORANGE JUICE
Salade de Carottes au Jus d'Orange

SERVES 6

- 3 carrots, peeled
- juice of 1 orange
- 1 tablespoon sugar
- ½ teaspoon ground cinnamon
- 1 tablespoon orange flower water
- ¼ cup blanched almonds, chopped

1 Grate the carrots into a bowl, then toss with the orange juice. Add the sugar and cinnamon, and sprinkle with the orange flower water.

2 Transfer to a serving bowl, then garnish with the chopped almonds and serve.

TOMATO SALAD WITH GARLIC AND ARGAN OIL
Salade de Tomates à l'Ail et à l'Huile d'Argan

SERVES 6

3 large tomatoes
4 cloves garlic, minced
2 tablespoons argan oil
1 teaspoon salt
1 tablespoon flaxseed

½ bunch fresh mint, leaves chopped roughly
5 black olives

1 Cut the tomatoes lengthwise in half, remove the seeds, and dice the flesh.

2 To make the dressing, combine the garlic, argan oil, salt, and flaxseed in a salad bowl. Add the diced tomatoes and toss well. Garnish with the mint leaves and black olives.

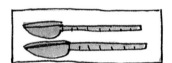

NUTMEG-ZUCCHINI SALAD
Salade de Courgettes Crues à la Noix de Muscade

SERVES 6

¼ teaspoon salt
¼ teaspoon ground nutmeg
¼ teaspoon ground cumin
2 cloves garlic, finely chopped
1 tablespoon lemon juice
2 tablespoons olive oil
  freshly ground black pepper
4 zucchini, grated

1 To make the dressing, combine the salt, nutmeg, cumin, garlic, lemon juice, olive oil, and black pepper, to taste, in a salad bowl.

2 Just before serving, add grated zucchini to the bowl and toss with the dressing.

ORANGE AND CUMIN SALAD
Salade d'Oranges au Cumin

This recipe was inspired by the delicious and beautifully presented salads we ate at Dar Moha restaurant in Boulogne-Billancourt, one métro stop outside of Paris. Dar Moha is the French annex of the trendy restaurant of the same name in Marrakech, Morocco. For a special occasion, borrow Dar Moha's idea of serving individual portions in hollowed-out orange halves.

SERVES 4

2   teaspoons cumin seeds
4   navel oranges
¼   cup olive oil
1   tablespoon harissa
½   onion, thinly sliced
½   cup pitted black olives
4   romaine lettuce leaves
     salt and freshly ground
     black pepper

     snipped fresh chives

✳ RESTAURANT
DAR MOHA
1, rue de Billancourt
92100 Boulogne-sur-Seine
tel: 01 46 03 61 65
métro: Jean Jaurès

1 Heat a small heavy sauté pan. Add the cumin seeds and toast until fragrant. Grind in a spice blender or crush with a mortar and pestle.

2 Grate the zest from 1 of the oranges and set aside. Peel the oranges, carefully removing all the bitter white pith. Cut out the individual segments of the oranges, working over a bowl to catch the segments and the juice. Discard any seeds.

3 To make the dressing, whisk together the oil, harissa, and roasted cumin. No more than 30 minutes before serving, add the onion and olives to the orange slices and toss with the dressing. Season to taste with salt and pepper.

4 To serve, arrange the lettuce leaves in a shallow bowl and spoon the orange salad on top. Garnish with the reserved orange zest and snipped chives.

MOROCCAN EGGPLANT SALAD
Zaalouk

A few carefully chosen spices make all the difference. Using most of the same ingredients that go into French ratatouille, the Moroccans make a more fragrant version of cooked eggplant and tomatoes. This recipe is adapted from Oum El Banine restaurant in the 16th arrondissement, where they prepare it in the morning so that the flavors have time to develop.

RESTAURANT

OUM EL BANINE
16, rue Dufrenoy 75116 Paris
tel: 01 45 04 91 22
metro: Porte Dauphine

1 Preheat oven to 350°F (180°C). Rinse the eggplants and prick all over with a fork. Place on a baking sheet, along with the garlic, and roast, turning frequently, until tender, about 40 minutes.

2 While the eggplant and garlic are cooking, place the chopped tomatoes and the tomato paste in a saucepan and simmer over low heat until reduced to a thick sauce, about 20 minutes. Remove from heat and let cool slightly.

SERVES 6

- 1½ pounds (700 g) eggplant
- 5 cloves garlic, skin on
- 1½ pounds (700 g) tomatoes, chopped
- 1 tablespoon tomato paste
- juice of 1 lemon
- 1 teaspoon harissa
- 1 teaspoon ground cumin
- ¼ bunch fresh parsley, leaves chopped
- ¼ bunch fresh coriander, leaves chopped
- salt and freshly ground black pepper to taste
- ¼ cup argan or walnut oil

3 Once the vegetables are roasted, slip the garlic cloves out of their skins, place in a medium bowl, and mash with the back of a fork; set aside. Transfer the eggplant to a colander, split them in half, and let the juices drain off. Working in the colander, scrape the flesh away from the skin with a fork, pressing out as much liquid as possible; discard the skin. Add the flesh to the garlic.

4 Transfer the cooled tomatoes to the bowl of a food processor. Add the eggplant and garlic, and then the rest of the ingredients except the oil. Pulse to a coarse puree. With the motor running, slowly add the oil in a thin, steady stream through the feed tube. Check for seasoning.

5 Serve at room temperature, with crusty bread for scooping.

Arbre d'argan

EARTHY DELIGHTS
1161 East Clark Road, Suite 260
DeWitt, Michigan 48820
tel: 517 668 2402
fax: 517 668 1213
www.earthy.com

ARGAN OIL

For centuries, the Berber women of the southwest corner of Morocco have extracted the oil from the nuts of the knotted and thorny argan tree, using it for cooking and medicinal purposes. The tree grows exclusively within a 140-mile radius between the Atlas Mountains, the Western Sahara, and the Atlantic Ocean. Almost a third of the argan forest was destroyed in the last century. Today the tree is a protected species and the oil is produced by a Moroccan women's cooperative. The oil's prized taste of nuts and mild spices has made it a star among Parisian chefs. Used in salads or with meat and vegetable dishes, it adds a new dimension in flavor. In Morocco, it is combined with ground almonds to make *amalou*, a spread that is delicious on morning toast. The oil is available in gourmet food stores and by mail order (see left).

TUNISIAN GREENGROCERS

"Shopkeepers from our island started coming to Paris in the 1950s," says Kaïs Ben Salem, beaming from his fruit and vegetable shop in the 14th *arrondissement*. Kaïs works with owners Hassen Karouia and Ridah Ben Mansour, all from the Tunisian island of Djerba, birthplace of a large percentage of today's Parisian greengrocers. Tunisian shops are as familiar to Parisians as Korean markets are to New Yorkers. Kaïs says there are at least 100 people from his small village, Oued Zebib, working in various shops throughout Paris.

Besides the regular fare of apples, oranges, and pears, there are pyramids of mangoes, litchis, and fresh walnuts towering next to bunches of coriander, parsley, and basil. Boxes of mesclun salad and fresh new potatoes are neatly aligned adjacent to purple artichokes and crisp fennel. Bottles of orange blossom water line the shelves alongside olive and walnut oil. There are dates on branches and almond-stuffed dates, fresh almonds, pistachios, olives, and figs.

When there is a lull in business, Ridah disappears into the back of the shop, where he fixes lunch for himself and his co-workers on a simple gas stove (see page 30).

"Ridah makes us everything," says Kaïs. "Couscous, tagines, and briks."

Reassuring fixtures in the neighborhood, Kaïs, Ridah, and Hassen shake hands with passersby, distribute strawberries to children, and keep people's keys for them. When they occasionally close on a Monday, their Parisian neighbors feel a little lost and may grumble about not being able to pick up a bag of clementines on their way home from work.

BEET SALAD WITH HARISSA
Salade de Betteraves à l'Harissa

Roasted beets have a depth of flavor you just don't get with boiling. While this recipe features beets, any root vegetable will taste delicious roasted and tossed with harissa and argan oil.

SERVES 6

- 4 large beets
  olive oil
- 3 scallions, chopped
- 1 clove garlic, minced
- ¼ bunch fresh parsley, leaves chopped
  grated zest and juice of 1 lemon
- 1 teaspoon harissa
- 2 tablespoons argan oil or olive oil
  salt and freshly ground black pepper

1 Preheat the oven to 350°F (180°C). Trim, wash, and dry the beets, then rub all over with olive oil. Place in a baking pan and roast until tender, about 1½ hours. Remove and let cool slightly.

2 Peel the beets and cut into large chunks. Toss them in a bowl with the scallions, garlic, and parsley.

3 To make the dressing, whisk together the lemon juice, lemon zest, harissa, and argan or olive oil. Drizzle over the beets and season with salt and pepper to taste.

TUNISIAN CHILI PASTE
Harissa

Harissa is the fiery-hot chili paste of North Africa, used as a table condiment or as an ingredient to spice up sauces and salads. There is no one true version of harissa—it differs from country to country and from one cook to the next. But all versions are based on red chilies, pureed with garlic, olive oil, and at least one of several of the most common spices found in North Africa: cumin, coriander, fennel seeds, and caraway seeds. You can use any hot red chili pepper, but for the most flavorful results, try anchos, New Mexican, or guajillo, either individually or in combination. This recipe uses reconstituted dried red chilies, but harissa can also be made with steamed fresh chilies.

MAKES 1 CUP

12 dried chilies

4 cloves garlic

1 tablespoon lemon juice

ground cumin, coriander, fennel seeds, and/or caraway seeds to taste

1 teaspoon salt

extra virgin olive oil

1 Remove the stems and seeds from the chili peppers. Soak in warm water for 20–30 minutes, or until softened. Drain and squeeze out as much liquid as possible.

2 Place the chilies in a blender or food processor, along with the garlic, lemon juice, spices, and salt, and blend to a smooth paste. With the motor running, add olive oil teaspoon by teaspoon until a thick paste forms. Spoon into a jar, top with a layer of olive oil, and store in the refrigerator. Harissa should be made at least a day in advance for the flavors to blend; it also freezes well.

IDEAS FOR HARISSA

• Stir harissa and smoked Spanish paprika into pureed red peppers for a spicy dip for vegetables or a spread for crusty bread.

• Mix chopped preserved lemons, garlic, and olive oil with harissa to make Tunisian relish. It's delicious tossed with cold steamed vegetables.

• Rub harissa into meat, chicken, or fish, then marinate for 30 minutes before grilling.

• To turn a jar of plain black or green olives into something special, drain and combine with 1 tablespoon harissa, 3 fresh bay leaves, and 1 teaspoon each of roasted cumin, coriander, and fennel seeds. Return the olives to the jar, top off with olive oil to cover, and refrigerate for a week. Bring to room temperature before serving.

• To make a spicy vinaigrette, whisk together 2 teaspoons of harissa, 1 teaspoon honey, ⅓ cup lemon juice, and salt and pepper to taste. Add ¾ cup olive oil. Toss with a simple salad of tomatoes, black olives, fresh chopped coriander, and mint.

SPICY BRIK PASTRIES
Rouleaux de Brik aux Epices

The following recipe is typical of the many different savory brik pastries that can be found in North African restaurants all over Paris. These are folded into triangles or rolled like cigars.

MAKES 45

FILLING

1	teaspoon vegetable oil
8	ounces (225 g) ground beef or lamb, or a combination
1	onion, minced
2	cloves garlic, minced
½	cup fresh parsley, leaves chopped
1	bay leaf
1	medium potato, grated
½	teaspoon salt
1	teaspoon paprika
½	teaspoon ground nutmeg
½	teaspoon ground mace
	juice of 1 lemon
3	tablespoons water
1	teaspoon ground cumin
½	teaspoon cayenne pepper

1 To make the filling, heat the oil in a large skillet over medium heat. Add the ground meat and cook until browned. Stir in the onion and garlic and cook until softened.

2 Add all of the remaining filling ingredients except the cumin and cayenne and simmer gently, stirring occasionally, until the liquid has evaporated and the mixture is quite dry.

3 Remove the bay leaf and add the cumin and cayenne. Transfer the mixture to a food processor or blender and blend to a smooth paste. Taste for seasoning, and cool.

4 If using brik pastry, gently peel away the wax paper from each individual round, lay on a work surface, and cut into 4 triangles, like a pie.

TO ASSEMBLE

12 sheets brik or filo pastry

1   egg white, lightly beaten

vegetable oil for deep-frying

Position the wider end toward you and place a cigar shape of filling horizontally across the bottom edge. Fold in the sides to enclose the ends of the filling, then roll up the pastry toward the narrow point. Repeat with the remaining brik and filling. Seal the cigars with the beaten egg white and place seam side down on a baking sheet.

5 If using filo, cut each sheet into 3 strips, then proceed as for the brik pastry.

6 Heat the oil in a deep heavy saucepan. Cook the pastries, in batches, turning occasionally, for 3 minutes, or until nicely browned. Drain on paper towels and serve warm. The cigars can also be baked in a preheated 400°F (200°C) oven for 10–12 minutes.

BRIK PASTRY

The wheat pastry used throughout the Maghreb is known as *ouarka* in Morocco, *dioul* in Algeria, and *malsouqa* in Tunisia.

In Paris, it's called *brik*, the Tunisian word for wrapped pastry, and is found in the fresh foods sections of most supermarkets. It is paper-thin and generally sold in packages of 10 round leaves separated by sheets of waxed paper. It is more elastic than filo dough, but filo can be substituted if brik is not available. Baked or fried, it comes out light and crunchy. Brik pastry is very easy to use; the only tricky part is peeling it away from the wax paper.

Once the brik is stuffed with a sweet or savory filling, it can be rolled into cigar shapes, as in our recipe, or folded into triangles or square packages (see illustration). These wrapped packets. like the pastry itself, have different names: *briouat* in Morocco, *bourek* in Algeria, and *brik* in Tunisia.

BRIK PASTRIES WITH FRESH SARDINES
Brik aux Sardines

In this recipe, fresh sardines are used to make this very popular version of brik, but tuna or any other fresh, firm-fleshed fish could be substituted. These briks are an adaptation of the all-time favorites served at 404 restaurant.

SERVES 6

4   small tomatoes
1   clove garlic, minced
1   teaspoon ground cumin
½   teaspoon red pepper flakes
    juice and zest of 1 lemon
½   cup fresh parsley, chopped
½   bunch fresh coriander,
    leaves chopped
½   bunch fresh mint, leaves
    chopped
    salt and freshly ground
    black pepper
12 fresh sardines, gutted and
    scaled

1   Preheat the oven to 375°F (190°C). Cut the tomatoes lengthwise in half, remove the seeds, and dice the flesh. Place in a bowl and add the garlic, cumin, red pepper flakes, lemon juice and zest, and mix well. Add the chopped fresh herbs and toss to combine. Season with salt and pepper.

2   Season the sardines with salt and pepper. Heat 1 tablespoon of olive oil in a sauté pan and quickly sear the fish on both sides. Drain on paper towels.

3   If using brik pastry, gently peel away the wax paper from one sheet and lay flat on a work

olive oil for sautéing and
brushing

6 sheets brik or filo pastry

1 tablespoon sesame seeds

salad greens and vinaigrette

RESTAURANT

LE 404
RESTAURANT FAMILIAL

69, rue Gravilliers 75003 Paris

tel: 01 42 74 57 81

métro: Arts et Métiers

surface. Brush lightly with oil. Place 2 sardines in the center of the round, and heap a generous tablespoon of the herb and tomato mixture on top. Fold the edges of the pastry over the filling to enclose it and form a square package, and brush with olive oil to seal. Put seam side down on a baking sheet, then sprinkle with sesame seeds. Repeat with the remaining sheets and filling.

4 If using filo pastry, cut each sheet in half. Brush one half with oil and place the other on top. Proceed as for the brik pastry to enclose the filling and seal.

5 Bake for 15 minutes, or until the pastry is golden. Serve atop a green salad dressed with vinaigrette.

SARDINES

For the population along the coast of the Mediterranean, fresh sardines are standard fare. In season during the spring and summer, they are simply grilled or fried or used in salads. Fresh sardines are a delightful and delicious change of pace for those of us who have only tasted sardines from a can. For centuries throughout the Mediterranean, the summer catch of sardines was preserved with oil and salt in clay pots. Napoleon I is responsible for getting sardines into a more modern container. At the beginning of the 19th century, his government offered 12,000 francs to anyone who could develop a way to preserve food for his roving armies. It didn't take long for sardines to show up in a can.

"Sardine" is actually a generic word for any tiny fish with fragile bones that can be preserved in oil. In the Mediterranean, pilchards are used. They are no longer than a finger and eaten whole. In Paris, these fresh sardines are only available in the spring.

TUNISIAN FISH SOUP
Chorba bil Hout

Ridah Ben Mansour is from Djerba, an island situated off the southern coast of the Tunisian mainland, where locals eat a great deal of freshly caught seafood. Ridah cooks fish in Paris on a gas stove in the storage room of his fruit and vegetable store. He gave us his recipe for chorba bil hout, a Tunisian fish soup similar to bouillabaisse. The delicious soup uses the fish from the day's catch that is unsuitable for simple cooking. Any nonoily fish and shellfish can be used. Use the trimmings and frames to make the fish stock.

SERVES 6-8

- 3 tablespoons olive oil
- 2 onions, diced
- 1 bird's-eye chili, minced, or 1 teaspoon red pepper flakes
- 3 cloves garlic, minced
- 2 teaspoons harissa
- 2 teaspoons ground cumin
- pinch of saffron threads
- 1 fennel bulb, trimmed and diced
- 2 cups diced potatoes
- 3 tablespoons lemon juice
- 6 cups Fish Stock or water
- 1 large can diced tomatoes
- 1 teaspoon salt, or to taste
- freshly ground black pepper
- 4½ pounds (2 kg) mixed fish and shellfish, cleaned
- ½ cup chopped fresh coriander
- ½ cup chopped fresh parsley
- 1 lemon, cut into wedges

1 Heat the olive oil in a large heavy saucepan, over medium heat. Add the onions, chili, and garlic and cook until the onions are translucent.

2 Add the harissa, cumin, saffron, fennel, potatoes, lemon juice, and fish stock or water. Bring to a boil, then reduce heat, cover, and simmer until the potatoes are tender, about 10 minutes.

3 Add the tomatoes, salt, and pepper to taste. Cover and simmer another 15 minutes. Add the fish and shellfish and cook until tender, about 10 minutes. Adjust seasoning.

4 Before serving, stir in the fresh herbs. Ladle into bowls and serve with the lemon wedges.

BASIC FISH STOCK

This is a very basic fish stock, without wine or seasonings, slowly simmered for several hours. French fish stock, based on flatfish, will turn bitter if cooked for longer than 20 minutes, but here no flatfish is used and the long cooking time makes a rich stock.

MAKES 8 CUPS

5 pounds (2.25 kg) trimmings and frames from nonoily fish

1 Rinse the trimmings and frames under cold running water. If using heads, cut out the gills and rinse thoroughly to remove any blood.

2 Put the trimmings and frames in a large stockpot and cover with water. Bring to a boil, then lower the heat and gently simmer for at least 2 hours. Remove any scum that forms on the surface. If not removed, the scum will give the broth a sour flavor.

3 Strain and use the stock immediately, or cool, refrigerate, and use within 2–3 days. The stock can also be frozen for up to 6 months

IMANE'S HARIRA
L'Harira d'Imane

The backbone of the Moroccan peasant's diet, harira is traditionally eaten to break the fast at the end of the day during Ramadan. A mix of grains infused with spices, it is a complex and savory blend. Harira is often accompanied with dates and fried pastries.

SERVES 6–8

- 1 cup dried chickpeas
- ¼ teaspoon baking soda
- 2 teaspoons olive oil
- 1½ pounds (680 g) boneless shoulder lamb, cut into 2-inch (5 cm) cubes
- 1 large onion, chopped
- 1 stalk celery, chopped
- 1½-inch (4 cm) piece ginger, peeled and finely minced
- 1 teaspoon ground turmeric
- ½ teaspoon ground cinnamon
- ½ teaspoon grated nutmeg
- 1 teaspoon salt, or to taste

1 Toss the chickpeas with the baking soda in a bowl. Cover with cold water and soak overnight. Drain and rinse.

2 The next day, heat the olive oil in a large pot and brown the lamb, in batches, 10–15 minutes. Add the onion, celery, and ginger and cook until the vegetables are soft. Combine the turmeric, cinnamon, nutmeg, salt, and black pepper in a small bowl, then stir these ingredients into the pot, along with the tomato paste.

3 Pour enough water into the pot to cover the ingredients and bring to a boil, skimming off any scum that rises to the surface. Reduce the heat,

1   teaspoon freshly ground black pepper, or to taste

2   teaspoons tomato paste

½   bunch chopped flat-leaf parsley, leaves chopped

3   tablespoons butter

¼   cup short-grain rice

1½ cups crushed tomatoes

½   bunch fresh coriander, leaves chopped, plus shredded leaves for garnish

add the parsley and butter. Simmer 1½ hours, or until meat and chickpeas are tender.

4 Meanwhile, rinse and drain the rice. Puree the crushed tomatoes and chopped coriander in a food processor or blender.

5 Twenty minutes before serving, add the rice and tomato puree. Continue cooking at a low simmer, stirring occasionally, until rice is just tender. Serve hot, garnished with the fresh coriander leaves.

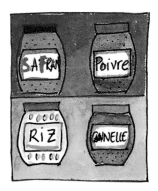

IMANE BELGHITI

Imane Belghiti studies management at a university in Paris. One of an estimated 24,000 Moroccan students living in France, she cooks whenever she has time: eating well is something she learned at home, where her mother makes everything from scratch. Moroccans are the largest body of foreign students in France, and they often cook together to relieve homesickness. It's hard to imagine Imane, enthusiastic and bright-eyed,

feeling blue, but she admits that preparing her mother's harira is a ritual that makes her feel instantly better when Paris's gray winter days are getting the better of her. Gathering together the ingredients, chopping, and stirring are all gestures she finds comforting. Imane shared this lip-smacking recipe with us (stressing the fact that each family makes its own special concoction), and when we first tasted it, we immediately felt reassured, too!

MAIN COURSES

LAMB STEW WITH TURNIPS AND CHICKPEAS
Ragoût d'Agneau aux Navets et aux Pois Chiches

Leila Marouane has been called one of the most talented Algerian novelists of our time. Her first book was published in Paris in 1996, and she has been writing steadily ever since. She lives in the Montparnasse area of Paris and regularly gets together with her girlfriends to cook Algerian dishes, often an enormous couscous or a lamb specialty. Leila gave us this recipe for lamb with turnips, which she has fond memories of eating for the first time at her friend Souhila's grandmother's house in the capital city of Algiers.

SERVES 4

- 2 tablespoons vegetable oil
- 3 pounds (1½ kg) lamb from the shoulder or leg, cubed
- 2 onions, grated
- 1 tablespoon salt
- ½ teaspoon freshly ground black pepper
- 2 teaspoons ground cumin
- 2 teaspoons cumin seeds
- 1 teaspoon paprika
- 8 ounces (225 g) turnips, peeled and cut into quarters
- 2 small cans chickpeas, drained and rinsed
- 1 jalapeño pepper, finely sliced
- ½ bunch fresh parsley or coriander, leaves chopped

1 Heat the oil in a large heavy casserole over medium heat. Add the lamb, onions, salt, and pepper and sauté until the lamb is brown and the onions are soft, about 10 minutes. Add the ground cumin, cumin seeds, paprika, and enough water to barely cover the meat. Bring to a boil, cover, then reduce heat, and simmer 30 minutes.

2 Add the turnips and simmer another 40–45 minutes, or until the vegetables and meat are tender. Add the chickpeas and jalapeño pepper and simmer 5–10 minutes to heat through.

3 Using a slotted spoon, transfer the meat and vegetables to a serving dish; cover to keep warm. Taste the sauce and, if necessary, reduce over high heat to intensify the flavors. Pour the sauce over the meat and vegetables and sprinkle with the fresh herbs.

COUSCOUS ROYAL

Couscous is the traditional Friday meal in the homes of most North Africans. When we feel in need for this comfort food, we head straight for the Taghit in the 14th arrondissement, where they have three types of semolina grain from which to choose. In France this dish is presented with the broth, meat, and vegetables in one bowl and the couscous and grilled merguez served separately. The couscous is spooned into soup plates and then the meat and vegetables are ladled on top, moistened with the broth.

SERVES 6–8

3 pounds (1.4 kg) boneless lean lamb, cut into cubes, or substitute equal amount chicken quarters

2 onions, cut into large pieces

2 cloves garlic, minced

1½ cups dried chickpeas, tossed with 1 teaspoon baking soda and soaked overnight in water

3 quarts (3 liters) water

3 tablespoons olive oil

1 teaspoon salt, or to taste

pinch of saffron threads

1 teaspoon ground cinnamon

1 teaspoon ground coriander

½ teaspoon ground ginger

1 large can tomatoes, diced

2 carrots, peeled and halved lengthwise, then in half again

2 turnips, peeled and quartered

2 zucchini, cut lengthwise in half, then in half again

2 stalks celery, cut into 4-inch (10 cm) pieces

¼ cup raisins

1 Put the meat (or chicken, if using) in a large pot with the onions, garlic, and drained chickpeas. Add the water, olive oil, salt, saffron, cinnamon, coriander, and ginger. Bring to a boil, then reduce heat, cover, and let simmer for 1 hour.

2 Add the tomatoes, carrots, and turnips and continue cooking for another 30 minutes, or until the meat is tender.

3 Add the zucchini, celery, raisins, and parsley, and more water if necessary so that all the vegetables are covered; you want to have plenty of broth. Continue cooking for another 30 minutes. Taste for seasoning.

4 While the lamb and vegetables are cooking, grill the merguez over a charcoal or gas fire or cook under a preheated broiler.

5 Just before serving, transfer a ladle of simmering broth to a small bowl, and dissolve the harissa in the liquid.

½ bunch fresh parsley, chopped

8 *merguez* (spicy lamb sausages)

2 teaspoons harissa

RESTAURANT

TAGHIT

63, rue de l'Ouest 75014 Paris

tel: 01 43 20 25 57

métro: Pernety/Gaîté

FLUFFY COUSCOUS

3 cups chicken stock or water

2 tablespoons unsalted butter

1 teaspoons salt

2¼ cups couscous

¼ cup golden raisins (optional)

¼ cup slivered almonds, toasted (optional)

6 Serve as described above: broth, vegetables, and meat in one bowl, grilled merguez and couscous served separately—all accompanied by lots of harissa sauce.

1 Bring the stock or water, butter, and salt to a boil in a small pot. Stir in the couscous, remove from heat, and cover. Leave for 5 minutes. Add the raisins and almonds, and fluff with a fork.

ATLAS COUSCOUS

Ordering in is not part of Parisian daily life, although times are changing. One of the first take-out businesses in the capital was for couscous. There are now several companies that deliver the North African staple, but we prefer Atlas Couscous, which brings not only couscous to your kitchen, but also briks, tagines, *pastilles*, and desserts. The smiling delivery boys transfer the couscous and the fresh vegetable broth from their *couscoussière* into your serving bowls and explain how to reheat the other dishes if necessary. When you have no time to cook, this is a great way to get together with friends for a real Moroccan dinner.

ATLAS COUSCOUS

tel: 01 45 41 22 22

Open 10AM to midnight every day except Monday

YAMOU'S GRILLED FISH WITH CHERMOULA
Grillade de Poisson au Chermoula

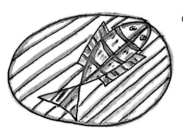

Chermoula could almost be called Moroccan pesto. There are many variations, but the basic ingredients are listed below. Meat and fish can be either marinated in chermoula and grilled or coated with it and baked. Pureed tomatoes may be added to the mixture, which can then be tossed with a variety of cooked vegetables.

SERVES 4

CHERMOULA

4	cloves garlic
2	bunches fresh coriander, leaves chopped
1	tablespoon ground cumin
1	teaspoon hot pepper flakes
1	tablespoon paprika
¼	cup lemon juice
½	cup olive oil
	salt and freshly ground black pepper
4	whole fish, bass, snapper, or red mullet, about 10 ounces (280 g) each, cleaned and scaled
1	lemon, cut into wedges

1 To make the chermoula, combine the garlic, coriander, cumin, hot pepper flakes, paprika, and lemon juice in a food processor and process until coarsely chopped. With the motor running, slowly add the olive oil in a steady stream and process until smooth. Season with salt and pepper.

2 With a sharp knife, cut two deep slits in thickest part of both sides of each fish. Rub the fish with the chermoula, working it well into the slashes. Place in the refrigerator for 1 hour to marinate.

3 Prepare a hot grill fire or preheat the broiler. Grill or broil the fish about 3 minutes each side. Serve with lemon wedges and any unused chermoula sauce.

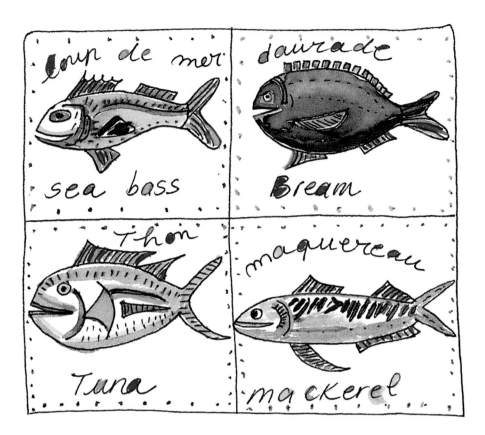

YAMOU, PAINTER AND COOK EXTRAORDINAIRE

Abderrahim Yamou, one of Morocco's leading painters and sculptors, has lived in France for more than 20 years. When he's not painting or sculpting, he's busy concocting mouthwatering meals for family and friends, and it's always Moroccan food. "It's what I cook best," he says simply. "There may be an element of nostalgia involved, but it's mostly because it's delicious!"

Yamou began cooking in his teens, when he went hiking with friends in the Atlas Mountains. He would bring along bags of flour and make bread, and he and his friends would stuff chickens with couscous and grill them on a spit. He learned to cook from watching his mother, but he wasn't allowed to help in the kitchen—it was her territory and his sister's. Once in France, Yamou was free to cook in his own kitchen. "There was a comfort to cooking; I was exploring my culinary identity—and enriching it."

Yamou has no trouble finding the requisite ingredients for his creations: "One used to have to walk around the block to find coriander, now I find it right downstairs."

His two favorite dishes are a tagine with artichokes and freshly shelled peas, and fish served with his delectable chermoula sauce.

LAMB TAGINE WITH ARTICHOKES AND PEAS
Tagine d'Agneau aux Artichauts et Petits Pois

Albert Lahyani, an architect from Casablanca who has lived in Paris since his student days, is the primary cook in his family. He introduced his French wife to the flavors of Moroccan cuisine, and he very often cooks tagines for dinner. This is one of his favorites.

SERVES 6

- 2 tablespoons vegetable oil
- 3 pounds (1½ kg) lamb from the shoulder or leg, cut into large cubes
- 2 onions, sliced
- 2 cloves garlic, minced
- 1 small lemon, seeded and diced
- 1½ cups fresh peas or frozen peas, defrosted
- 1 teaspoon ground ginger
- 2 teaspoons ground cumin
- ½ teaspoon saffron threads
  salt and freshly ground black pepper
- 2 9-ounce (250 g) packages frozen artichoke bottoms, defrosted and rinsed
- 1 tablespoon olive oil
- ½ cup celery leaves, coarsely chopped

1 Heat the vegetable oil in a large heavy saucepan over high heat. Add the meat, onions, and garlic and cook, turning the meat to brown on all sides, about 10 minutes. Add the lemon, fresh peas (if using), and enough water to barely cover. Bring to a boil, reduce heat and simmer, skimming off any scum that forms on the surface. Combine the ginger, cumin, saffron, salt, and pepper in a small bowl. Add a ladle of simmering broth and mix well. Stir back into the pot, cover, and cook 45 minutes, or until the meat is tender.

2 Ten minutes before the meat is done, place the artichoke bottoms in a single layer on top of the other ingredients in the pot. (If using frozen peas, add them at this point.) Cook until the artichokes are easily pierced with a knife.

3 Spoon the lamb and vegetables into a warm serving bowl. Taste the broth and reduce, if necessary, before adding to the bowl. Serve drizzled with the olive oil and garnished with the celery leaves.

TAGINE

Tagine is the name both of the dish and of the earthenware vessel in which it is cooked. The dish is a stew of meat, poultry, or fish that is gently simmered with a variety of vegetables or fruits and assorted spices. The ingredients are generally matched in contrasting sweet and pungent flavors.

The cooking receptacle is a heavy, round, shallow earthenware dish with a tight-fitting conical lid. The design of the lid traps steam from the cooking, which falls back on the ingredients, keeping everything tender and moist. These stews are meant to be cooked over a low flame on top of the stove, as the height of the lid would make it impractical to place in an oven. The lid has a very useful knob on the top, which allows you to remove it easily during cooking to check the braising liquid or add additional ingredients.

In Paris, there are several stores specializing in wares from North Africa where you can find tagines of all sizes, painted in bright colors and decorated with intricate and imaginative patterns.

These tagines are quite beautiful but are better suited for serving, and not actual cooking. Heavy cast-iron, lead-free clay, or ceramic tagines, more practical for modern kitchens, are now regularly produced and are easily found in kitchen supply stores.

CHICKEN TAGINE WITH PRUNES AND ALMONDS
Tagine de Poulet aux Pruneaux et aux Amandes

Tagines are often characterized by contrasting flavors in perfect equilibrium. In this recipe given to us by chef/owner Ghenima Agaova of Le Numide restaurant, sweet plays off savory.

SERVES 4

- 3 tablespoons olive oil
- 1 chicken, cut into 8 pieces
- 2 onions, 1 minced, 1 thinly sliced
- 2 teaspoons ground coriander
  pinch of saffron threads
- 1 teaspoon ground cinnamon
- 1 teaspoon salt
- ½ teaspoon freshly ground black pepper
- 1 tablespoon sugar
- 1 teaspoon orange flower water
- 18 prunes
- ¼ cup raisins
- 1 cup fresh coriander leaves, finely chopped
- ¼ cup toasted almonds
- 2 tablespoons toasted sesame seeds

Tagines

1 In a heavy casserole, heat 2 tablespoons of the oil over medium heat and sauté the chicken until brown on all sides. Add the minced onion and cook until soft, about 10 minutes. Add the ground coriander, cinnamon, saffron, salt, and pepper and sauté 1 minute. Pour in enough water to barely cover, bring to a boil, reduce the heat, cover, and simmer until the chicken is just tender.

2 Meanwhile, heat the remaining 1 tablespoon olive oil in a small saucepan and add the sliced onion, sugar, and orange flower water. Cover, and cook over low heat until the onions are tender and beginning to caramelize. Remove from heat.

3 About 15 minutes before the chicken is done, add the prunes, raisins, fresh coriander, almonds, and caramelized onions. When cooked, transfer the chicken to a serving dish, cover, and keep warm. Taste the braising liquid and reduce if necessary. Pour the sauce over the chicken, and sprinkle with the sesame seeds.

LE NUMIDE

75, rue Vasco de Gama
75015 Paris
tel: 01 45 32 13 13
métro: Porte de Versailles/Lourmel

LE NUMIDE

Ghenima Agaoua, wearing a white chef's jacket and a purple turban wrapped around her head, has just finished the lunch service at her restaurant, Le Numide. Customers are satiated and happy, not a speck of couscous is visible in her shining kitchen, and a lamb barbecue is marinating for the dinner service. Agaoua is a Berber from the Kabylia area of Algeria. She came to France as a child with her father, who ran several couscous restaurants, and she returned to Algeria as an adult. In 1990, as the political situation there deteriorated, she moved back to Paris with her husband, Merzouk, and opened Le Numide, named for the ancient northwest African country that was roughly situated in what is now Algeria.

The care Mrs. Agaoua puts into the quality and preparation of her food is obvious. From the artichoke, fava bean, and lamb tagine or the lamb couscous flavored with oranges and cinnamon to the Kabylian specialty *amakfoul* (a dry couscous with steamed vegetables), each dish is gloriously seasoned. Mint and coriander are ordered from Morocco—Mrs. Agaoua finds the leaves thicker than the Asian variety sold in Paris. She rolls the couscous herself and flatly refuses to serve anything she doesn't deem fresh or seasonal.

"When you're introducing a foreign cuisine to a host country, you have a moral responsibility to serve people the best," says Mrs. Agaoua, who unquestionably feels that she is an ambassador for her country's cooking. "France is a gastronomic country. I don't adapt my cooking to the French palate, but I always find the time to explain to people what they're eating."

CHICKEN TAGINE WITH PRESERVED LEMONS
Tagine de Poulet aux Citrons Confits

This is probably one of Morocco's best-known tagines. Its popularity is due to the flavor of bitter cracked olives offset by the tangy preserved lemons. In Morocco, half-ripened olives that range in color from brick red to violet are used, but any good quality salt or brine-cured olives, such as Italian Gaetas or Greek Kalamatas, can be substituted. This dish is relatively simple—its success lies in the quality of the ingredients.

SERVES 4

- 3 tablespoons olive oil
- 1 2.5-pound (1 kg) chicken, cut into 8 pieces
- 2 onions, grated
- 2 cloves garlic, minced
  large pinch of saffron threads
- 1 cinnamon stick
- 1 tablespoon minced fresh ginger
  salt and freshly ground black pepper
- 1 tomato, diced
- ½ bunch fresh parsley, chopped, plus extra for garnish
- ½ bunch fresh coriander, leaves chopped
- 3 cups water
- 1 cup Moroccan cracked purple olives or good-quality salt- or brine-cured olives
- 1 preserved lemon, diced

1 In a heavy casserole, heat the oil over medium heat and sauté the chicken until brown on all sides, about 10 minutes. Add the onion, garlic, saffron, cinnamon, ginger, salt, and pepper to taste, and cook until the onions are soft, about 10 minutes. Add the tomato, parsley, coriander, and water and bring to a boil. Cover, reduce to a simmer, and let cook 35–40 minutes, or until the chicken is tender.

2 Meanwhile, add a ladle of the braising liquid, and gently simmer. Place the cracked olives and preserved lemon in a small pot, and then simmer over a low heat until most of the liquid has evaporated.

3 When the chicken is done, transfer to a serving dish, cover, and keep warm. Return the braising liquid to a simmer and stir in the lemon mixture. Taste; if the flavors need concentration, bring to a boil and reduce. Pour the sauce over the chicken and sprinkle with parsley.

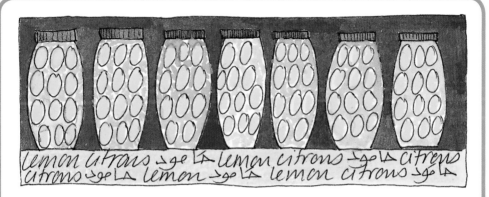

PRESERVED LEMONS

Preserved lemons are an indispensable ingredient that gives Moroccan cuisine its unique flavor. In Morocco, small thin-skinned Doqq and Boussera lemons are used, but these are difficult to find outside of North Africa. Meyer or Eureka lemons make good substitutes, but any lemon, small and heavy for its size (indicating juiciness) and with a relatively thin skin, will produce good results. There are various methods for preserving the lemons. Moroccan Jews use olive oil to cover the lemons, removing them after six days. Other recipes call for adding herbs or spices. Here is a simple recipe that results in perfectly preserved lemons.

6 lemons
¼ cup salt, preferably sea salt
Freshly squeezed lemon juice
Sterilized 1 pint glass jar

Wash the lemons thoroughly to remove any dirt or wax. Holding a lemon lengthwise between index finger and thumb, cut deep vertical slits at ½-inch (1 cm) intervals with the point of a knife all the way around the lemon. Push down on the fruit with your finger and thumb until the slits spread apart, and press as much salt as possible into the openings, then begin layering the lemons into the sterilized jar, packing them in tightly and sprinkling more salt in between layers. When all the fruit has been pressed into the jar, add enough lemon juice to cover completely. Place the jar in a cool place and gently turn every day for 1 month.

To use, rinse the lemons under cold running water. Usually the pulp is discarded and just the peel is used. Preserved lemons will keep up to a year, but they must remain covered with the pickling juice.

KABYLIA LAMB AND SEMOLINA DUMPLINGS
Agneau Kabyle et Boulettes de Semoule

Hakim Mazouz, co-owner with his brother Mourad (of Momo in London) of the celebrated 404 restaurant, is Algerian, originally from the Berber village of Sidi Aich, in eastern Algeria. Kabylia is the mountainous region in the north of Algeria known for its harsh conditions. The cuisine from this area is characterized by the use of tomatoes and very few spices.

  The Mazouz brothers serve essentially Moroccan dishes at the 404. But Hakim pines for his mother's cooking, and when he's too busy to go to Algeria, he pops in to visit his sister, Samia, who learned to cook all their mother's dishes when she was a girl. The following recipe is Zahra Mazouz's, by way of her daughter Samia, who is a passionate cook and lives in Lyons, France.

SERVES 4

- - - - - - - - - - - - - - - - - - - -

LAMB STEW

2	tablespoons olive oil
3	pounds (1½ kg) of lamb from the shoulder or leg, cubed
1	onion, grated
2	cloves garlic
2	tablespoons tomato paste
2	carrots, peeled and diced
2	turnips, peeled, and cut into eighths
2	stalks celery, diced
1	potato, peeled and diced
1	teaspoon paprika
1	teaspoon ground coriander
	salt and freshly ground black pepper

SEMOLINA DUMPLINGS

2	cups coarse semolina
1	large egg
2	tablespoons olive oil
1	small onion quartered
1	clove garlic
1	tomato, quartered
½	bunch fresh coriander, leaves finely chopped
½	bunch fresh mint, leaves finely chopped
1	teaspoon salt
1	teaspoon ground coriander
½	teaspoon freshly ground black pepper
2	teaspoons baking powder
½	bunch fresh coriander, leaves finely chopped

1 To make the stew, heat the olive oil in a large casserole over medium heat. Add the meat, onion, and garlic and cook, turning the meat to brown evenly, about 10 minutes. Stir in the tomato paste and cook 2–3 minutes. Add the vegetables, paprika, coriander, salt and pepper to taste, and enough water to cover the ingredients. Simmer, covered, until the meat is tender, 45–50 minutes.

2 While the meat is cooking, prepare the dumplings: In a medium bowl, combine all the ingredients except the baking powder, mixing well. Add ½ cup of the lamb cooking liquid and stir to blend well. Set aside for 20 minutes to allow the semolina to soak up the moisture from the liquid ingredients. Stir in the baking powder, then form the dumplings by pinching off large teaspoonfuls of the semolina mixture. Roll between your palms to make small balls roughly the size of walnuts (they expand as they cook). Set aside on a plate.

3 When the meat is cooked, use a slotted spoon to remove the meat and vegetables to a deep serving platter or bowl. Cover and keep warm. Return the broth to a low simmer. Gently place the dumplings in the simmering broth in a single layer (you may have to work in batches). The dumplings should be submerged in liquid and not touching; add water if necessary. Cover and cook 15–20 minutes.

4 Using the slotted spoon, place the dumplings on the warm meat and vegetables, then pour over the hot broth. Garnish with the coriander.

LAMB WITH RAS EL HANOUT AND HONEY
Agneau au Ras el Hanout et au Miel

Ras el hanout, which means "the best in the shop," refers to a combination of the best spices the vendor can provide. Recipes range from simple to complex, and there are many versions of this aromatic blend. Moroccans have a fondness for combining fruit with meat and even boost the sweetness by adding honey, as in this dish. You can adjust the quantities of honey and raisins according to taste.

SERVES 6

- -

3   pounds (1½ kg) lamb shoulder meat, cut into large cubes

3   tablespoons *ras el hanout*

     salt and freshly ground black pepper

¼   cup olive oil

1   large onion, chopped

3   cups water

¼   cup honey

2   cinnamon sticks

¾   cup raisins, plumped in warm water and drained

1   cup toasted whole almonds chopped fresh parsley

1 Preheat the oven to 325°F (170°C). Place the lamb in a bowl and sprinkle with the *ras el hanout* and salt and pepper, tossing to coat. Heat the oil in an ovenproof casserole and cook the onion until soft. Add the meat and brown lightly. Pour the water over and stir in the honey and cinnamon. Cover tightly, transfer to the oven, and bake for 3–4 hours, or until the lamb is fork-tender.

2 Using a slotted spoon, remove the meat to a bowl; keep warm. Skim off excess fat from the broth, then place the casserole over low heat and add the raisins. Reduce the liquid until it has a syruplike consistency. Add salt and pepper if necessary. Return the lamb to the pot and add the toasted almonds. Stir to coat with the sauce, then transfer to a serving dish and sprinkle with parsley.

SPICE SHOPS

When we first moved to Paris years ago, it was difficult to find exotic spices. A special trip had to be made to a neighborhood where there was a North African, Armenian, or Lebanese store. Today it seems that just around any corner there is either a grocery store or a market in which you can find all the spices and ingredients you need to make a chicken tagine, for a start. Some of the best shops in which to find spices are:

AHGA
21, rue Montorgueil
75001 Paris
tel: 01 42 33 72 39
métro: Etienne Marcel

IZRAEL
30, rue François Miron
75004 Paris
tel: 01 42 72 66 23
métro: Hotel de Ville

MAISON SAFRAOUI
31, boulevard de la Villette
75010 Paris
tel: 01 42 40 91 12
métro: Belleville

PALAIS DES EPICES
20, rue de la Charbonnière
75018 Paris
tel: 01 42 55 80 80
métro: Barbès-Rochechouart

MARCHE DE BARBES
(the most popular and least expensive market in Paris)
boulevard Rochechouart
75018 Paris
métro: Barbès-Rochechouart

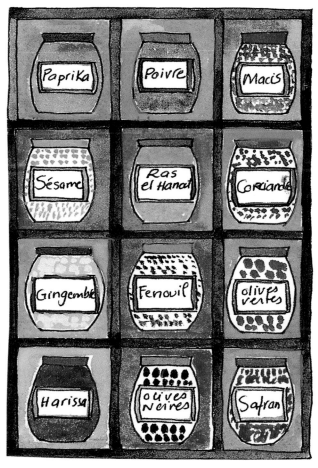

DESSERTS

FRIED HONEY AND ALMOND BRIK PASTRIES
Cigares au Miel

Our friend Imane Belghiti, a Moroccan student in Paris, introduced us to these North African pastries. She learned how to make them from her mother, who regularly produces a delicious variety of Moroccan sweets for friends and family.

MAKES 20–30 PASTRIES

FILLING

- 2 cups ground almonds
- 1 cup of confectioners' sugar
- 2 tablespoons orange flower water
- ½ teaspoon ground cinnamon
- ½ teaspoon almond extract

TO ASSEMBLE

- 10 sheets brik or filo pastry
- 2 cups honey, diluted with 1 cup of water
- 2 tablespoons orange flower water
- 2 tablespoons butter, melted
  oil for deep-frying

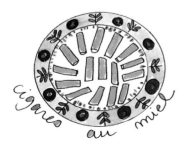

1 To make the filling, combine all the ingredients in a bowl. Stir in cold water, 1 teaspoon at a time, until the mixture comes together and forms a smooth paste.

2 Cut the sheets of brik or filo into 9 x 4 inch (22 x 10 cm) bands. Place 1 heaping teaspoon of filling at a short end and use your fingers to press into a sausage shape slightly shorter than the width of the pastry. Roll into a cigar shape, folding in the long sides as you go. Brush with the melted butter to seal and place seam side down on a baking sheet. Repeat with the remaining filling and sheets, then refrigerate for 10 minutes so the butter hardens.

3 Place the honey and orange flower water in a small pot and bring to a very low simmer.

4 Heat 3 inches (7.5 cm) oil in a heavy saucepan and deep-fry the pastries, in batches, until golden brown. While still warm, quickly dip the pastries in the simmering honey, then remove with a slotted spoon. Place on a flat dish to dry. Once cool, the pastries can keep in an airtight container for a week.

GAZELLE'S HORNS
Cornes de Gazelle

These are very popular pastries throughout the Maghreb. Although the shape is reminiscent of a crescent, it actually represents a gazelle's horn, hence the name. These pastries are always served on festive occasions, particularly at wedding banquets. The almond filling, scented with orange blossom water, is perfectly complemented by a glass of mint tea.

Cornes de Gazelles

MAKES 16 PASTRIES

FILLING

2 cups ground almonds

1 cup confectioners' sugar

2 tablespoons orange flower water

2 tablespoons butter, melted

½ teaspoon ground cinnamon

PASTRY

2 tablespoons butter, melted

2 tablespoons orange flower water

1 large egg yolk

1¾ cups all-purpose flour

½ teaspoon salt

1 large egg yolk, beaten with 1 tablespoon water for egg glaze

confectioners' sugar for dusting

1. To make the filling, combine all the ingredients in a bowl. Knead with your hands until the mixture comes together and forms a smooth paste.

2. To make the pastry, combine the flour and salt in a small bowl. In a medium bowl, combine the butter, orange flower water, and egg yolk, then add the flour mixture. Mix and let stand 20 minutes.

3. Preheat the oven to 350°F (180°C). Butter and flour a large baking sheet. Place half the dough on a floured work surface and roll out to a very thin rectangle. Cut into 8 strips 4 inches (10 cm) wide. Repeat with remaining dough.

4. Divide the filling into 16 pieces and roll each into a 3-inch (7.5 cm) cylinder. Place a cylinder on each strip of pastry, 1 inch (2.5 cm) from the bottom edge, spacing them 1½ inches (4 cm) apart.

5. Dampen the other end of each pastry strip with a little water, then fold over the filling. Press around the filling with your fingertips to seal.

6. Use a fluted pastry cutter to trim the pastries: Place half of the cutter around the filling and cut out half-moons. Push in the middle folded edge of each one to form a crescent.

7. Place the crescents on the prepared baking sheet. Brush the egg glaze over the top of each pastry.

8. Bake for 12–16 minutes, or until lightly golden. Remove from the oven and cool on a rack. Sprinkle with confectioners' sugar before serving.

dattier

DATES STUFFED WITH ALMOND PASTE
Dattes farcies à la Pâte d'Amande

Almonds show up everywhere in the Maghreb, as a fruit, a condiment, and even a seasoning. Almonds belong to the same family as the rose; together they are among to the world's oldest seasonings and scents.

MAKES 16

16 large dates

5 ounces (140 g) almond paste

1 tablespoon orange flower water

⅓ cup sugar

1 Pit the dates, leaving the fruit intact: Push on one end and force the pit out the other end.

2 Combine the almond paste and orange flower water, and spoon into a pastry bag fitted with a medium plain tip. Pipe the paste into the dates, then roll the dates in the sugar to coat.

ALMOND PASTE WITH ARGAN OIL
Amalou

Spread on pancakes for breakfast or on a piece of hot toast in the afternoon with mint tea, this combination of argan oil, almonds, and honey is ambrosial.

MAKES 2 CUPS

1   teaspoon vegetable oil
1½ cups blanched whole almonds
½   cup argan or walnut oil
     pinch of salt
¼   cup honey
     pinch of ground cinnamon
     (optional)

1 Heat the vegetable oil in a large skillet and lightly brown the almonds. Drain on paper towels and cool.

2 Transfer the almonds to the bowl of a food processor and grind to a fine powder. With the motor running, slowly add the oil in a steady stream and process to form a smooth, creamy paste. Add the honey, salt, and the cinnamon, if desired, and process until well blended.

3 Pour into a jar, cover, and refrigerate. The paste will keep for up to 2 months.

"TOWARD NOON AN ODOR OF ANISETTE AND ABSINTHE PERVADED THIS STREET IN ALGIERS. IN BISKRA'S MAURESQUE CAFES, ONLY COFFEE, LEMONADE, AND TEA WERE SERVED. ARAB TEA; PUNGENT SWEETNESS, GINGER.."

—Andre Gide, "Les Nourritures Terrestres"

KENZA'S FINGERS
Doigts de Kenza

These pretty sweets are adapted from La Bague de Kenza's cookbook. Usually served at civil marriages along with tea, they are elegant looking and deliciously crunchy.

  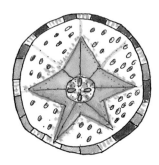

MAKES 20–25 PASTRIES

2½ cups ground almonds

½ cup sugar

2 large eggs

grated zest of 1 orange

1 teaspoon baking powder

1 cup slivered almonds

confectioners' sugar

1 Preheat the oven to 350°F (180°C).

2 Mix the almonds and sugar together in a bowl. Make a well in the center of the ingredients and add the eggs, orange zest, and baking powder. Using your fingertips, mix the ingredients in the well, then slowly incorporate the dry ingredients to make a firm dough.

3 Sprinkle the slivered almonds onto a clean work surface.

4 Wet your hands, pinch off a generous tablespoon of the dough, and roll it into a thin finger shape. Roll and press the dough in the slivered almonds, sprinkle with confectioners' sugar, and place it on a baking sheet. Repeat with the rest of the dough.

5 Bake for 15 minutes. Let cool before serving.

LA BAGUE DE KENZA

It is well known that North Africans have a considerable sweet tooth. Ambrosial or cloying, depending on your taste buds, pastries made with ground almonds, dried dates, and figs, flavored with orange blossom or rose petal water and then soaked in honey, are carefully stacked on silver trays in *pâtisseries*. Brik pastry shows up as a crunchy wrapper for sweetmeats, rolled into cigar shapes or folded parcels, then fried and dipped in simmering honey. Sheets of brik are also fried in butter and layered with confections of almonds, cinnamon, and sugar.

Until recently, these sweets were only served in wealthy homes and were out of reach for most people. Today, while too rich to be eaten on a daily basis, they have become an essential element or any family occasion. They are generally served with tea or before the fresh fruit that concludes all meals.

La Bague de Kenza is the Parisian pastry shop in which to taste delicacies from Algiers. Sumptuous pyramids of stuffed dates and pastries made with almonds, walnuts, pistachios, honey, and essence of orange blossoms and rose petals are piled high on decorative platters. Samira Fahim and l'Hassen Rahmani, self-avowed gourmands and gourmets, opened their first Bague de Kenza in 1996. Ten years later, there are four Bague de Kenza shops and a cookbook called *Les Douceurs de Kenza* (*Kenza's Sweets*). Samira says she is proud to be treating the French to sweets from her hometown city of Algiers and hopes one day to open a pastry school in which there will be students with names like "Bernard, Frédéric, or David...not just students of North African origin!"

Pastry shop and restaurant
LA BAGUE DE KENZA
106 rue St. Maur
75011 Paris
tel: 01 43 14 93 15
métro: St. Maur

ORANGES WITH CINNAMON
Oranges à la Cannelle

From mid-January until March, Maltese oranges from Tunisia flood the Paris markets. Thin-skinned and juicy, they are excellent when eaten sliced and lightly dusted with cinnamon powder and sprinkled with fresh mint. Navel oranges or blood oranges from Italy are good alternatives.

SERVES 4

6   navel oranges
1   tablespoon orange flower water
1   tablespoon sugar
    cinnamon powder for dusting
    fresh mint, leaves chopped

1 Using a sharp knife, peel away the skin and white bitter pith from the oranges. Cut horizontally into thin slices, removing any seeds with the tip the knife.

2 Arrange the orange slices in a single layer on a large plate or shallow serving dish. Sprinkle with the orange flower water and sugar, then dust lightly with cinnamon. Garnish with the mint.

BUTTER COOKIES WITH CINNAMON
Ghribia

These butter cookies melt in your mouth and are a favorite at the Bague de Kenza Algerian pastry shop. Not too sweet and with just the right amount of crispness, they are perfect to serve with tea or as an afternoon snack. Ghribia are fairly simple and quick to mix together, a great recipe for children to make by themselves. Do not overbake the ghribia—they should remain white.

MAKES 24

- 4 cups all-purpose flour
- 1⅓ cups unsalted butter, melted
- 1¼ confectioners' sugar
- ½ cup ground almonds
- 2 teaspoons baking powder
  ground cinnamon for sprinkling

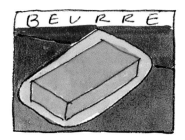

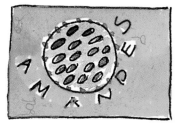

1 Preheat the oven to 325°F (170°C). Grease a baking sheet.

2 In a medium bowl, combine the flour and butter with your fingertips until completely blended. Continuing with your hands, mix in the sugar, almonds, and baking powder to form a very stiff dough. If the dough is too dry, add water, a teaspoon at a time, until it comes together. If the dough is too soft, add a little more flour.

3 Pinch off pieces of dough roughly the size of walnuts and roll them between your palms to form balls. Flatten the bottom of each ball, then mold the tip into a high round peak. Place on the baking sheet and sprinkle with cinnamon. Repeat with the remaining dough.

4 Place the baking sheet in the oven and bake 20–30 minutes, or until firm. Let cool completely on a rack before removing the cookies to a serving plate.

HONEY CREPES FROM THE 404
Les Crêpes au Miel du 404

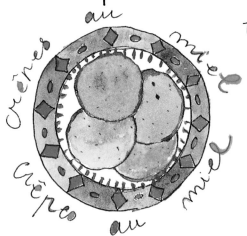

These pancakes are eaten for breakfast in Morocco, but they also make a delicious dessert. This recipe comes courtesy of the 404 Restaurant in Paris, where we always order them at the end of a meal.

SERVES 6

1½ teaspoons active dry yeast
2 tablespoons warm water
1 teaspoon sugar
1 cup plus 2 tablespoons semolina flour
1⅔ cups all-purpose flour
½ teaspoon salt
1 large egg
1½ cups warm milk
1½ cups warm water
vegetable oil

1 cup slivered almonds
½ cup honey

1 In a small bowl, combine the yeast, 2 tablespoons warm water, and sugar. Set aside in a warm place for 10–20 minutes. The yeast mix should then be full of bubbles; if not, the yeast is old and should not be used. Start again with fresh yeast.

2 Sift together the flour, semolina flour, and salt into a large bowl. Make a well in the center of the dry ingredients and add the egg, yeast, warm milk, and warm water. Whisk lightly with a fork to blend, then, using your fingers, slowly incorporate the dry ingredients to form a smooth batter. Cover the bowl with a cloth and put it in a warm place to allow the dough to rise for 2 hours, or until doubled in volume.

3 Spread out a clean damp dishcloth on a large plate. Pour a 4-inch (10 cm) diameter crepe onto a hot griddle, lightly greasing it between each batch. The crepes are cooked on one side only. When the bottom is golden brown and little bubbles have formed on the surface, the crepes are done. Remove to the damp dish towel, which will keep them nice and moist, and continue with the rest of the batter. (Do not stack the crepes while they are warm.)

4 The crepes can be served warm (if necessary, reheat with a little butter in a warm pan) or at room temperature, garnished with the slivered almonds and honey.

"I ATE TWO FOR PRACTICE, ENJOYING THE SENSUALITY OF EATING SOMETHING SO RICH AND DANGEROUS, AND THEN A THIRD BECAUSE IT TASTED SO GOOD. THE EGG WAS SITTING ON A BED OF VEGETABLES MIXED WITH CHILE-RICH HARISSA, AND EACH TIME THE YOLK CAME SHOOTING OUT BETWEEN THE CRACKLING LAYERS OF PASTRY IT CREATED AN INCREDIBLE SENSATION."

—Ruth Reichl on eating brik in Tunisia, *Tender at the Bone*

TUNISIAN HONEY CAKE
Gâteau Tunisien au Miel

In this traditional cake, honey is used to sweeten the batter. Baked goods made with honey are moist and dense and color quickly. The taste of honey is subtle and varies according to where it is harvested.

SERVES 6–8

- ½ cup sugar
- 2 large eggs
- 5 tablespoons honey
- 1 cup plus 1 tablespoon all-purpose flour
- 2 teaspoons baking soda
- 4 tablespoons butter, melted
- 2 tablespoons pine nuts
- 1 tablespoon honey, diluted with 1 teaspoon water

1 Preheat the oven to 375° F (190°C). Butter a 9-inch (23 cm) round cake pan.

2 In a medium bowl, whisk together the sugar and eggs until the sugar is dissolved. Stir in the honey.

3 In a separate bowl, stir the flour and baking soda with a fork to combine. Slowly add the dry ingredients to the sugar and egg mixture, then add the melted butter.

4 Pour the batter into the prepared pan and bake for 30–40 minutes, or until a toothpick inserted in the center comes out clean.

5 Remove the cake from the oven; let stand for 5 minutes then invert onto a serving plate. In a small sauté pan, dry roast the pine nuts until lightly golden, then add the diluted honey. Spread the mixture evenly over the warm cake. Cool completely before slicing.

MINT TEA
Thé à la Menthe

Mint tea is the national beverage in Morocco, where atay (in Moroccan dialect) or thé a la menthe is a serious matter. Referred to as "Moroccan whiskey," it is the symbol of hospitality and served whenever an opportunity arises. It is poured with flair from a great height, so that it will be frothy on top, into beautifully colored and decorated tea glasses. But tea is a relatively new arrival, introduced by the English in the 19th century. In fact, the richly engraved silver teapots that many of us associate with tea in North Africa are actually hybrids of ancient coffeepots from Yemen and Andalusia, often made in Manchester, England!

SERVES 4

2　teaspoons Chinese green gunpowder tea

4　sprigs fresh mint, preferably spearmint

　　sugar to taste

1 Rinse a teapot with boiling water. Spoon the loose tea into the pot, pour in some boiling water, swirl it around to moisten the tea, then carefully drain it off, leaving the tea. Crush the fresh mint with your hands and add to the teapot, along with sugar to taste. Pour in 4 cups of boiling water and allow the tea to infuse for 5 minutes.

2 Before serving, stir the tea. Serve Moroccan-style in small tea glasses.

UN PETIT PEU DE CHINE
CAMBODGE
LAOS
VIETNAM

Bahn-Mi

PORC

SOYA SAUCE

HUILE OLIVE

Salade de Calamars
aux poivrons rouges

Gingembre

HUILE DE SESAME

SHAOXING

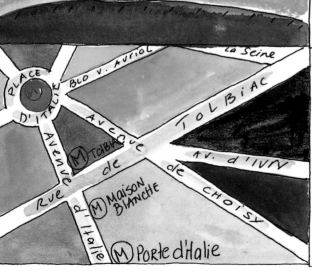

PLACE D'ITALIE
BLD V. AVRIOL
La Seine
AVENUE DE TOLBIAC
AVENUE DE CHOISY
M TOLBIAC
Av. d'IVRY
M MAISON BLANCHE
Rue d'Italie
M Porte d'Italie

lait de coco

LISERONS D'EAU

Les trois tr

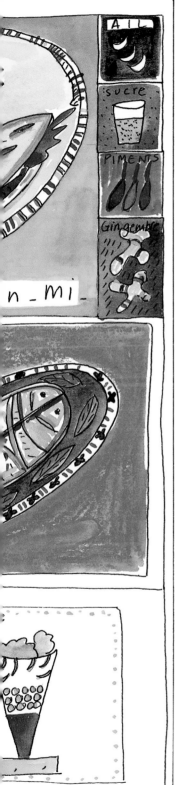

BO BUN BUSINESS:
VIETNAM, CAMBODIA, LAOS, and CHINA

"...maybe that's youth; to believe that the world is made of inseparable things. Men and women, mountains and plains, humans and gods, Indochina and France."—French actress Catherine Deneuve, narrating at the beginning of Regis Wárgnier's 1993 Academy Award-winning film "Indochine."

YIN-YANG FUSION

The word *Indochine* triggers for many French a selective memory process of romanticized images of their former colony—teak steamers on the Mekong River, mangoes, and white linen suits.

French Indochina may have collapsed more than 50 years ago, but Parisians are still intimately involved with the Southeast Asian countries of Vietnam, Cambodia, and Laos, and that connection is food.

Southeast Asian restaurants, ranging from trendy and minimalist to crowded holes-in-the-wall, are fixtures of Paris's restaurant scene. Some of the finest examples of this Asian cuisine can be found in several neighborhoods where immigrants from France's former colonies have settled, such as the 13th *arrondissement* in southern Paris and the Belleville area to the north. Plates of velvety noodles, tender strips of grilled meat, crisp bean sprouts, baskets of aromatic herbs, and crunchy roasted peanuts grace the tables. Customers noisily enjoy a typical Laotian dessert drink—ice, fruit, and green vermicelli in a tall glass filled with coconut milk—or guzzle Vietnamese beer.

Scores of traditional *traiteurs,* or delicatessens, selling *carottes rapées* and a *plat du jour* have been replaced by Asian delis, which for the most part offer variations of Vietnamese dishes. These days it is not uncommon to see people walking down the street munching on a Vietnamese *rouleau de printemps* (spring roll) as a snack instead of a *pain au chocolat*.

France's recent history is intricately linked to Vietnam, Laos, and Cambodia—countries once grouped under the name Indochina—first as a colonial power, then as a safe haven for those fleeing wars and repressive political regimes. These regimes were often run by heads of state who were educated in France. Several of the most emblematic figures of Southeast Asia's tumultuous 20th century history studied in Paris: Bao Dai, the last emperor of Vietnam; Ho Chi Minh, the Vietnamese communist revolutionary; Cambodian king Norodom Sihanouk; and the leaders of the infamous Khmer Rouge.

In the 21st century, Asian immigrants are less political and more cultural. Paris is now a base for Asian publishing, filmmaking, and the music industry. French writers have often used a fictional Indochina in their novels and films: Marguerite Duras' *The Lover* (which was later adapted to film by Jean-Jacques Annaud) and Régis Wargnier's *Indochine* are among the better known.

Vietnamese, Laotians, and Cambodians began arriving in Paris during the early part of the 20th century. During World War I, nearly 100,000 men from French Indochina were enlisted in the French army, and throughout the first half of the 20th century, France recruited manpower from the region.

CHINATOWN

The first important wave of immigration into Paris came in the 1950s during and just after the end of French rule in Indochina. These

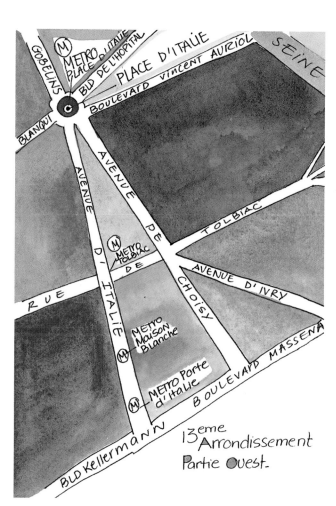

13ᵉᵐᵉ Arrondissement
Partie Ouest.

arrondissement becoming Europe's largest, and most dynamic Chinatown.

More than 200,000 Asians live in the Paris area (these figures do not include numerous Asians who have acquired French nationality), and over 35,000 of them live in the 13th. The name "Chinatown" is misleading because its population is so complex. Most Asians in this neighborhood come from former Indochina and it is this particular group that went into the food sector and the restaurant business. The 13th and part of Belleville, besides providing for the needs of the entire Asian population in France, are now among the principal suppliers of Asian food products in Europe. Surprisingly, for a country with such a grand culinary tradition, there are relatively few "real" Chinese (from the People's Republic of China) restaurants. This can be explained by a historically smaller Chinese presence in Paris (although today this is very rapidly changing); the fact that the food sector is firmly in the hands of Southeast Asians; and, finally, the fact that newer immigrants from China come, in large part, from poor rural areas and tend to go into clothing manufacturing or import/export, or to open restaurants of lesser quality.

immigrants, who were often students, settled mainly in the Latin Quarter. The second wave arrived in the 1970s, when Vietnamese, Laotians, and Cambodians came en masse (approximately one fourth of the Vietnamese boat people ended up in France) fleeing war and communism. A great number were of Chinese origin, although their families had been living in Southeast Asia for several generations. This advent changed the Parisian landscape definitively, with the 13th

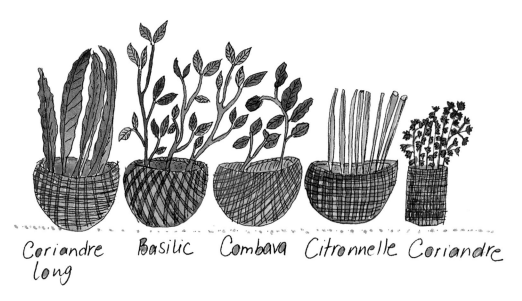

Coriandre long   Basilic   Combava   Citronnelle   Coriandre

Southeast Asian cooking has earned tremendous popularity over the past decade, not only for its delectable and colorful dishes but also for its nutritious yet light aspect. These are cuisines that use a minimum amount of oil and lots of fresh vegetables. Meat is an accompaniment rather than the principal ingredient in a main course.

The shared tropical climate and proximity to seacoasts and rivers have resulted in certain similarities among Southeast Asian cuisines. Rice is a staple and fish a vital component in many dishes, even when simply in the form of fish sauce. All three countries use an abundance of herbs and vegetables in their cooking. Each country does, however, retain its own distinct cuisine.

THRICE VIETNAMESE

Vietnam was occupied at various points in its history by two countries with grand culinary traditions: China and France. Many influences from these cuisines are evident in Vietnamese cooking.

Didier Corlou, a French chef and cookbook author, fell in love with Vietnam and its cooking and moved to Hanoi over a decade ago. He describes three types of Vietnamese cuisine. In the south, coconut, lemongrass, chili pepper, and tropical fruit are used. Dishes are often sweet-and-sour. In the center of the country, the cooking is spicier and more seafood is eaten. In the north, where the climate is more seasonal, there is an abundance of vegetables, fresh herbs, and freshwater fish.

From the French, the Vietnamese inherited coffee, pastries, and bread, which they integrated into their cuisine with snacks such as *banh mi cha lua*, a sandwich made on a baguette with pâté, deli pork, pickled vegetables, and other delicacies. Laotian and Cambodian cuisines are heavily influenced by Thai (and, more remotely, Indian) cooking.

STICKY AND BITTER

Laotian cuisine is characterized by the presence of sticky rice. A spicy mix of marinated meat or fish with lime juice, green onions, mint, and chili called *laap* is a staple. In contrast to the Vietnamese, who will often combine sweet and sour, Laotians prefer more bitter tastes. A big bowl of fresh raw greens and herbs is always served, undressed, on the side. As in Thai cuisine, hot chilies, ground peanuts, tamarind juice, ginger, and coconut are often used. A French touch is present in the breads and pastries.

KHMER CUISINE

Cambodian cuisine, also known as Khmer cuisine, is similar to Thai cooking but not as spicy. Curries and stews show ties to Indian cooking by way of Java. As in Vietnam and Laos, French bread is a lasting legacy, as are dishes made with frog's legs. Salads are flavored with cilantro, mint, and lemon thyme. Cambodians are known for having a sweet tooth, but Western-style desserts are uncommon. Instead, they may snack on confections made from sweetened rice products and coconut milk or tropical fruit.

UPSCALE AFFORDABLE

Chinese cuisine in Paris is usually Cantonese (or Zheijiangese, specifically from the port of Wenzhou, a city south of Shanghai). A few restaurants do justice to the delicately balanced stir-fried or steamed food of Canton, and a handful of others offer specialties from Zhejiang Province, famous for its various fish dishes.

The French are still relatively unfamiliar with high-quality Chinese cuisine—most associate Chinese food with fast, cheap meals. While there are numerous low-end Chinese dining spots, there are also, curiously, two Michelin one-star Chinese restaurants in the city (Chen Soleil d'Est in the 15th *arrondissement* and Tang in the 16th), an indication that there is room for more upscale yet affordable Chinese eateries.

All in all, there are more than 4,500 Asian restaurants in Paris. Among these there are many examples of outstanding food from Vietnam, Cambodia, and Laos. It is possible to discover a few authentic and delicious Chinese meals, and that is a trend very likely to develop over the next decade.

APPETIZERS

GREEN PAPAYA SALAD
Salade de Papayes Vertes

This is a favorite in virtually every Laotian and Cambodian restaurant in Paris. Unripe, green papaya is used to make a grated salad much like coleslaw but without any added oil or fat. Deliciously refreshing on its own, the salad's pungent flavors can also complement grilled meat or fish. Since the salad dressing is made with Laotian quantities, adjust spiciness according to your own taste. Look for small green papayas the size of cucumbers; they are fleshier than larger ones.

SERVES 6

- 1 green papaya, peeled, cut in half, and seeded
- 2 carrots, peeled
- 1 tablespoon salt
- 30 dried shrimp (optional)
- 1 cup fresh mint leaves, chopped
- 1 cup coriander leaves, chopped

DRESSING

- ½ cup lime juice
- 2 bird's-eye chilies, seeded and finely chopped
- 2 cloves garlic, crushed
- ¼ cup *nuoc mam*, or more to taste
- ¼ cup sugar
- salt, if needed

- 8 cherry tomatoes, halved
- 2 tablespoons finely chopped roasted peanuts

1 Grate the papaya and carrots on a box grater or in a food processor or julienne using a mandoline. Place in a bowl and sprinkle with the salt. Leave for 10 minutes to soften, then rinse and drain in a colander.

2 If using dried shrimp, place in a bowl, cover with boiling water, and let sit for 5 minutes. Drain, then crush, using a mortar and pestle.

3 Combine all the ingredients for the dressing except the salt in a bowl large enough to hold the salad. Add the papaya, carrot, chopped herbs, and dried shrimp, if using, and toss with the dressing. Taste for seasoning, adding salt if needed. Let sit for 20 minutes before serving to allow the flavors to develop.

4 Garnish with the halved cherry tomatoes and chopped roasted peanuts.

VIETNAMESE DIPPING SAUCE
Nuoc Cham

This "salt and pepper" of Southeast Asian cuisines is used as a dipping sauce or a dressing. It enhances the flavor of food without masking the other ingredients. Don't be put off by the large quantity of nuoc mam in this sauce; its fishy aroma blends into the other flavors. The sauce needs resting time, so make it at least 30 minutes before you need it. It will keep for up to a month in the refrigerator.

MAKES 1 CUP

1   bird's-eye chili
1   clove of garlic
2   tablespoons sugar
¼   cup lime juice
¼   cup *nuoc mam*
¼   cup warm water
1   tablespoon thinly shredded carrot (optional)

1 Roughly slice the chili and garlic and then put in a mortar, along with the sugar. Pound into a paste and transfer to a bowl. If you do not have a mortar, finely mince the chili and garlic before adding to the sugar. Add the other ingredients (except the carrots) and stir well until the sugar dissolves. Add the shredded carrots, if using. Let the sauce stand for at least 10 minutes for the flavors to fully develop.

NUOC MAM: SMELLY AND ADDICTIVE

What is the culinary link between ancient Rome and Southeast Asia? It's the delicate gold liquid found in every kitchen from Vietnam, Laos, and Cambodia to Thailand, Myanmar, and the Philippines. Known as *garum* in Rome and *nuoc mam* in Vietnam, fish sauce is still made as it was in ancient times by layering anchovies and salt in a barrel and letting the mixture ferment. The liquid that forms after three months is drained off and poured back over the top. Six months to a year later, the mixture is considered ready and the first run of pale gold *nuoc mam* is drained off. The extra virgin olive oil of the *nuoc mam* world, it is labeled *nhi*.

A *nuoc mam* of lesser quality, which is deeper in color and stronger in taste and smell, is obtained from pressing once again on the fermented fish.

Nuoc mam is used much like soy sauce. While both are salty, *nuoc mam* brings out very different flavors when paired with the same ingredients. Its strong fish smell magically disappears when added to dishes, and it gives complexity and depth without masking other flavors. High in vitamin B and protein, *nuoc mam* is considered a flavoring as well as a condiment. Most chefs find it quite addictive.

Vietnamese *nuoc mam* is considered more fragrant and not as salty as the more commonly found Thai brands, but oxidation can be a problem and thus Vietnamese brands tend to change character very quickly. In France, Vietnamese *nuoc mam* is easier to find but, on the whole, Thailand remains the principal exporter of this essential and delicious Southeast Asian ingredient.

BO BUN

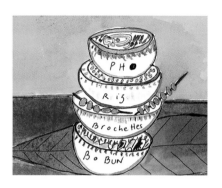

This Vietnamese salad is a mixture of temperatures, textures, and tastes that's healthy and satisfying. Perfect as a light summer meal, it's easy to make when you're entertaining, since all of the ingredients can be prepared in advance and kept in the refrigerator until time to stir-fry the marinated beef and assemble the salad. Dress with Nuoc Cham sauce. Nathalie Leroy, chef and owner of La Baie d'Halong restaurant, where her bo bun is a favorite with regular customers, uses beef for this recipe, but stir-fried pork, chicken, or shrimp would work just as well.

SERVES 4

BEEF AND NOODLES

- 1 pound (450 g) boneless steak, sliced into thin 2-inch (5 cm) strips
- 2 cloves garlic, finely minced
- 1 scallion, sliced
- 1 teaspoon finely minced lemongrass
- 2 tablespoons *nuoc mam*
- ½ teaspoon sugar
- 8 ounces (225 g) rice vermicelli
- 2 tablespoons vegetable oil
- 1 onion, sliced into thin rings

1 Combine the sliced beef, minced garlic, scallion, lemongrass, *nuoc mam,* and sugar in a bowl and marinate 30 minutes.

2 To cook the rice vermicelli, bring a large pot of water to a rolling boil. Add the noodles and cook 3 to 5 minutes, giving the pot a stir from time to time. The noodles are done when soft and white but still firm. Drain and rinse in cold water until cool. (The vermicelli can be cooked in advance and kept at room temperature for several hours.)

3 Right before serving, heat the vegetable oil in a large skillet or a wok and sauté the sliced onion until translucent. Add the marinated beef and quickly stir-fry to brown, about 1 minute. Remove from heat.

SALAD AND GARNISHES:

2   cups fresh mung bean sprouts

2   cups shredded red or green lettuce leaves

1   cucumber, peeled, seeded, and cut into julienne strips

1   carrot, peeled and shredded

    handful each of fresh mint, coriander, and Asian basil

2   tablespoons roasted peanuts, crushed

1   recipe *Nuoc Cham* (page 72)

4 To serve, the different elements of the dish can be arranged on a platter and guests can create their own salads. *Bo bun* can also be prepared in individual portions: To assemble, first place some of the bean sprouts, lettuce, cucumber, and carrots in the bottom of each bowl, then add a handful of herbs and cool vermicelli noodles. Top the whole thing off with slices of the caramelized beef and garnish with a sprinkle of crushed peanuts before drizzling over the *Nuoc Cham* sauce.

LA BAIE D'HALONG

164, avenue de Versailles 75016 Paris
tel: 01 45 24 60 62
métro: Porte de St. Cloud

One of Paris's most innovative Vietnamese restaurants is located on a nondescript avenue in the well-heeled 16th *arrondissement*. Vietnamese-born Nathalie and Roger Leroy (who chose new names when they adopted their French nationality) have created a little gastronomical treasure far from the city's Chinatown.

"The day we opened, Catherine Deneuve walked in. She became one of our most faithful customers," says Nathalie Leroy, who was born in southern Vietnam but uses recipes from all regions of the country. "We also have lots of clients who lived in Vietnam when it was a French colony. They're nostalgic for the food."

Leroy learned to cook when she was a university student, working in the kitchen of a Vietnamese restaurant near Place Maubert for five years. Leroy and Roger, her husband, opened La Baie d'Halong in 1975; she took charge of the kitchen, he mans the floor. They both take tremendous pride in their ability to keep the restaurant in constant evolution. Roger often redecorates the interior, while Nathalie enjoys inventing new dishes within the framework of traditional Vietnamese cuisine. She travels frequently to the Far East and Southeast Asia to keep up with culinary trends there.

Leroy was one of the first Parisian chefs preparing Vietnamese food to move away from presenting dishes in a conventional style. She uses French and even Japanese decorative effects to make her food look more contemporary. Her impeccably fresh and delicious *bo bun* salad has a somewhat architectural aspect, and the vegetables are artfully arranged to show their bright colors.

The Leroys' children are studying the hotel and restaurant business in the United States, and they foresee opening a restaurant there in the near future. Their home base, however, will remain La Baie d'Halong. Roger Leroy explains their success by saying, "You have to love what you do."

VIETNAMESE SPRING ROLLS WITH LIME-PEANUT SAUCE
Rouleaux de Printemps

It's hard to go wrong with these spring rolls, a fixture in Parisian take-outs, which resemble individually wrapped salads. It takes practice to get nice tight rolls, but once they're in a package, they are neat and easy to eat, healthy, and delicious, with just the right balance of crunchy vegetables and lightly seasoned shrimp. Some of the peanut sauce goes inside the rolls to add punch, but be sure to save enough to serve alongside for dipping.

SERVES 5

LIME-PEANUT DIPPING SAUCE

½   cup crunchy peanut butter

¼   cup unsweetened coconut milk

¼   cup lime juice

¼   cup soy sauce

1   tablespoon Asian chili sauce

1   teaspoon Asian sesame oil

1   teaspoon *nuoc mam*

1   clove garlic

1   shallot

    1-inch (2.5 cm) piece of ginger, peeled and minced

1   bird's-eye chili

1   teaspoon vegetable oil

¼   cup roasted peanuts, crushed

1. To make the lime-peanut dipping sauce, combine all the ingredients in the bowl of a food processor and blend until smooth. The sauce can be made 1 day ahead and kept covered in the refrigerator.

2. For the filling, heat the oil in a large skillet over high heat and stir-fry the shallots and garlic until soft, about 30 seconds. Add the shrimp and cook until just pink, about 1 minute. Spoon in the *nuoc mam* and sesame oil and cook, stirring, until the sauce is slightly reduced and the shrimp are well coated, about 1 minute. Transfer to a bowl.

3. To cook the rice vermicelli, bring a large pot of water to a rolling boil. Add the noodles and cook 3 to 5 minutes, giving the pot a stir from time to time. The noodles are done when soft and white but still firm. Drain and rinse in cold water until cool. Transfer to a bowl and, using scissors, cut the noodles into 4- to 5-inch (10–12 cm) pieces.

FILLING

2　tablespoons vegetable oil

2　large shallots, minced

1　clove garlic, minced

1　pound (450 g) shrimp, shelled, deveined, and sliced lengthwise in half

1　tablespoon *nuoc mam*

2　teaspoons Asian sesame oil

5　ounces (140 g) rice vermicelli

VEGETABLE MARINADE

¼　cup rice wine vinegar

1　tablespoon sugar

1　tablespoon salt

1　small seedless cucumber, peeled

1　small carrot, peeled

1　small green papaya, peeled, halved, and seeded (or substitute jicama)

10　6-inch (15 cm), round rice papers

1　head red or green leaf lettuce handful each of fresh mint, coriander, and Asian basil leaves

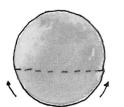

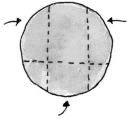

4 In a small saucepan, combine the ingredients for the vegetable marinade and heat over medium heat, stirring until sugar and salt have completely dissolved, 1 to 2 minutes. Pour into a medium bowl and let cool completely.

5 Cut the cucumber, carrot, and papaya into large chunks, then grate on a box grater or in a food processor or julienne using a mandoline. Toss with the cooled marinade. Set aside.

6 To assemble, slip a rice paper into a shallow bowl of warm water. Remove after 10 seconds; it should be moist but still slightly stiff. Lay flat on a work surface lined with a paper towel. Tear off a piece of lettuce leaf the size of your palm and place it on the bottom half of the rice paper. Arrange 3 pieces of shrimp on top of the lettuce, then layer ¼ cup of marinated vegetables, a heaping tablespoon of noodles, and several leaves of mint, coriander, and Asian basil. Last, dribble a tablespoon of lime-peanut sauce over the ingredients. Fold up the bottom of the rice paper over the filling as tightly as possible, then bring in the sides and roll up to form a tight cylinder. Repeat with the rest of the rice papers and filling.

7 The rolls can be prepared 2 hours in advance and kept at room temperature on a tray lined with slightly damp paper towels, covered with plastic wrap. The rolls should not be refrigerated, because this would toughen the rice paper.

8 Slice each roll crosswise in half on a diagonal and arrange on a platter lined with lettuce leaves. Serve with the remaining lime-peanut dipping sauce.

SQUID SALAD WITH RED PEPPERS AND TAMARIND DRESSING
Salade de Calamars aux Poivrons Rouges

Salade de calamars aux poivrons rouges

Served as a starter or a main course, this salad is a flavorful mix of delicate squid and acidic tamarind. Crisp mung bean sprouts add texture. Bright red peppers are a vibrant contrast to the pale squid. This can be largely prepared in advance, adding fresh raw vegetables and herbs before serving. Take care when cooking squid, since it becomes rubbery if overcooked.

SERVES 4

- - - - - - - - - - - - - - - - - - -

2   tablespoons tamarind paste

2   tablespoons sugar

3   tablespoons warm water

3   tablespoons *nuoc mam*

2   tablespoons lime juice

1   bird's-eye chili, seeded and sliced

1   clove garlic, minced

1   pound (450 g) cleaned fresh or frozen squid, thawed if frozen

2   tablespoons vegetable oil

1   red bell pepper cut into julienne strips

2   shallots, minced

½   cup fresh Asian basil, chopped

½   cup fresh coriander, chopped

2   cups fresh mung bean sprouts lettuce leaves for serving

1 To make the dressing, combine the tamarind paste, sugar, and warm water in a bowl. Stir until the sugar has dissolved. Add the *nuoc mam*, lime juice, chili, and half the garlic. Set aside.

2 If using fresh squid, rinse in cold water, then pat with paper towels. Remove the ring of tentacles from each body and cut in half. Slice long tentacles crosswise into 2-inch (5 cm) pieces. Cut the flaps away from the body and slice them into wide strips. Cut the bodies crosswise into ½ inch (1¼ cm) rings.

3 Heat oil in a large skillet until it is hot but not smoking. Quickly stir-fry the strips of red pepper until they start to go limp, about 3 minutes. Remove with a slotted spoon and set aside. Add the squid to the pan, and stir-fry until cooked through, about 2 minutes. Return the red peppers to the pan, add the rest of the garlic and shallots, and cook until the shallots are translucent, about 1 minute. Remove from the heat and immediately pour the dressing over the squid and toss. Set aside to cool. The squid can be prepared up to 6 hours in advance, covered, and kept in the refrigerator until ready to serve.

4 To assemble, toss the chopped herbs and mung bean sprouts with the dressed squid. Serve immediately on a platter or plates lined with lettuce leaves.

WARM LAOTIAN BEEF SALAD
Laap

Manola Jouanneaux, an elegant Franco-Laotian acquaintance, learned to cook in Laos and in France. Her recipes are a perfect fusion of French and Laotian cultures, which she constantly juggles when she entertains. Manola shared the following recipe for beef laap with us after consulting with her Laotian cousin to make sure it was authentic. Laap is one of the national dishes of Laos—a Laotian steak tartare (the meat can be briefly cooked or served raw; in this recipe, the meat is cooked). Laap may be made with fish, chicken, or game, but it is most commonly made with beef. Rice and a basket of fresh vegetables accompany it.

SERVES 6

vegetable oil for frying

4 shallots, 2 thinly sliced, 2 finely minced

1 pound (450 g) ground beef

3 tablespoons *nuoc mam*

juice of 2-3 limes

1 teaspoon salt

1-inch (2.5 cm) piece of galangal (see Glossary), peeled and minced

3 stalks lemongrass, thinly sliced

3 scallions, thinly sliced

2 kaffir lime leaves, veins removed and finely minced

2 bird's-eye chilies, or more to taste

2 cups fresh coriander leaves, roughly chopped

2 cups fresh mint leaves, roughly chopped

5 leaves fresh saw grass (see Glossary), roughly chopped

3 tablespoons roasted rice powder (see Glossary)

GARNISHES

celery stalks (long stalks cut lengthwise in half)

sliced cucumber

Belgian endive leaves

trimmed radishes

Romaine lettuce leaves

1 To fry the sliced shallots, pour oil into a small skillet to a depth of about 2 inches. Heat until hot but not smoking. Sprinkle the shallots over the oil and stir with a slotted spoon to separate and turn. As soon as the shallots become golden brown, remove and drain on paper towels. When cool, transfer to a plate until ready to use.

2 In a large dry skillet, or using a minimum amount of oil, briefly cook the meat, breaking it apart and leaving it rare. Transfer to a bowl and allow the meat to cool just slightly, then stir in the *nuoc mam*, lime juice, and salt.

3 Combine the minced shallots, galangal root, lemongrass, scallions, kaffir leaves, and bird's-eye chilies and mix well. Stir into the warm beef then toss the seasoned meat with the fresh chopped coriander, mint, and saw grass leaves.

4 Transfer the beef salad to a serving bowl. Sprinkle with the ground rice and scatter the fried shallots over the top. Arrange the garnishes on a platter and serve alongside the salad.

SHRIMP AND SUGARCANE SKEWERS
Chao Tom

This wildly popular street food has made its way onto restaurant menus and even into the frozen section of most Asian stores in Paris. Shrimp paste is first grilled on sugarcane skewers, then removed, wrapped in lettuce leaves, and garnished with vegetables and herbs. The sugarcane is not just a substitute for bamboo skewers—its flavor is important to the overall enjoyment of the dish. It should be chewed on (but not actually swallowed), to release sweet cane juice, a perfect balance for the shrimp. While traditionally the shrimp skewers are grilled, they can also be browned in a pan and finished in the oven with similar results.

Chao Tom.

Pâte de tamarin

Sauce d'arachide

1   In a medium bowl, toss the shrimp with the salt. Set aside for 10 minutes. Rinse well with cold water and blot dry.

2   To prepare the sugarcane skewers, rinse the sugarcane well under cold water. Using a large heavy knife, split the sugarcane lengthwise into halves and then again into quarters. Continue slicing the stalks lengthwise until you have 16 skewers. Using a paring knife, carefully peel away the bark from each skewer and trim to a ½-inch (1¼ cm) diameter.

3   Place the garlic, shallots, and bird's-eye chilies in the bowl of a food processor and process to blend. Add the shrimp, ham, lime zest and juice, coriander, rice powder, *nuoc mam*, sugar, and black

MAKES 16 SKEWERS

. . . .

SHRIMP PASTE

1	pound (450 g) shrimp, shelled and deveined
1	teaspoon salt
1	8-inch (20 cm) section sugarcane
2	cloves garlic
2	shallots
2	bird's-eye chilies, seeded and minced
2	tablespoons diced ham
	grated zest of 2 limes
3	tablespoons lime juice
½	cup fresh coriander leaves
1	tablespoon roasted rice powder (see Glossary)
1	tablespoon *nuoc mam*
1	teaspoon sugar
1	teaspoon freshly ground black pepper
1	egg white, beaten until slightly frothy
	vegetable oil for forming skewers and frying vegetable platter: lettuce leaves, cucumber strips, fresh mung bean sprouts, and fresh mint and coriander leaves

PEANUT DIPPING SAUCE

2	cloves garlic
2	teaspoons sugar
1	bird's-eye chili, halved and seeded
½	cup soy sauce
2	tablespoons smooth peanut butter
1	tablespoon tamarind paste
1	teaspoon *nuoc mam*
2	tablespoons lime juice
2	tablespoons roasted peanuts, crushed

pepper and process to a smooth paste. Pour in beaten egg white and process until completely blended.

4 Dip your fingers in a small amount of oil, pinch off about 2 tablespoons of the shrimp paste, and mold evenly into a cylinder around the upper end of a sugarcane skewer, leaving the bottom half exposed for a handle. Repeat with the remaining shrimp paste and sugarcane. Place the skewers on a tray, cover tightly with plastic wrap, and refrigerate for 1 hour.

5 To make the peanut dipping sauce, place all of the ingredients, except for the roasted peanuts, in a blender or food processor and pulse until smooth. The sauce can be made a day ahead and kept covered in a jar in the refrigerator.

6 The traditional method of cooking the skewers is to steam them first for 7 minutes, then grill over medium coals, turning frequently, until browned on all sides (about 7 minutes). For equally good results, preheat the oven to 375°F (190°C). Heat 1 tablespoon oil in a wide skillet and brown the skewers; cook them in several batches so that the skewers are not crowded and can be turned to color evenly. Transfer the skewers to a baking sheet and finish cooking in the oven, 5 to 8 minutes.

7 Meanwhile, pour the dipping sauce into a small bowl and sprinkle with the crushed peanuts. Serve the skewers with the vegetable garnish and dipping sauce.

SALT AND PEPPER SHRIMP WITH COGNAC
Crevettes Sel et Poivre au Cognac

Mei Kwai Lou restaurant is a landmark in the 13th arrondissement. One of the first Chinese restaurants to open, it is now an institution in Chinatown. Peter Cheng, the owner, moved to Paris from Hong Kong with his family as a boy. He learned to cook when his mother was running the restaurant. Monthly trips to London were necessary to buy ingredients unavailable in French markets. Peter now has no trouble finding what he needs just a few streets away. The following recipe is adapted from Peter's salt and pepper shrimp.

SERVES 4

- 1   pound (450 g) medium shrimp in shells
- 2   cloves garlic
- 4   bird's-eye chilies
- 1   teaspoon sugar
- 1   teaspoon Chinese 5-spice powder (see Glossary)
- ¼   teaspoon salt
- ¼   teaspoon freshly ground black pepper
- ¼   cup vegetable oil
- 3   tablespoons Cognac or Shaoxing wine, Chinese rice wine (see Glossary)

1   To prepare the shrimp, using a sharp paring knife, split the shrimp down the backs through the shell, cutting about a ¼ inch (½ cm) into the flesh. Devein with the sharp tip of a knife.

2   Using a mortar and pestle, crush the garlic and chilies to a paste, or blend to a paste in a food processor.

3   Combine the sugar, 5-spice powder, salt, and pepper in a small bowl.

4   To cook, heat the oil in a large skillet. When hot but not smoking, throw in the shrimp and

RESTAURANT

MEI KWAI LOU

1, rue du Moulinet 75001 Paris

tel: 01 45 80 09 95

métro: Place d'Italie

cook 1 to 1½ minutes, or until they just begin to turn pink. Remove the shrimp with a slotted spoon and drain on a paper towel. Drain the oil from the skillet, then return the pan to the heat and add the chili and garlic paste. Cook for 30 seconds, or until fragrant.

5 Return the shrimp to the skillet. Sprinkle liberally with the salt and pepper mixture, shaking the pan to coat well, about 1 minute. Spoon the Cognac or wine over the shrimp, give the pan a swirl to distribute the liquid evenly, and then tilting the skillet away from you, light the alcohol with a match and let it burn until the flame dies out. (If you are using a hood fan above your stovetop, turn it off before flambéing the shrimp.) Serve immediately.

TANG FRERES

Tang Frères began as a modest grocery store in the 1970s. The Rattanawans, a Laotian family originally from China, saw the potential in opening a supermarket in the 13th *arrondissement* catering to the needs of the newly arrived Asian immigrants. Thirty-odd years later, Tang Frères has 500 employees and yearly sales of 150 million euros.

The mammoth supermarket in the 13th is frequented not only by the entire Asian community, but also by anyone looking for succulent mangoes, exotic fresh herbs, innumerable sorts of Chinese soups or sauces, frozen shrimp, dim sum ready for steaming, every variety of rice imaginable, kitchenware, or bonsai—all at unbeatable prices.

There are seven more Tang stores in Paris and its suburbs, along with two Tang restaurants and bakeries. The formidable enterprise regularly sponsors the annual Parisian Chinese New Year festival. The main supermarket boasts 10,000 clients a day.

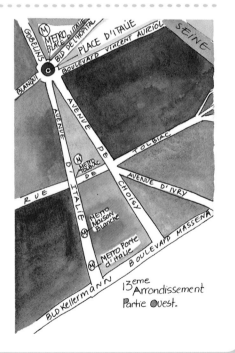

13ème Arrondissement Partie Ouest.

SIZZLING CREPES
Banh Xeo

The best banh xeo we have eaten in Paris are served in a tiny restaurant called Nhu Yen. Similar to omelettes but used like crepes, banh xeo are warm, golden, and crisp on the outside, soft and chewy on the inside. They are cooked with a filling, wrapped in cool crunchy lettuce leaves, and dipped in Nuoc Cham sauce. It's rare to find banh xeo in restaurants, because they must be cooked slowly over a low flame and most kitchens won't sacrifice a burner for making just one dish. Ready-made mixes are available in Asian stores, but if you have the ingredients on hand, happily, they are a snap to make yourself. Made with rice flour and coconut milk, without eggs, these crepes get their warm ocher color from turmeric. The following recipe is inspired by the sizzling crepes at Nhu Yen.

✱ RESTAURANT
NHU YEN
11, rue Philibert Lucot
75013 Paris
tel: 01 45 85 78 44
métro: Tolbiac

1 If using the dried mung beans, soak them in cold water for 2 hours; drain. Steam for 15 to 20 minutes, or until soft.

2 To make the batter, put all the ingredients in a blender and process to mix. Strain through a sieve into a bowl. Set aside. The batter can be

MAKES 6 CREPES

BATTER

⅔ cup cornstarch

1⅔ cups rice flour

1⅓ cups water

1⅔ cups unsweetened coconut milk

1 teaspoon powdered turmeric

½ teaspoon salt

FILLING

¾ cup dried yellow mung beans (optional)

6 ounces (170 g) boneless pork shoulder, cut into thin slices

18 medium shrimp, peeled, deveined, and sliced lengthwise in half

2 tablespoons *nuoc mam*

2 cloves garlic, finely minced

2 shallots, finely minced

1 tablespoon sugar

1 teaspoon freshly ground black pepper

1 onion, thinly sliced

2 cups fresh mung bean sprouts

2 cups thinly sliced mushrooms

vegetable oil for cooking

FOR SERVING

lettuce leaves, fresh Asian basil and coriander leaves

1 recipe *Nuoc Cham* Dipping Sauce (page 72)

made the day ahead and kept covered in the refrigerator; whisk thoroughly before using.

3 For the filling, place the pork and shrimp into separate bowls. Divide the *nuoc mam*, garlic, shallots, sugar, and pepper between them and toss to mix. Cover and let marinate in the refrigerator for 30 minutes.

4 Combine the sliced onion, bean sprouts, mushrooms, and cooled steamed mung beans, if using, in a bowl. Set aside.

5 Heat 1 tablespoon of oil in a 10-inch (25 cm) frying pan over high heat. Add the marinated pork and shrimp and stir-fry until just cooked through, about 2 minutes. Remove to a plate and divide into 6 equal portions.

6 Return the frying pan to the heat, add another tablespoon of oil, and heat until it is hot but not smoking. Whisk the crepe batter, then pour about ½ cup into the pan and swirl the pan to spread the batter evenly. Scatter ⅙ of the pork mixture over the batter and sprinkle about ½ cup of the mixed vegetables on top. Reduce the heat to low, cover and let cook for 5 minutes. Uncover and check the crepe by lifting up one side of it; the bottom should be brown and crispy. Fold the crepe in half like an omelet and slide onto a serving platter. Repeat with the remaining batter and filling.

7 To eat, tear off bite-sized pieces of the crepe, wrap in lettuce leaves with the herbs, and then dunk in the *Nuoc Cham* sauce.

VIETNAMESE SANDWICHES
Bahn Mi

At Thieng Heng, a small hole-in-the-wall, crispy baguette sandwiches are lined up a foot high awaiting the noontime rush. But customers don't come here looking for jambon/gruyère sandwiches; instead, the crush is for the backbone of French meals—the humble baguette—combined with the yin-yang flavors of Vietnam. Spread with mayonnaise and hot chili paste, stuffed with roasted meats or Vietnamese cold cuts, and topped with cool cucumbers, pickled shredded carrots, and citrusy coriander, bahn mi are a perfect fusion of culinary cultures that would make a delicious surprise in a lunch box or on a summer picnic. You can easily assemble them at home.

SERVES 4

PORK

¼ cup sugar

½ cup water

2 tablespoons *nuoc mam*

2 tablespoons soy sauce

2 shallots, coarsely chopped

1 clove garlic, coarsely chopped
   1-inch (2.5 cm) piece of ginger,
   peeled and chopped

2 tablespoons vegetable oil

1½ pounds (675 g) pork tenderloin

VEGETABLES

½ cup sugar

½ cup white vinegar

¼ teaspoon salt

1 seedless cucumber, peeled
   and cut into thin strips

1 carrot, peeled and cut into this
   strips

1 small red onion, thinly sliced

2 baguettes, cut lengthwise
   into 6-inch (15 cm) pieces
   mayonnaise

12 fresh coriander sprigs

2 jalapeño peppers, sliced
   Asian soy sauce (Maggi)

* RESTAURANT

THIENG HENG

50, avenue d'Ivry 75013 Paris

métro: Porte d'Ivry

1 Place the sugar and ½ cup of water in a small heavy saucepan and stir to combine. Bring to boil over medium heat and cook until the mixture has caramelized, turning dark brown, but not burnt, about 10 to 12 minutes. Prepare a cup of hot water and place near the pot. When the caramel is ready, remove the pot from the heat and, holding it away from you to avoid being splattered, add 4 tablespoons of the hot water. This will cool the caramel and stop further cooking. Once the caramel has stopped sputtering, add the *nuoc mam* and soy sauce, swirling the pot to combine. Let cool.

2 Puree the shallots, garlic, and ginger in a blender. Add the oil and caramel mixture and blend to a paste. Place the pork in a dish and brush the caramel paste all over it. Cover with plastic wrap and marinate at room temperature for 30 minutes.

3 Meanwhile, combine the sugar, vinegar, and salt in a large bowl and stir until the sugar dissolves. Add the cucumber, carrot, and onion and marinate at room temperature for 30 minutes. Drain.

4 Preheat the broiler or light a hot fire in a charcoal or gas grill. Place the pork on a broiler pan or on the grill and cook until just done, about 10 minutes on each side. Transfer the cooked pork to a plate, cover with foil, and let rest for 10 minutes. Slice thinly.

5 Lightly toast the cut side of the baguettes. Spread mayonnaise on one half of the bread and top with the grilled meat. Garnish with vegetables, coriander sprigs, and peppers and sprinkle with soy sauce. Press down on the top of the sandwich to compact and serve.

STIR-FRIED GREEN BEANS WITH CHINESE OLIVE PASTE
Haricots Verts avec Pâte Chinoise

This is not a strange fusion of French Provençal and Chinese cuisine, as olives do grow in China in the Canton region, birthplace of so many of the recent Chinese immigrants in Paris. The olive paste, a mixture of pounded olives and mustard greens, is sold in jars in Asian stores. This is a popular vegetarian dish at Sinorama, a large, bustling Chinese restaurant on the border of Chinatown in the 13th arrondissement, but the paste is also delicious combined with stir-fried chicken or pork.

SERVES 4

2   tablespoons oil
1   pound (450 g) green beans, trimmed
½   shallot, finely minced
1   clove garlic, finely minced
2   tablespoons water
3   tablespoons Chinese olive paste with mustard greens
     salt if needed

1 Heat the oil in a wok or large skillet over high heat until hot but not smoking. Add the green beans, shallot, and garlic and stir-fry for 2 minutes. Add water, cover, and let steam 3 minutes.

2 Remove the lid, add the olive paste, and toss well to coat. Taste for seasoning and add salt if necessary. Serve immediately.

RESTAURANT

SINORAMA
135, avenue de Choisy
75013 Paris
tel: 01 44 24 27 81
métro: Tolbiac

MAIN COURSES

HANOI BEEF SOUP
Phô

The list of ingredients is long and there are lots of little steps, but there is nothing technically difficult about making phô. And as the exotic, spice-laden aromas start to waft from the stockpot, you'll realize you're on to something that was well worth the effort. Vietnamese food is all about contrasts, and in this version of phô, long-simmered flank steak, fragrant with cooking spices, is placed in juxtaposition with slices of raw marinated sirloin steak, rapidly cooked to tender perfection by the steaming broth ladled into the bowls.

1 For the broth, place the bones, oxtail, and flank steak in a 12-quart (12-liter) stockpot. Add enough water to cover and bring to a boil. Cook for 5 minutes. Remove from heat; drain the bones and meat in a colander and rinse well with cold water. This initial cooking removes impurities and scum; the flavor of the bones and meat is extracted during the long cooking.

2 Wash the stockpot to remove any residue. Return the bones and meat to the pot, add the 6 quarts (6 liters) water, and bring to a boil. Immediately lower the heat and let simmer, skimming the surface of any fat or scum. The stock should not boil again during the cooking process, or it will become cloudy.

3 Dry-roast the cloves, star anise, cardamom, fennel, coriander seeds, and white peppercorns in a large skillet until they begin to release their fragrance. Remove from the heat and

THANH BINH GROCERY STORE

Thanh Binh
18, rue Lagrange (just off Place Maubert)
75005 Paris
tel: 01 43 54 66 11
métro: Maubert-Mutualité

Just across the river from Nôtre Dame Cathedral, on the Place Maubert, an uneven flight of steps leads down to a small Vietnamese grocery store. It's a place one might easily overlook, but in Vietnamese-Parisian grocery lore, Thanh Binh is a historical monument. When large numbers of Vietnamese students first came to Paris, they settled near Place Maubert, not far from the Sorbonne university. Thanh Binh was the first Vietnamese grocery store to open in a neighborhood that had become symbolic of Vietnamese immigration in the late 1950s.

On each side of the narrow shop are shelves piled high with packages of Vietnamese coffee, tea, Asian sauces, noodles, and canned goods. Sacks of rice are neatly stacked in the back, and a rickety rack containing papayas, mangoes, chili peppers, and other exotic fruit and vegetables creates a division between the two aisles.

Over the years, the astonishing amount of products the small shop managed to cram on its shelves became overwhelming and the family opened another store across the street called Thanh Binh Jeune. They recently converted the second floor of the original shop into a small boutique where they sell elegant silk Vietnamese *ao dai* dresses, pillow covers, and ceramics. The shop also provides a visa service for those traveling to Vietnam.

Thanh Binh Ngo Thi, one of seven siblings, helps run the store that one of her brothers opened in the 1960s. The rest of the family became involved when they arrived in Paris in 1968, fleeing the war in Vietnam. The store was called Thanh Binh because her name means "peace" in Vietnamese.

"These days everyone goes to the 13th to shop!" says Thanh Binh Ngo Thi, smiling. "We have to renew ourselves in order to keep up with the competition."

SERVES 6–8

BROTH

4	pounds (2 kg) beef marrow bones
2	pounds (1 kg) oxtail, cut into 4-inch (10 cm) pieces
1	pound flank steak
6	quarts water
8	whole cloves
5	whole star anise
1	tablespoon fennel seeds
2	tablespoons coriander seeds
2	tablespoons white peppercorns
1	whole black cardamom pod, slightly crushed
2	medium onions, peeled, cut into quarters
2	4-inch (10 cm) pieces of ginger, sliced lengthwise in half
1	whole nutmeg, grated
2	cinnamon sticks
2	stalks lemongrass, bulb end bruised with the side of a heavy knife
2–3	tablespoons *nuoc mam*
2	tablespoons sugar
1	teaspoon salt

BOWL GARNISHES

1	pound (450 g) boneless sirloin beef
	1-inch (2.5 cm) piece of ginger, grated
1	pound (450 g) rice vermicelli
¼	cup sliced scallions
¼	cup fresh coriander leaves
2	medium onions, thinly sliced

ADDITIONAL GARNISHES

sprigs of fresh mint, Asian basil, and saw grass

fresh mung bean sprouts

sliced bird's-eye chilis

lightly crush with the side of a heavy knife or using a mortar and pestle. Set aside.

4 Place the onion quarters and ginger cut side down in the same skillet, set over high heat, and leave to blacken, about 10 minutes. Remove the ginger and set aside. Turn the onions and blacken the other cut surfaces. Remove from heat. Rinse both the onions and ginger under cool water.

5 Place onion and ginger with crushed spices and grated nutmeg in a cheesecloth and tie up into a bundle. Add to the simmering stock, along with cinnamon sticks, bruised lemongrass, 2 tablespoons of *nuoc mam*, sugar, and salt. Let the broth simmer for 1 hour.

6 Test the flank steak—as soon as it is fork-tender, remove and let cool. Continue simmering the broth for 3–4 more hours. If the liquid falls below the bones, add more water.

7 Meanwhile, thinly slice the uncooked beef sirloin. To get really fine slices, put the meat into the freezer for 1 hour; partially frozen, it will be much easier to cut. Rub beef slices with the grated ginger and reserve in the refrigerator until needed.

8 Slice the cooked flank steak into thin, bite-sized pieces. In a bowl, cover the rice noodles with boiling water and leave to soak 10 minutes, or until soft. Drain, then add a little cold water to keep them from sticking.

9 Strain the broth through a fine sieve lined with a double layer of cheesecloth into a clean pot. Adjust the seasoning with additional *nuoc mam*, salt,

and sugar as needed and return to simmer. Keep in mind that the garnishes are not seasoned, so the broth should be boldly flavored.

10 To serve set out 6 to 8 large soup bowls. Brush the ginger off the beef sirloin and divide it and the cooked flank steak among the bowls and top with the sliced scallions, coriander leaves, and thinly sliced onions. Bring the broth up to a rolling boil, then ladle into the bowls. Guests should garnish their own bowls with fresh herbs, mung bean sprouts, chilies, and lime juice to taste.

PHÔ: VIETNAM IN A BOWL

For many, the essence of Vietnamese food is contained in a steaming bowl of *phô*: a simple beef broth with the heavenly aromas of cinnamon, ginger, and star anise. This quintessential Vietnamese dish reflects the strong influences from the country's colonial past. It is said that *phô* was created in Hanoi during the French occupation in the 1880s. Traditionally the Vietnamese ate pork, chicken, and fish. Cows and water buffalo, used in the fields as beasts of burden, were seen as too valuable for daily consumption. But the French appetite for beef meant that red meat began to show up in the markets. Thrifty Vietnamese cooks collected the beef bones left over from steak and *boeuf bourguignon*, threw them into a pot, and cooked up a beef broth to which they added noodles. The name *phô*, which is pronounced like *feu* in French, is thought to come from the name of the broth-based French classic *pot-au-feu*.

Over time, using a French technique to give broths flavor, a little roasted ginger and onion were incorporated in the brew. The last-minute addition of thinly sliced raw meat cooked in the hot broth, as well as the combination of spices, was China's contribution to *phô*.

Eating *phô* is a national pastime in Vietnam and a veritable cult in Hanoi. Paris has its share of *phô* restaurants; we suggest the following locations.

PHÔ 14
129, avenue de Choisy
75013 Paris
tel: 01 45 83 61 15
métro: Tolbiac

RESTAURANT PHÔ BIDA VIETNAM
36, rue Nationale
75013 Paris
tel: 01 53 79 01 61
métro: Nationale

DONG HUONG
14, rue Louis-Bonnet
75011 Paris
tel : 01 43 57 18 88
métro: Belleville

FISH STEAMED IN BANANA LEAVES
Poisson en Papillote de Feuilles de Bananes

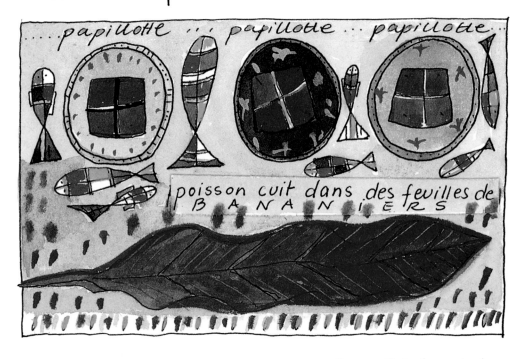

Long before the French invented the term "en papillote," people in other cultures cooked their food wrapped in little packages. Banana leaves are used throughout Southeast Asia for simple steaming. The trick is to make them pliable so they don't tear: cut the leaf into the shape you need, then quickly run it over the heat of a flame— the gas burner on a stovetop works well. The leaf will change color and texture instantly. Wrap up the filling as you would a gift and secure it with toothpicks. Nathalie Leroy, chef and owner of La Baie d'Halong restaurant, makes her fish this way.

SERVES 4

- - - - - - - - - - - - - - - - - - - -

4 white-fleshed fish fillets, weighing about 7 ounces (200 g) each

1 banana leaf

2–3 bunches of bok choy or Chinese broccoli, cut into large bite-sized pieces

1 lime, cut into slices

MARINADE

1-inch (2.5 cm) piece of fresh turmeric or ½ teaspoon powdered turmeric

1 clove garlic, minced

1 shallot, minced

2 teaspoons *nuoc mam*

1 stalk lemongrass, minced

1 teaspoon honey

1 teaspoon vegetable oil

1 If using fresh turmeric, peel, roughly chop, and place it in a mortar with the garlic. Use a pestle to form a paste. Remove to a small bowl and mix with the rest of the marinade ingredients. If using powdered turmeric, simply combine with the other ingredients in a bowl.

2 Place the fish fillets in a shallow dish and rub all over with the marinade. Cover with plastic wrap and marinate in the refrigerator for 30 minutes.

3 In the meantime, wash the banana leaf and wipe dry. With a sharp knife, remove the thick spine of the leaf that runs along one edge. Cut 4 pieces of banana leaf just a little larger than the fillets and set aside. Cut 4 larger pieces big enough to wrap up each piece of fish and run them over a flame as described on the opposite page.

4 Place a handful of bok choy or Chinese broccoli on each of the small leaf squares, lay one of the marinated fillets on top, and garnish with the slices of lime. Spread out one of the larger sections of banana leaf on a work surface, shiny side down. Place a fillet on the large leaf, and then fold up the sides to completely encompass the fish. Secure with toothpicks. Repeat with the other fillets.

5 Cook the packets in a steamer for 15 minutes. To check for doneness, remove one packet and carefully open it. The fish is done when it flakes easily with a fork. Secure the package again with a toothpick and return to the steamer if it needs more cooking.

6 Transfer the packets to a warm platter and serve with sticky rice, noodles, or a salad.

STICKY RICE
Riz Gluant

Sticky rice is generally eaten with one's fingers, as it has the perfect kind of stickiness that adheres to food but not to fingers. The rice is often presented in small bamboo baskets with lids, and bite-sized amounts are pinched off and used to pick up bits of meat or vegetables or to soak up sauces. In Laos, sticky rice (klao niaw) is eaten at every meal.

Short-grained and milky in color, sticky rice is easily distinguished from other varieties. Making up less than 2 percent of the world's annual rice harvest, it is consumed as a staple mostly where it is grown: in Laos, Thailand, and certain areas of Cambodia and Vietnam. Outside of these regions, it is used more commonly as the base for sweet dishes and snacks and as an ingredient for brewing beer.

Sticky rice is not difficult to cook. It is steamed rather than cooked in water. In most Laotian homes, the rice is soaked overnight and set to steam in the morning. Laotians have a special conical bamboo steamer that sits over a pot specifically designed for this purpose. The soaked rice is placed in the steamer, then set over boiling water. Halfway through the cooking process the rice must be flipped, bringing the grains on the bottom up to the top and vice versa. This is not as complicated as it sounds, because the rice at this point can be lifted up in one lump. Sticky rice can also be cooked in an ordinary steamer with perfectly good results. If your steamer has holes larger than the rice, line it with wax paper pierced with holes.

MAKES 6 SERVINGS

1 Soak 2 cups rice in cold water for at least 2 hours, then drain and rinse.

2 Place the rice in a steamer container above boiling water and steam for 35 to 40 minutes. If you are using a traditional Laotian steamer, as described above, turn the rice over halfway through the cooking. If using a regular steamer, use a flat spatula to flip the rice. When properly cooked, the grains should be firm to the bite—the center of the rice should be resistant but not hard.

3 Spread the rice out (traditionally this is done on a bamboo mat) to rest for a few minutes. Fluff by hand before serving (traditionally in covered bamboo baskets).

LAOTIAN CHICKEN CURRY
Curry de Poulet du Laos

This is another of Franco-Laotian Manola Jouanneaux's recipes. It is an incredibly accessible curry, but don't be fooled by its simplicity. The rich coconut milk, strong aromatic herbs, and sweet potatoes give this dish a satisfying originality and great taste.

SERVES 4–6

- 1   cup unsweetened coconut milk
- 2   stalks lemongrass
- 2   tablespoons vegetable oil
- 1   3-pound (1.5 kg) chicken, cut into serving pieces, or 6 chicken thighs, preferably free-range
- 3   shallots, minced
- 3–4 tablespoons good-quality curry powder, to taste
- 2   cups chicken stock
- 3   kaffir lime leaves, torn to pieces
-     3-inch (8 cm) piece of galangal (see Glossary), cut into quarters
-     several coriander roots (or a handful of fresh coriander leaves)
-     salt
- 3   small sweet potatoes, peeled and cut into 2-inch (5 cm) chunks
- 2   tablespoons *nuoc mam*
- 1   cup fresh Asian basil leaves
- 1   cup fresh coriander leaves

1 In a small saucepan, bring the coconut milk to a gentle simmer over low heat and cook until slightly thickened. Remove from heat and set aside.

2 Meanwhile, trim the stalks of lemongrass, cutting away the grassy tips and leaving about 6 inches of stalk attached to the bulb. Using the side of a heavy knife, bruise the bulbs and set aside.

3 Heat the oil in a 5-quart (5-liter) pot until hot but not smoking. Place as many chicken pieces as will fit in the pot without crowding and brown on all sides. Transfer to a plate and repeat with the remaining chicken pieces.

4 Reduce the heat to moderately low, add the shallots, and cook, stirring so they do not burn, about 1 minute. Add the curry powder and cook for about 30 seconds, or until fragrant. Add the reduced coconut milk and the chicken stock and whisk to blend.

5 Return the chicken pieces to the pot, along with any juices that have accumulated. Add the lemongrass, kaffir lime leaves, galangal, coriander roots or leaves, and salt to taste.

Turmeric

galanga

Piments
Rouges.

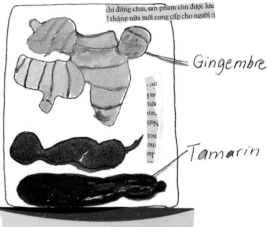

Gingembre

Tamarin

6 Bring to a boil, then reduce the heat to maintain a gentle simmer, cover, and cook for 20 minutes.

7 Remove the cover and, using a slotted spoon, push the chicken pieces aside so you can slide the sweet potatoes under them. Do not be tempted to add more liquid at this point. Let the curry simmer for another 10 minutes and then check; if you feel more liquid is needed, add ½ cup of water. Continue cooking another 15 to 20 minutes or until the potatoes are just tender.

8 Taste for seasoning and add the *nuoc mam*. Garnish with the Asian basil and coriander leaves and serve with sticky or basmati rice.

BEEF TENDERLOIN WITH CRUSHED PEPPER
Filet de Boeuf au Poivre

When researching recipes for this chapter, we kept coming across Maggi soy sauce as an ingredient. Our initial reaction was to dismiss this seasoning hailing from Switzerland, but we eventually realized what a common household item this is in Asia—it is as much of a staple as hoisin sauce or hot chili paste. Used as a condiment, it is sprinkled on everything from steamed dumplings to Vietnamese banh mi sandwiches. Stirred into sauces, it brings complexity to the flavors of the overall dish. In this popular dish served at the restaurant, Sinorama, Maggi soy sauce is quite simply paired with beef.

SERVES 2

- 2 tablespoons vegetable oil
- 1 pound (450 g) beef tenderloin, cut into bite-sized cubes
- 1 tablespoon minced shallots
- 1 teaspoon finely minced garlic
- 2 teaspoons crushed black pepper
- 3 tablespoons Maggi "Taste of Asia" soy sauce

*RESTAURANT

SINORAMA

118, avenue de Choisy
75013 Paris

tel: 01 53 82 09 51

métro: Tolbiac or Place d'Italie

1 Heat the oil in a wok or large skillet until hot but not smoking. Toss in the cubed tenderloin, shallots, garlic, and crushed pepper. Stir-fry 1 to 2 minutes, searing the meat evenly on all sides. Spoon over the Maggi sauce and stir the meat to coat. Let cook 1 more minute, or more according to taste.

2 Remove from heat and let the meat rest 1 minute in the pan. Spoon the meat and sauce into a shallow bowl and serve accompanied by steamed rice.

MONKFISH COOKED IN CARAMELIZED NUOC MAM
Lotte en Caramel de Nuoc Mam

Philippe Tran, chef and owner of the Vietnamese restaurant Le Lai, gave this wonderfully simple recipe to us as we were finishing lunch one day. The flavors of the caramel perfectly complement the dense and meaty monkfish.

SERVES 4

2 tablespoons *nuoc mam*

2 tablespoons sugar

2 pounds (1 kg) monkfish fillet, cut into large bite-sized pieces

1 clove garlic, minced

2 scallions, finely sliced
   freshly ground black pepper

✳ RESTAURANT

LE LAI
24, rue de Javelot 75013 Paris
tel: 01 45 83 83 33
métro: Tolbiac

1 Put the sugar and *nuoc mam* in a wok or large skillet and caramelize slowly over low heat (see method on page 89). When the caramel sauce has reached a rich brown color, raise the heat and add the monkfish. Shake the pan to toss the pieces and coat them with the sauce as they cook, for 7–10 minutes. Add the garlic, scallions, and black pepper to taste.

2 Serve immediately accompanied by a steamed green vegetable and rice.

PARIS CHINOIS

Red lights lit up the Eiffel Tower in 2004 for the Chinese New Year, commemorating the 40th anniversary of Franco-Chinese diplomatic relations. The relationship between the French and the Chinese has waxed and waned over many centuries. Back in 1667, Louis XIV dressed up in Chinese clothing for a costume ball at Versailles. *Chinoiserie,* a style of decoration inspired by Asian themes, was *le dernier cri* in France at the end of the 17th century and for most of the 18th century. This fashion spilled over to the rest of Europe, but France led the way, reproducing Chinese motifs in fabric, wallpaper, furniture, and other objects.

In the late 18th century, to satisfy Queen Marie Antoinette and the Marquise de Pompadour's passion for Far Eastern designs, the royal porcelain manufacturer created a great number of dinner services inspired by Chinese pieces, including exotic teapots with spouts in the shape of serpents.

In 1849, France obtained a concession in the city of Shanghai (which was known at the time as the Paris of the East), and it maintained a French administration there until 1946. The inaugural meeting of the Chinese Communist Party was held in the French Quarter, a neighborhood that today is lined with the leafy plane trees, one of the hallmarks of French colonialism.

Chinese in France

During World War I, more than 140,000 Chinese laborers were brought to Europe, many of them to France. Two thousand lost their lives during the war, and there is even a Chinese cemetery near the Somme River. A fraction of these laborers remained in Paris, establishing the first Chinese community. Immigrants from the Zhejiang region continued to trickle in until the rise of the Communist Party in China put an end to the movement. Other than

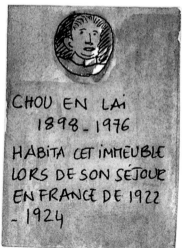

CHOU EN LAI
1898 - 1976

HABITA CET IMMEUBLE
LORS DE SON SÉJOUR
EN FRANCE DE 1922
- 1924

17, Rue Godefroy, Paris 13ᵉᵐᵉ

the arrival of Southeast Asians of Chinese origin, Paris didn't see much immigration from the People's Republic of China until the mid-1980s, when the number of arrivals skyrocketed. Currently, the French government is still struggling to get illegal Chinese immigration under control and is developing a recruitment policy that would be more selective, aiming to attract highly educated immigrants.

During the 1920s, future leaders Zhou Enlai and Deng Xiaoping lived in Paris; it was during this time that Deng Xiaoping joined the Chinese Communist Party. Throughout the 20th century, Chinese artists and intellectuals came to Paris. Painter Zaou Wou Ki has lived in Paris since 1948; Gao Xingjian, the Nobel Prize–winning writer, is now a French citizen; and in 1989, I. M. Pei, the Chinese-American architect, completed what has become an integral part of the Louvre—the pyramid.

The Best Cooks

On the culinary front, Franco-Chinese relations are expanding in leaps and bounds. The Chinese Cultural Center opened in Paris in 2002 and just a year later organized a successful gastronomic festival. This relationship can only have a positive effect on the food-loving capital, which until recently remained the least likely international city in which to find a wide choice of Chinese culinary specialties. This dearth may have been, in part, because as Françoise Sabban, a French historian and cookbook author, writes, "The Chinese and the French, each in their way, have managed to make the entire world believe that they are the only ones who know how to eat and cook."

STEAMED SEA BASS WITH GINGER AND SPRING ONIONS
Poisson à la Vapeur à la Cantonnais

This traditional dish from Canton is one of designer and boutique owner Patricia Wang's favorites when she's cooking for both Chinese and French friends. She finds the combination of flavors equally pleasing to Asian and French palates. A whole fish makes a dramatic presentation, but the dish can also be made with fillets.

SERVES 4

- 1   3-pound (1.35 kg) whole fish (sea bass, turbot, or bream) cleaned and scaled, head left on, or 2 fillets weighing approximately 1½ pounds (675 g) each, with skin
- 3   tablespoons Shaoxing wine
- 2   tablespoons soy sauce
- ½   teaspoon sugar
- ¼   teaspoon freshly ground black pepper
- 1   4-inch (10 cm) piece of ginger, peeled and julienned
- 2   scallions, julienned
- ¼   cup peanut oil
      handful of fresh coriander sprigs

1 Rinse the fish under cold running water and pat dry with paper towels. If using a whole fish, score the skin in a crosshatch pattern. Place the fish in a shallow dish—if using fillets, arrange in a single layer, skin side down. Sprinkle with salt and pepper. Pour 2 tablespoons of the wine over the fish, turning to coat well. Marinate in the refrigerator for as little as 10 minutes, or as long as overnight.

2 Place 2 cups of water in the bottom of a steamer and bring to a boil.

3 Combine the remaining 1 tablespoon wine, the soy sauce, sugar, and black pepper in a bowl.

4 When ready to cook, remove the fish from the marinade and place in the steamer. Cook for 10 to 15 minutes or until the fish flakes easily with a fork. Remove the fish to a shallow heatproof serving dish; if using fillets, arrange skin side up. Pour the soy sauce mixture over the steamed fish, then scatter with the julienned ginger and scallions.

Gingembre

Shaoxing

Huile de sésame

5 Heat the oil in a small saucepan until it is smoking; it is essential that the oil be very hot.

6 Slowly pour the hot oil evenly over the fish. The oil should make a hissing sound as it fries the garnishes and crisps the skin of the fish. Sprinkle the fish with coriander leaves and serve immediately, accompanied by steamed rice.

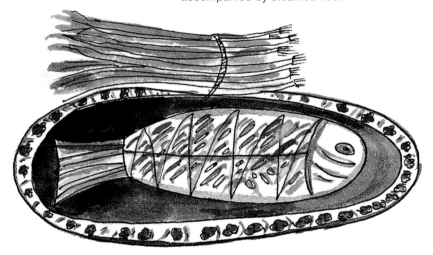

PATRICIA WANG

Patricia Wang was 18 months old when her parents arrived in Paris from the Chinese port of Wenzhou. As Parisian as can be, her stylish boutique, Haili (named after her daughter), is in the Montparnasse area of Paris and carries colorful, hippie-chic women's clothing, bags, and jewelry.

Patricia may be Parisian on the outside, but if the Chinese maxim that you are what you eat is to be believed, then Patricia's inner being is firmly rooted in Wenzhou. Her parents owned several Chinese restaurants and as a child, Patricia and her brother were brought up exclusively on Chinese food.

"We ate rice every day," she says. "Sometimes my brother would say he was tired of eating Chinese food and that he was going to go out and have pizza, but he'd always end up eating Chinese food."

When Patricia left home and started to cook for herself, she realized that she remembered a lot of the gestures she had watched the women in her family make when they were in the kitchen. Her mother still owns a restaurant in Paris and Patricia often stops by for a meal or for culinary advice. She regularly cooks Chinese food but not exclusively.

"I really like couscous, too," she says.

VIETNAMESE SPICED BEEF ROLLED IN LA LOT LEAVES
Bo La Lot

Le Lai restaurant is located on the esplanade of the mammoth Olympiades housing complex in Chinatown. Like most businesses in the neighborhood, it's a family affair, with Philippe Tran's sister helping out in the kitchen. Most dishes served by the Trans are from southern Vietnam, including the following recipe, which is commonly found either in restaurants or as street food in Ho Chi Minh City.

La lot leaves are often sold in Asian shops under their Thai name, cha plu. If you cannot find la lot leaves, substitute grape leaves packed in brine or Japanese shiso leaves; the taste of the dish will differ only slightly, because it's the assertive spices in the beef that dominate. If using grape leaves, be sure to rinse them to remove the taste of the brine. Serve as finger food or as a main course.

MAKES 24 ROLLS

- 1 pound (450 g) ground beef
- 1 teaspoon Chinese 5-spice powder (see Glossary)
- ½ teaspoon ground cinnamon
- ½ teaspoon curry powder
- ½ teaspoon powdered turmeric
- 1 teaspoon finely minced garlic
- 1 teaspoon minced lemongrass
- 1 teaspoon salt
- 1 teaspoon sugar
- 1 teaspoon freshly ground black pepper
- 2 tablespoons roasted peanuts, crushed
- 24 la lot leaves, grape leaves packed in brine, or Japanese shiso leaves
   vegetable oil for brushing
- 1 recipe *Nuoc Cham* (page 72)

RESTAURANT

LE LAI

24, rue de Javelot 75013 Paris
tel: 01 45 83 83 33
métro: Tolbiac

1 Place the ground beef in a bowl with all the ingredients except the la lot leaves. Using your hands or a wooden spoon, mix to thoroughly combine the ingredients. Cover and let marinate for several hours, or overnight, in the refrigerator.

2 To make the rolls, place a la lot leaf shiny side down on a work surface. Pinch off 2 tablespoons of filling, roll into a cigar shape, and place on the bottom half of the leaf. Roll up the leaf, pressing down on the filling with the palm of your hand to form a neat cylinder. If the leaves are large, fold in the edges as you roll them up; with smaller leaves, some of the meat may extend beyond the edges. Thread three rolls at a time crosswise onto skewers, securing the tips of the leaves. Repeat with the remaining leaves and filling.

3 To cook, prepare a medium-hot fire in a grill or preheat the broiler. Grill or broil about 3 minutes per side, or until filling is cooked through.

4 Serve accompanied by the *Nuoc Cham* sauce for dipping.

TAO PORK BRAISED IN COCONUT JUICE
Porc Braisé au Jus de Coco

Tao Restaurant makes this simple yet elegant dish. It is Vietnamese comfort food, as you will discover when the aromas begin to fill your kitchen. Braising requires a long cooking time but very little attention, resulting in perfectly moist and tender pork. The recipe calls for coconut juice, the clear liquid found in the interior of an immature coconut—not to be confused with coconut milk, a liquid made from strained boiled coconut milk and water. Coconut juice, generally packaged with a bit of pulp, can be found canned or in the frozen foods section of stores specializing in Asian products.

RESTAURANT

TAO RESTAURANT
248, rue St. Jacques
75005 Paris
tel: 01 43 26 75 92
métro: Luxembourg

1 Preheat the oven to 325°F (170°C). Place the garlic, shallots, ginger, star anise, and chilies in an ovenproof casserole large enough to hold the meat in one layer. Arrange the pork on top, and set aside.

2 To make the caramel, combine the sugar and water in a heavy pot and bring to a boil. Let the mixture cook until it becomes a golden brown caramel, about 6 to 8 minutes.

SERVES 4

· · · · · · · · · · · · · · · · · ·

3   cloves garlic, halved

2   shallots, halved

    3-inch (8 cm) piece of ginger,
    peeled and cut into quarters

3   whole star anise

2   bird's-eye chilies, halved

2   pounds (1 kg) pork shoulder,
    cut into serving pieces

⅓   cup sugar

½   cup water

3   cups coconut juice

½   cup *nuoc mam*

1   teaspoon Chinese 5-spice
    powder (see Glossary)

    fresh coriander leaves

3 Remove from heat and, holding the pot away from you to avoid being splattered, slowly add the coconut juice and *nuoc mam*. Return to heat and bring to a boil, stirring to dissolve any bits of caramel. Whisk in the 5-spice powder, then pour the hot caramelized liquid over the pork. Cover the dish, place in the center of the oven, and cook for 2 to 3 hours, turning the meat about halfway through the cooking time. The pork is done when it is fork-tender and falling off the bone.

4 To serve, remove the meat to a warm serving bowl and strain over the braising liquid, discarding the solids. Sprinkle with fresh coriander leaves and serve accompanied by steamed rice.

TAO RESTAURANT

· ·

Tao is a small, sleek restaurant near the Luxembourg Gardens. Black banquettes and tables run the length of the room. The walls are decorated with large color photographs of Vietnamese landscapes.

Truong Thanh Tri overlooks the kitchen staff and his customers with engaging grumpiness. In the boat-people exodus, Truong left Hue, Vietnam, as a young man and spent several years in Hong Kong in a refugee camp. He came to Paris in 1989, sponsored by the French government, and began working in Vietnamese restaurants.

Truong has been managing Tao for six years. The menu is a mix of family-style cooking and some typical Vietnamese street food specialties. Dishes are simple and clean tasting, lightly perfumed, and in some cases adapted to the French palate, such as the fresh shrimp salad with mustard vinaigrette and crushed peanuts. *Phô* soup and *bo bun*

salad are offered either as first courses, in small bowls, or as main courses in big bowls.

Truong has had fun with his desserts—besides the usual sticky rice and mango sweets, he offers a first-rate selection of ice cream and sorbets. "Femme Fatale" is grapefruit and passion fruit ice cream with coconut sauce, "Le Général" is coconut ice cream sprinkled with rice alcohol, and "Double Force" is ginger ice cream topped with candied ginger.

DESSERTS

Glace pilée

lait de Coco

Liserons D'EAU

Perles de tapioca

Les trois trésors.

POTIRON.

OEUFS

COCO NUT MILK

BANANAS COOKED IN COCONUT MILK
Nam Van

Ching Mouscadet, a painter, grew up in Laos, lives in Paris, and makes frequent trips to Southeast Asia, where she practices art therapy with underprivileged children. She is also a fervent cook. For the following recipe, which Ching generously gave us, she likes to use the more aromatic small finger or manzano bananas, found in Asian and Hispanic specialty stores. Heating bananas enhances their natural sweetness. Since they are a tender fruit, they cook quickly. Choose slightly underripe bananas for this recipe, because they will hold together better during cooking.

SERVES 6

- 2½ cups unsweetened coconut milk
- 2 tablespoons tapioca pearls, rinsed
- 6–8 small finger bananas or 3–4 medium regular bananas
- ½ cup sugar
- ½ teaspoon salt
- ¼ cup canned corn
- 2 tablespoons sesame seeds

1 In a large saucepan, bring the coconut milk to a boil. Add the tapioca, reduce the heat, and simmer until the tapioca is soft, about 10 minutes.

2 Meanwhile, peel and slice the bananas lengthwise in half. Cut each section crosswise in half if using small bananas, or into thirds if using regular bananas.

3 Once the tapioca is cooked, add the sugar, salt, and corn and mix well. Gently fold in the bananas and continue cooking at a low simmer for 10 minutes. Remove from the heat.

4 Dry-roast the sesame seeds in a small pan until golden brown. Remove and lightly crush in a mortar with the pestle. Ladle the bananas into bowls and serve warm, sprinkled with the seeds.

LAOTIAN PUMPKIN CUSTARD
Flan de Potiron Laotien

Another of Ching Mouscadet's recipes, in which she uses familiar ingredients to turn out an unusual dessert. Coconut custard is baked in hollowed-out pumpkins and then sliced like a cake—the rich yellow custard provides a beautiful contrast to the orange pumpkin and is a delicious surprise when sliced in front of your guests. This dessert is eaten throughout Southeast Asia. If you can't find Asian pumpkins or kabocha squash, small sugar pumpkins work just as well.

SERVES 6

- 1 cup unsweetened coconut milk
- 1 vanilla bean split in half
- 1 cup soft or grated palm sugar (see Glossary)
- ¼ teaspoon of salt
- 5 large eggs
- 1 small Asian pumpkin or kabocha squash, about 2½ pounds (1 kg)

1 Preheat the oven to 325°F (170°C). Wash and dry the pumpkin. Trim the stem, then turn it upside down and cut out a hole about 3½ inches (9 cm) in diameter from the bottom; reserve the cut-out section. The top of the pumpkin, which will now serve as the base, is generally thicker and will hold together better during cooking. Remove the seeds and membranes from the interior, scraping them out with a spoon. Wrap the pumpkin in two layers of aluminum foil, leaving the hole at the top open.

2 In a small saucepan, heat the coconut milk with the split vanilla bean until warm. Remove from heat, add the palm sugar and salt. Stir until the sugar is completely dissolved. In a bowl, whisk the eggs then gradually add the coconut milk and sugar.

3 Set the pumpkin in a deep baking dish. Remove the vanilla bean and pour the custard into the pumpkin, leaving a 1-inch (2.5 cm) gap at the top since the custard will expand while cooking. Replace the top.

4 Pour enough hot water into the baking dish to reach halfway up the side of the pumpkin. Place in the oven and cook for 1¼ hours, or until the custard has set—test this with the tip of a knife.

5 Remove the pumpkin from the baking dish and allow to cool completely, then refrigerate for at least 2 hours, or overnight.

6 To serve, remove the aluminum foil from the pumpkin and slice into wedges.

THREE TREASURES COCONUT DRINK
Boisson à la Noix de Coco des Trois Trésors

Sweetened coconut milk serves as the base for a variety of drinks throughout Southeast Asia. Our favorite, served at the Vietnamese restaurant Le Lai, is a colorful concoction, almost substantial enough to be called a dessert—in fact, it's served with both spoon and straw. As in Vietnamese cuisine in general, beverages play with contrasting flavors and textures—chewy tapioca strips, soft mung beans, and crunchy colored water chestnuts are layered with crushed ice in tall glasses, which are then filled with sugary sweet coconut milk. A colorful paper umbrella is optional.

SERVES 2–4

- ½ cup sugar
- 1 cup boiling water
- 1 cup unsweetened coconut milk
- 1 cup colored tapioca sticks
- 8 canned water chestnuts, rinsed and roughly chopped
- ½ cup of water, colored with 2–3 drops of red food coloring
- 2 tablespoons tapioca flour
- ½ cup canned sweetened mung bean paste
- crushed ice

1 Put the sugar in a small bowl and add the boiling water, stirring to dissolve. Set aside to cool, then use to sweeten the coconut milk to taste.

2 Soak the tapioca in water for 30 minutes; drain. Heat a small pot of water to a gentle simmer. Add the tapioca and cook 10 to 15 minutes, until soft. Stir occasionally to prevent sticking.

3 Soak the water chestnuts in the colored water 20 to 30 minutes, until they are pink. Drain and roll in the tapioca flour. Place coated pieces in a sieve and shake off excess flour.

4 Bring a small pot of water to a boil. Add the water chestnuts and cook until they float, 2 to 3 minutes. Remove with a slotted spoon to a small bowl of cool water and leave for 10 minutes. Drain.

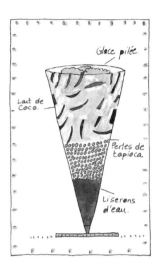

Glace pilée.

Lait de Coco.

Perles de tapioca

Liserons d'eau.

5 To serve, layer the ingredients into tall glasses as follows: 2 tablespoons water chestnuts, crushed ice, 2 tablespoons mung bean paste, crushed ice, ¼ cup tapioca, and crushed ice. Pour the coconut milk over, and serve immediately.

SWEET STICKY RICE WITH COCONUT AND MANGO
Riz Gluant Sucré et Parfumé Manques

Sweet sticky rice with fresh fruit is a classic dessert from a region not known for elaborate sweets. In this recipe, we have paired the sweet rice with mangoes, but any tropical fruit will do. The cream isn't authentic, but it gives a nice French touch.

SERVES 6

- ½ cup sticky rice
- 2 cups unsweetened coconut milk
- 2 tablespoons plus 1 teaspoon of sugar
  pinch of salt
- 1 vanilla bean, split in half
- 3 tablespoons heavy cream
- 1 teaspoon light brown sugar
- 1 ripe mango, peeled and pitted

1 Soak the rice in cold water for 2 hours, or overnight. Drain, rinse, and steam as described on page 99. Remove to a large bowl.

2 Put the coconut milk, sugar, salt, and vanilla bean in a small pot and heat until boiling. Pour over the cooked rice and stir to mix, then cover and let stand for 15 minutes. Stir the cream into the rice. Let cool. To serve, remove the vanilla bean, spoon rice into a bowl, sprinkle with the brown sugar, and garnish with slices of the mango.

JAPON

TOFU

F DAMAME

PÂTE de MISO

NOUILLES SOBA AVEC TRANCHES DE MAGRET DE CANARD FUMÉ

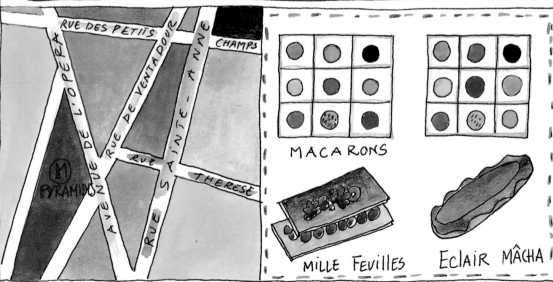

RUE DES PETITS CHAMPS

RUE DE VENTADOUR

RUE SAINTE-ANNE

AVENUE DE L'OPÉRA

RUE SAINTE-THÉRÈSE

PYRAMIDES

MACARONS

MILLE FEUILLES

ECLAIR MÂCHA

CHO

OCHO

HOCHO

BENTO

AVETS

UMON

Dinah Diwan 2006

WAITING FOR WAGASHI: JAPAN

"No Japanese, however humble, would think of serving food on just any old plate, relying on flavor alone to please. Each item is an artistic composition in which the receptacle, the food, and its arrangement are all carefully brought together to complement one another. The whole meal is a composition too—a symphony of carefully orchestrated flavor, color, texture, and seasonal appropriateness."

—Shizuo Tsuji, "Japanese Cooking: A Simple Art"

THE LOVE OF JAPONISME

Why include a separate chapter on Japanese food in Paris? The French capital is an axis around which revolves a very special 35-year-old culinary relationship that developed between the two countries and that was the catalyst for French nouvelle cuisine. The French and the Japanese are mutually fascinated by each other's cooking, in part, perhaps, because their cuisines are diametrically opposed and each has so much to learn from the other.

Furthermore, Paris has always represented a mythical city for the Japanese, containing the key to cultural knowledge. Japanese began coming to France in the 19th century, and in turn, the French became enthralled with all that was Japanese. "Japan had recently been opened to Europeans. Japan was fashionable; all they talked about was Japan, it was a real craze. So the idea of writing a Japanese piece occurred to us," French composer Camille St.-Saëns wrote in his *Musical Memories*, on why he composed the operetta *La Princesse Jaune* (*The Yellow Princess*) in the 1870s.

Impressionist and post-Impressionist painters were greatly influenced by *Japonisme*, and it was during this time that the Paris landmark La Pagode was built. The director of Le Bon Marché department store commissioned an architect to build an exact replica of a Japanese pagoda for his wife, who then held lavish balls in the ornate structure. Newly renovated, La Pagode has been a mythical cinema for years, with a quiet bamboo-filled garden.

In the 1920s and '30s, Japanese artists such as the painter Foujita and the photographer Nakayama Iwata, as well as writers and intellectuals, settled in Paris. Most of the Japanese community left at the onset of World War II but returned in the 1950s. Paris remained a cultural beacon for the Japanese. In an article written in 1946, the novelist Naoya Shiga recommended that Japan adopt French as its national language.

In the 1960s and '70s, Japanese fashion designers took Paris by storm with Kenzo, Issey Miyake, and Kansai Yamamoto at the

DEBA HOCHO

NAKiri HOCHO

SASHiMi HOCHO

forefront. At the same time, both countries became interested in each other's cuisine.

UNDER THE SPELL

In Japan, French cuisine is venerated, and working in a French restaurant has become almost a rite of passage for young Japanese chefs. There are myriad French restaurants in Japan now, run by French-trained Japanese chefs, as well as branches of Paris restaurants such as Alain Ducasse's Spoon and Joël Robuchon's l'Atelier. Didier Chantefort, an executive chef at the Cordon Bleu headquarters in Paris, says that in 50 years, the best French cuisine will come out of kitchens in Japan. "French food is at its best in Japan now," asserts Elisabeth Takeuchi, who co-authors cookbooks with her Paris-based husband, and *kaiseki* (a cuisine for grand occasions) specialist, chef Hisayuki Takeuchi.

Paris, too, is under the spell of the Japanese chefs who are, in the words of the *New York Times*, "out-Frenching the French."

Chefs Hiroyuki Hiramatsu of Hiramatsu restaurant and Tateru Yoshino of Stella Maris are both passionate about French cuisine. Hiramatsu and Stella Maris rival the top French restaurants in Paris, with Yoshino's restaurant winning a coveted Michelin star last year. The winner of the 2006 French dessert championship was none other than a Japanese woman: the Plaza-Athenée's pastry chef, Mari Tanaka.

JAPANESE TECHNIQUES

French chefs, in turn, searching for something new, discovered Japanese cuisine 30-odd years ago when they traveled to Japan, but they also learned from the young Japanese chefs in their own kitchens. Parisian chefs began to adopt Japanese techniques, arranging food aesthetically and in tiny portions: Japan became the primary source of inspiration for contemporary French gastronomy.

The French continue to integrate Japanese ingredients and style into their cooking. Recently a group of young French chefs belonging to an association called Generation C made a trip to Japan to learn secrets from chefs in Kyoto. Paris has also enabled resident Japanese chefs the freedom to invent personal styles, taking the best from both French and Japanese cuisine. For Hisayuki Takeuchi, his cooking has no label—it's a highly personal cuisine, one that he dreams up while snacking on green tea madeleines.

Mariko Ueno, a Cordon Bleu graduate, created a new concept: *wa-fumi*—Japanese dishes adapted to French palates. Ueno uses

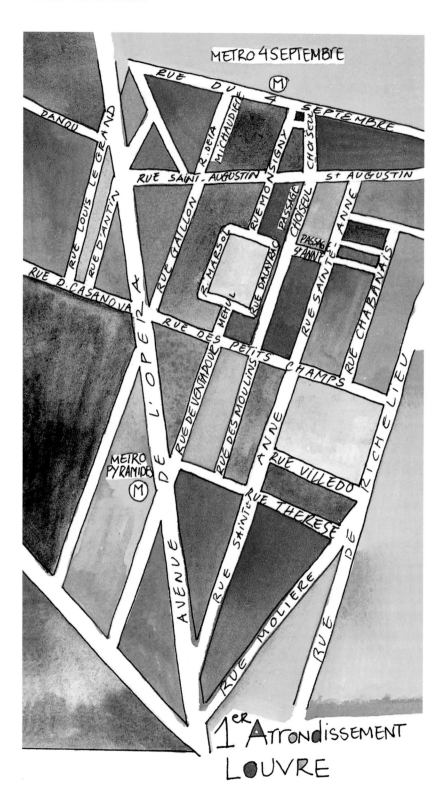

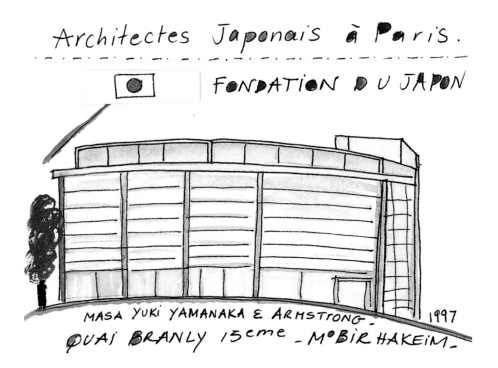

Architectes Japonais à Paris.

FONDATION DU JAPON

MASA YUKI YAMANAKA & ARMSTRONG.   1997
QUAI BRANLY 15eme - M° BIR HAKEIM.

French and Japanese products together, producing dishes like *magret de canard* with a shoyu flavoring, or figs with port and oshiruko sauce.

JAPANESE RESIDENTS

Approximately 25,000 Japanese live in France today, about three quarters of them in the greater Paris area. Unlike many immigrants, the Japanese who have decided to settle in Paris live here by choice, not for economic reasons, or were sent to work in France by their companies. The Japanese neighborhood in Paris is not far from the Opéra Garnier, in the 1st and 2nd *arrondissements*, where real Japanese restaurants abound, as opposed to "Japanese" restaurants owned and operated by Chinese, which are all over the city.

The 11th *arrondissement* has become the center for manga bookstores. France is paradise to comic-book lovers, and Japanese mangas fit right in, with certain streets in the neighborhood packed with manga-crazy Parisians.

The French are increasingly interested in Japanese culture. With the opening of La Maison de la Culture du Japon à Paris in 1997, right by the Eiffel Tower, and the Paris guidebook *Paris Nippon*, focusing on all that is Japanese in the city, well into its third edition, it's certainly a trend that shows no sign of abating.

APPETIZERS

TOFU THREE WAYS:
Hiyayakko, Yudofu, et Atsuage-tofu

If you live in a community with a large Asian population you may be able to find high-quality handmade tofu, like Akira Suzuki's in Paris. Freshly made, tofu has a custardlike texture and a delicate, nutty taste best appreciated when served simply. Akira Suzuki chose the following recipes for us as the best ways to enjoy the soft and subtle flavors of tofu.

WARM WINTER TOFU Yudofu

When the weather turns cool, tofu is simmered in a simple broth, then dipped in sauce. Japanese cooks prepare this dish in an earthenware pot that is heated at the table. A fondue pot works just as well.

SERVES 4

1   6-inch piece konbu (see Glossary)
2   blocks firm tofu, about 14 ounces (400 g), each cut into 5–8 pieces
5   cups water

DIPPING SAUCE

2   cups dashi (page 129)
⅓   cup soy sauce
1   tablespoon mirin

TOPPINGS

     chopped scallions
     dried bonito flakes

1 Wipe the konbu with paper towel to remove any sand, leaving any white powdery substance: this adds flavor to the braising liquid. Place the clean konbu in the bottom of a fondue pot along with the tofu pieces. Gently pour the water over the tofu. Bring to a low simmer.

2 Combine ingredients for dipping sauce. When the tofu is hot, diners should remove the pieces one by one, dip into sauce, and garnish with the various toppings.

COLD SUMMER TOFU Hiyayakko

In the summer months, fresh tofu is seasoned with various garnishes and served ice-cold. Feel free to use all or just some of the toppings.

SERVES 4

2 blocks firm tofu, about 14 ounces (400 g)

GARNISHES

2 scallions, chopped
1 teaspoon grated ginger
   thinly sliced shiso leaves
   handful of bonito flakes
   soy sauce

1 Taking care not to break the blocks, place the tofu in a bowl of cold water. Refrigerate to chill completely.

2 When ready to serve, drain the tofu and transfer to a serving plate. Slice each block in half and scoop out a hole in the top of each piece. Fill the holes with a bit of each of the garnishes and sprinkle with soy sauce.

FRIED TOFU WITH GRATED GINGER Atsuage-tofu

For this recipe, firm tofu is drained and pressed to remove excess moisture. After frying, the tofu can be eaten on its own or tossed with stir-fried vegetables.

SERVES 4

- 2 blocks firm tofu, about 14 ounces (400 g)
  vegetable oil for deep-frying
  soy sauce
  grated ginger

1 Wrap the tofu in paper towels and place on a slightly inclined cutting board or flat plate, set in a shallow pan to catch the runoff liquid. Place another plate on top of the tofu and top with a weight to press out the excess liquid. Leave for 1 hour in a cool place, or refrigerate overnight. The tofu will be compressed and several ounces lighter.

2 Remove the paper towels and blot the tofu dry. Cut each block in half.

3 To deep-fry, pour 2 or 3 inches (6 cm) of oil into a deep saucepan and heat to 350°F (180°C). Slide the pieces into the hot oil and cook until golden brown, about 2 minutes. Drain on paper towels and serve, garnished with a sprinkling of soy sauce and grated ginger.

SUZU TOFU

A few years ago, an intrepid 60-year-old Japanese businessman, Akira Suzuki, had concluded that there were no Japanese making tofu in France. He wanted to create additive-free and delicious tofu. After taking tofu-making courses in Japan, it took him 250 tries and 1½ tons of soy to get the curdling process just right.

The sole employee of Suzu Tofu, Suzuki produces about 400 blocks of tofu a week, which he sells to two Japanese grocery stores and two restaurants in Paris. Suzuki's tofu is expensive, since he imports all his ingredients from Japan. But those who buy it swear by it, and Suzuki is confident that he will increase production to 3,000 blocks of tofu a month.

SAVORY EGG CUSTARD
Chawan Mushi

The Japanese eat a tremendous amount of dishes made with eggs, and chawan mushi is one of their favorites. Served at the beginning of a meal or as side dish, chawan mushi is considered a soup, but it has a soft, fluid texture somewhat between custard and a crème brûlée. Azabu restaurant, in the 6th arrondissement, serves this delicately flavored and elegant dish as an amuse-bouche garnished with seafood. This is based on their recipe.

chawan mushi

SERVES 4

- 4 medium shrimp, shelled and deveined
- 2 cups dashi (see page 129)
- 1 teaspoon light soy sauce
- 1 tablespoon mirin
- 1 teaspoon salt
- 3 eggs
- 2 shiitake mushrooms, stemmed and sliced

  sprigs of fresh parsley

1 Blanch the shrimp for 30 seconds in boiling salted water. Drain and pat dry.

2 Combine the dashi, soy sauce, mirin, and salt in a small bowl. Beat the eggs lightly in another bowl, trying to avoid forming air bubbles. Stirring gently but constantly, add the dashi mixture in a thin stream.

3 Divide the shrimp and sliced mushrooms among four individual ½-cup ramekins. Gently ladle the egg mixture into the cups, filling them to ½ inch (1½ cm) from the rim.

✳RESTAURANT

AZABU

3, rue André Mazet 75006 Paris

tel: 01 46 33 72 05

métro: Odéon

4 Place the ramekins over boiling water in a steamer, cover with a paper towel (which will absorb water droplets), and steam over high heat for 3 minutes. Reduce the temperature to low and continuing steaming for another 10 minutes, or until a toothpick inserted in the middle of the custard comes out clean.

5 The custards can be served warm or cool, garnished with sprigs of parsley.

DASHI STOCK

Dashi is one of the fundamental building blocks of Japanese cuisine, but fresh dashi, like fresh chicken stock, is rarely made today. Most people today use *dashi-no-moto* (instant dashi).

There are many different types of dashi, but the basic broth, *ichiban dashi*, is quickly made from konbu (dried kelp) and *katsuo-bushi* (dried bonito flakes). If you decide to make your own, the procedure is simple, but there are a few important tricks to remember:

• Always begin with cold water, and do not let it boil, because this would cause the stock to become murky or even slimy.
• Remove the stock from the heat before adding the bonito flakes. Strain the stock 3 or 4 minutes after adding the flakes, or it will have a bitter fishy taste.
• Dashi is best used the day it is made, but it can be kept refrigerated for up to 3 days.

To make fresh *ichiban dashi*, lightly wipe a 5-inch (12 cm) square of konbu to remove any sand and grit, leaving the white powdery substance, which will add flavor to the broth. Put the konbu in a pot with 6 cups of water and soak for 10 to 15 minutes.

Place the pot over medium heat and bring almost to a boil; take it off the heat as soon as small bubbles begin to break the surface of the water. Remove the konbu. Sprinkle 1 cup *katsuo-bushi* (dried bonito flakes) over the broth, but do not stir. The flakes will begin to sink to the bottom of the pot. After 3 to 4 minutes, strain the broth through a cheesecloth or coffee filter.

If you are using instant dashi, don't be surprised if the flavor is intense. To make the flavor taste less concentrated, boil the granules or liquid instant substitutes for at least 1 minute, skimming off the foam.

GREEN BEANS WITH SESAME-MISO SAUCE
Haricots Verts en Sauce Sésame et Miso

Slim, elegant haricots verts show up everywhere in France and there seems to be no limit to the variety of ways they can be dressed up. Hirohiko Awano, the creative chef and owner of Kirakutei restaurant, cuts his beans into bite-sized pieces and tosses them with this healthy, delicious dressing.

SERVES 4

1 pound (450 g) green beans, cut into bite-sized pieces

SESAME-MISO SAUCE

⅓ cup rice wine vinegar

2 tablespoons white miso

2 tablespoons dark miso

2 tablespoons ponzu sauce

2 teaspoons grated ginger

1 tablespoon sugar

2 tablespoons sesame seeds, lightly toasted, plus more for garnish

1 teaspoon Asian sesame oil

2 tablespoons mirin

1 tablespoon sake

1 Bring a large pot of salted water to a boil. Add the beans and cook, uncovered 4–6 minutes: the beans should be tender but still slightly crunchy. Drain in a colander and rinse with cold water to stop the cooking.

2 To make the sauce, combine all the ingredients in a blender and process until smooth.

3 Place the beans in a salad bowl, drizzle with the sauce, and gently toss. Taste for seasoning. Sprinkle with sesame seeds and serve.

✳ RESTAURANT

KIRAKUTEI
38, 40 rue Pernety 75014 Paris
tel: 01 45 42 33 15
métro: Pernety

38,40 Rue Pernety, 75014 Paris.

WAKAME SEAWEED SALAD
Salade d'Algues Wakame

The Japanese have a variety of vinegary salads called sunomono. These healthy salads, which do not use oil, can be composed with any variety of vegetables. Crab, shrimp, and calamari are popular additions. This version was given by Yugi Ishii, a Japanese hair stylist living in Paris, who spends his free time cooking.

SERVES 4

1½ pounds (750 g) cleaned squid
1 large seedless cucumber
1 teaspoon coarse salt
2 tablespoons dried wakame

VINAIGRETTE

⅓ cup rice vinegar
1 tablespoon soy sauce
1 tablespoon sugar
1 tablespoon cold dashi (optional, see page 129)
½ teaspoon grated ginger

2 teaspoons toasted sesame seeds

1 Rinse the squid in cold water, then pat dry with paper towels. Remove the rings of tentacles from the bodies and cut in half. Slice long tentacles crosswise into 2-inch (5 cm) pieces. Cut the flaps away from the body and slice into wide strips. Cut the bodies crosswise into ½-inch (1½ cm) wide rings.

2 Bring a large pot of salted water to a boil. Add the squid and cook 40–60 seconds, or until just opaque. Drain in a colander and rinse with cold water. When cool, pat dry and set aside.

3 Cut the cucumber lengthwise in half, then thinly slice. Transfer the slices to a bowl and toss with the salt. Let sit 10–15 minutes. Meanwhile soak the wakame in cold water for 10 minutes. Drain the wakame and chop.

4 To make the vinaigrette, mix the ingredients in a small bowl; stir well to dissolve the sugar.

5 Transfer the cucumber slices to a colander and rinse with cold water. Drain and press lightly to squeeze out excess liquid. Put the cucumber, wakame, and squid in a bowl. Toss with the vinaigrette and sprinkle with sesame seeds.

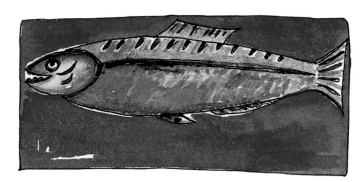

SPRING TURNIPS WITH SMOKED SALMON
Navets Primeurs au Saumon Fumé

Fresh, young turnips are a popular vegetable in Japan, often eaten raw with just a simple dressing. In Paris, small, tender turnips appear in the markets from February to June, sold in bunches with their bushy leaves still attached. Akiko Ida, one of France's top food photographers, gave us this recipe for a spring salad.

SERVES 4

1 pound (450 g) small turnips
1 teaspoon salt

VINAIGRETTE
3 tablespoons olive oil
3 tablespoons lemon juice
1 teaspoon grainy mustard
½ teaspoon minced garlic
½ teaspoon sugar
1 tablespoon chopped fresh parsley

3 ounces (125 g) smoked salmon, cut into small cubes
½ onion, thinly sliced

1 Peel the turnips and thinly slice. Place in a bowl, sprinkle with the salt, and leave for 10–15 minutes. Transfer to a colander to drain off any water.

2 To make the vinaigrette, whisk together all the ingredients in a serving bowl large enough to hold the salad.

3 Add the turnips, salmon, and onion to the bowl and toss well. Cover with plastic wrap and refrigerate for 30 minutes before serving.

AKIKO IDA MINIMIAMS

Akiko Ida wasn't a typical teenager. Her room, in the Gunma province of Japan, 125 miles northwest of Tokyo, was crammed with cookbooks. She would come home from school and bake—muffins, cakes, pastries, and bread. She experimented, learning that if she changed the proportions of the butter, sugar, or flour, the texture was different.

"I began to photograph the results as well as note the ingredients," says Akiko, seated in the Wepler Brasserie in northern Paris. "Soon I began to think more and more about the photographs, and I paid great attention to the lighting." Today Akiko is one of France's top food photographers, with more than 30 cookbooks for Marabout Editions to her credit in five years.

After high school, Akiko put her passion for cooking on hold to study sculpture in Tokyo. She then came to Paris, where she studied photography and met her Burgundian husband, Pierre Javelle, also a photographer. In 2002, Akiko and Pierre, gourmet and gourmand, respectively, created a concept in foodscape architecture, which they call the *minimiams*, or "miniyums." Using tiny hand-painted figurines from model railway stores, the couple assembles and photographs the *minimiams* to give a poetic and humorous vision of food: a shepherd, his dog, and a flock of sheep are assembled atop a cauliflower; monks perch in a circle on a *religieuse*, a French pastry often made with éclairs; tiny soldiers make their way through a forest of sea urchins; and a father pulls his child on a sled in a bowl of snow-white whipped cream.

GRILLED SEA SCALLOPS WITH SAKE AND SOY SAUCE
Coquilles Saint-Jacques au Sake

Hirohiko Awano, photographer, cameraman, and now chef, stands behind the tiny sushi counter in his squeaky-clean restaurant, Kirakutei (see page 130), creating dishes as appealing to the eye as to the palate. His specialty is sushi and this shows here in his delicate treatment of grilled scallops, lightly cooked with a minimum of ingredients, showcasing their sweet natural flavor. This recipe uses fresh scallops; look for those sold whole or prepared in the shell. Soy sauce can be too strong for certain seafood dishes. Seasoning soy sauce with mirin and sake mellows its intense flavor. The resulting brew can be used in any dish that calls for soy sauce.

SERVES 4

- 4 sea scallops with curved shell reserved, if available,
- ¼ cup sake
- shichimi (see Glossary)
- Seasoned Soy Sauce (see opposite page) or regular soy sauce

1 Preheat a broiler. With a very sharp paring knife, cut 4 deep crosswise parallel slices into each scallop, then turn the scallop and cut 4 more slices perpindicular to the first ones. The crosshatched scallops will open up like flowers.

2 Place one scallop in each of the reserved shells, or in ½-cup ramekins, cut side up. Spoon 1 tablespoon sake over each scallop and sprinkle with shichimi. Place on the broiler pan and cook 2–3 minutes, until just opaque.

3 Remove and sprinkle with soy sauce. Serve immediately.

SEASONED
SOY SAUCE

. . . .

1 cup sake

1¼ cups mirin

1 8-inch (20 cm) square konbu
(see Glossary)

1½ quarts (1½ liters) soy sauce

1 In a small saucepan, bring the sake and mirin
to a boil then reduce for 5–8 minutes.

2 Meanwhile, wipe the konbu with a soft cloth
to remove any sand and grit, leaving any white
powdery substance. Put the konbu and soy sauce
in a medium saucepan and bring almost to a boil;
take it off the heat as soon as small bubbles begin to
break on the surface of the liquid. Remove.

3 Pour the contents of the two pans into a bowls
and let sit overnight. Strain the soy sauce and
pour into a jar or other container. The soy sauce can
be kept refrigerated for up to 1 month.

POTATO KOROKKE
Croquettes de Pommes de Terre

This is Japanese comfort food, widely eaten in restaurants in Japan as well as in Paris. Potato korokke are also a mainstay of bento boxes, the Japanese lunchboxes. Sayuri Kigure, Cordon Bleu graduate and now chef at one of Paris's oldest Japanese restaurants, near the Opéra, suggests serving korokke with tonkatsu sauce (available in Asian markets) or mayonnaise for the full effect.

SERVES 4

- 1   pound (450 g) potatoes
- 1   tablespoon vegetable oil
- 1   onion, minced
- 4   ounces (110 g) ground pork
- 1   teaspoon salt
- ½   teaspoon freshly ground black pepper
- ½   teaspoons grated nutmeg
- 1   teaspoon soy sauce
- 1   egg
- ½   cup all-purpose flour
- 2   cups panko breadcrumbs (see Glossary)
       vegetable oil for deep-frying
       tonkatsu sauce

1 Boil the potatoes in their skins until tender. Drain and peel while still hot. Before they cool, press the potatoes through a ricer into a medium bowl; or mash with a fork or potato masher. (If you wait until the potatoes cool, they will become sticky.)

2 Heat the oil in a large skillet and sauté the onion until translucent. Add the ground pork and cook until browned. Season with the salt, pepper, and nutmeg. Take off heat and add to the mashed potatoes, then add the soy sauce and mix well. Let cool.

3 Oil your hands and divide the potato mixture into 8 parts. Pat each portion into an oval, a little larger than an egg.

★ RESTAURANT

TAKARA
14, rue Molière 75001 Paris
tel: 01 42 96 08 38
métro: Opéra

4 Beat the egg with 2 tablespoons of water in a shallow bowl. Spread the flour and panko onto separate plates. Dredge the croquettes in the flour, shaking off excess, dip in beaten egg, and roll in the panko breadcrumbs to coat evenly.

5 Heat the oil to 350°F (180°C) in a large deep pan. Add the croquettes and cook until golden brown. Remove with a slotted spoon onto paper towels. Serve warm, accompanied by tonkatsu sauce (see Glossary).

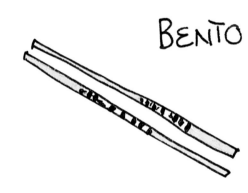

BENTO

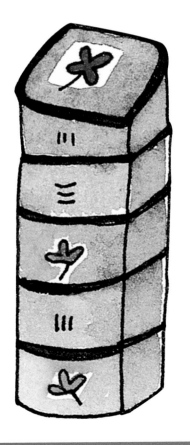

BENTO BOXES

Every day millions of Japanese pack their lunches for school or the office in bento boxes. These boxes range from plastic decorated with animated characters for children to ones that are functional or trendy. In some restaurants, meals are served in bento boxes as well. These are often lacquered, with many compartments, which might contain, as a typical lunch, rice, pickles, *potato korokke*, meat, and vegetables.

MAIN COURSES

SALMON HOT POT
Ishikari Nabe

Yugi Ishii, a Japanese gourmet who owns an elegant hairdressing salon in the Latin Quarter, gave us this recipe for a regional specialty he ate growing up. The Ishikari River in northern Hokkaido is known for its salmon. Nabe is a Japanese hot pot. Combine the two, and you get a delicious family dish that is eaten especially during the winter.

SERVES 4

- 4 ounces (100 g) udon noodles
- 2 quarts (1 liter) dashi
- 1 medium carrot, peeled and sliced into rounds
- 1 2-inch (5 cm) chunk of daikon, peeled and sliced thinly
- 5 napa cabbage leaves, sliced
- 4 ounces (100 g) spinach leaves, washed
- 6 shiitake mushrooms, stemmed and sliced
- 6 oyster mushrooms, sliced
- ¼ cup miso, white or red
- 1½ tablespoons sugar
- 3 tablespoons mirin
- 1 pound (450 g) skinless salmon fillet, cut into 1-inch (2.5 cm) cubes
- 1 pound (450 g) firm tofu, drained and cubed

1 Cook the udon noodles according to the package directions. Drain, rinse, and set aside.

2 Pour the dashi into a large pot and bring to a simmer over medium-high heat. Add the carrot and daikon and simmer for 10 minutes, or until almost tender. Add the cabbage, spinach, and mushrooms and simmer 2–3 minutes, until spinach is wilted.

3 Meanwhile, spoon the miso into a sieve and dip the sieve into the hot dashi to dissolve it into the soup. Miso can vary greatly in terms of saltiness and strength, so taste the broth as you add the miso and add it according to taste.

4 Stir in the sugar and mirin. Add the salmon and continue cooking until the salmon is cooked through. Add the tofu and remove from heat.

5 Divide the noodles among individual serving bowls. Using a slotted spoon, portion out the salmon, vegetables, and tofu over the noodles. Ladle the steaming broth into the bowls and serve.

GINGERED SALMON
Saumon au Gingembre

Hisayuki Takeuchi began his career as a chef cooking French food in Tokyo before moving to Paris, where he was chef in a variety of Japanese restaurants. French chefs were eager to work with him, but he remained on his own to develop a "futuristic cuisine without the confines of nationality." With his wife, Elisabeth, Hissa, as he's known, runs what he calls a "labo-resto," implying a laboratory within a restaurant. The following recipe was adapted from his website, www.kaiseki.com, on new Japanese cuisine.

SERVES 4

- 1½ pounds (600 g) skinless salmon fillet, cut into bite-sized pieces
- 1 ounce (30 g) dried bonito flakes
- 1 cup plus 2 tablespoons potato starch
- ¼ cup soy sauce
- 1 1-ounce (30 g) piece of ginger, peeled and finely grated
- salt and freshly ground black pepper
- vegetable oil for deep-frying
- lemon wedges
- sea salt

★ RESTAURANT

KAISEKI-SUSHI
7 bis, rue André Lefèbvre
75015 Paris
tel: 01 45 54 48 60
métro: Charles Michel ★

1 Place the salmon in a bowl. Sprinkle with the bonito flakes and 2 tablespoons of the potato starch, then add the soy sauce, ginger, and salt and pepper to taste. Mix well and let marinate 30 minutes to 1 hour.

2 Heat the oil to 350°F (180°C) in a large deep pot. Meanwhile, spread the remaining 1 cup potato starch on a plate. Roll the salmon pieces in it one by one so they are well coated, then shake to remove excess starch.

3 Cook the salmon in the hot oil until lightly browned, 1–2 minutes. Remove and drain on paper towels.

4 Serve with steamed rice and season with lemon wedges and sea salt.

SCALLOPS WITH A SHISO AND WASABI CRUST
Noix de Saint-Jacques Dorées en Croûte de Shiso et Wasabi

Chef Didier Chantefort has taught French cooking for years at Le Cordon Bleu, both in France and Japan. He offered us the following recipe, in which he demonstrates how to strike the right balance between French technique and Japanese ingredients. The recipe calls for clarified butter, which is butter that has had the milk solids and water removed. It has the advantage of being able to be heated to higher temperatures without browning or burning.

SERVES 4

MUSHROOM CREAM

2	tablespoons butter
¼	cup finely chopped shallots
	salt
3½	cups shimeji or oyster mushrooms (hard base removed, separated into smaller pieces if using shimeji or sliced if using oyster mushrooms)
2	cups shiitake mushrooms (stems removed and caps quartered)
2	cups chicken stock
	freshly ground black pepper
⅓	cup milk
1½	tablespoons heavy cream

GARNISH

1¼	cups shimeji or oyster mushrooms (hard base removed, separated into smaller pieces if using shimeji or sliced if using oyster mushrooms)
1	tablespoon butter
	sprigs of fresh chervil
1	sheet nori, cut into julienne

SHISO AND WASABI CRUST

4	tablespoons butter, softened
½	cup fresh bread crumbs
1½	tablespoons ground almonds
1	teaspoon potato starch
6	green shiso leaves, finely chopped
½	egg, beaten
½	teaspoon wasabi powder
	salt and freshly ground black pepper
2	tablespoons fresh bread crumbs

1 To prepare the mushroom cream, melt half the butter in a large saucepan over low heat. Add the shallots and a pinch of salt and cook until soft. Add the mushrooms and stir constantly for 3–5 minutes, until softened. Add the chicken stock, season with salt and pepper, and bring to a boil. Reduce the heat and simmer for 20 minutes.

2 Remove from heat and purée the mixture in a blender until smooth. Pour into a saucepan and whisk in the milk, cream, and the remaining butter and check the seasoning. Set aside.

3 Sauté the mushrooms for a garnish in the butter; keep warm.

4 To prepare the crust, combine the butter, 4 tablespoons of bread crumbs, almonds, potato starch, shiso leaves, beaten egg, wasabi, and salt and pepper to taste and blend to a spreadable paste.

5 Season the scallops with salt and pepper. Heat the clarified butter in a large skillet and rapidly sear the scallops on both sides for approximately 30 seconds. Place on a baking sheet and let cool. Using a spatula, spread a thin coat of the crust on top of each scallop. Using a small damp piece of plastic wrap, gently mold the crust into a slightly domed shape. Sprinkle the remaining bread crumbs over the scallops. Preheat the broiler. Broil for 1–2 minutes, until the crust is set and golden.

6 To serve, reheat the mushroom cream then ladle it into shallow bowls and add the sautéed mushrooms. Arrange 3 scallops in each bowl, and decorate with chervil sprigs and a sprinkling of nori.

SCALLOPS

12 sea scallops, tough side
   muscle removed

   salt and freshly ground
   black pepper

3 tablespoons clarified butter

CLARIFIED BUTTER

To make clarified butter, slowly melt unsalted butter, then remove from heat and let stand. Skim off any foam that has risen to the top, and gently pour the clarified butter into a bowl, leaving behind the milk solids, which will have settled to the bottom of the pan. One stick (8 tablespoons) of butter will produce about 6 tablespoons of clarified butter.

LE CORDON BLEU

One of the most astute business decisions André Cointreau made when he bought the venerable 112-year-old Le Cordon Bleu cooking school in 1984 was to ensure that the institute became more accessible to the Japanese. Le Cordon Bleu has always been in Japan's line of sight—the first Japanese student attended the school in 1905—and Japan's booming economy means that lovers of French food could indulge their passion. Cointreau hired Setsuko Shoai 17 years ago; today she still manages the Japanese students (and Asian students in general), handles admissions coming from Japan, and oversees frequent groups of visiting Japanese foodies. In 1991, Le Cordon Bleu opened the first of two cooking schools in Tokyo.

In Paris, Japanese make up roughly 12 percent of the student body, which is mostly non-French, since the majority of young French chefs enter the field via apprenticeship programs. Most Japanese students dream of being able to stay on in Paris, says Shoai, and the few who do obtain working papers are usually snapped up to work in prestigious restaurants.

"The Japanese students are among the most passionate," says Chef Didier Chantefort, executive teaching chef at Le Cordon Bleu and a former longtime resident of Japan. "They are serious, rigorous, and very interested."

Pastry diplomas are slightly more popular among the Japanese because it's easier to open up a small pastry shop back home rather than a restaurant, says Chantefort. "The Japanese love French food because they appreciate luxury, refinement, and aesthetics. There's a rigor in their work and they have the means to use the best ingredients possible. Some of the finest meals I ever made were in Japan. We didn't cut any corners and the freshness of the ingredients there is unbeatable. I shouldn't say this, but in 50 years, the best French cuisine may be eaten in Japan."

MISO-MARINATED FISH
Miso Zuke-yaki

Miso is a creamy, thick paste made from soybeans and a grain, most often wheat, barley, or rice. Sea salt and a yeastlike mold are added, then it is fermented for several months to several years. Miso varies in flavor and color depending on the grain used and the length of fermentation. Deeper-colored miso generally has a more intense flavor, while lighter-colored miso is milder and can even be slightly sweet. In the West, miso is known primarily as a base for soup; in Japan, it is a staple and is used to flavor sauces, dressings, and marinades. Azabu, a sleek, trendy restaurant in the St.-Germain neighborhood, serves traditional Japanese dishes like this one. The fish is marinated overnight in a combination of light and dark miso, then cooked on a teppan yaki grill.

SERVES 4

- 1 4-inch (10 cm) piece konbu (see Glossary)
- 1 cup mirin
- ½ cup white or *shiro* miso
- ½ cup red or *aka* miso
- 1½ pounds (700 g) white-fleshed fish fillets, cut into 8 equal pieces
- sea salt
- 1 tablespoon butter

1 Two days before serving, lightly wipe the konbu to remove any sand and grit, leaving the white powdery substance. Soak the konbu in the mirin for 12 hours, or overnight.

2 After the soaking period, place the mirin and konbu in a small saucepan and bring almost to a boil over medium heat; remove from heat as soon as small bubbles begin to break on the surface. Remove the konbu, then cook the mirin at a low boil for another 2 minutes to allow the alcohol to evaporate. Remove from heat and stir in the two types of miso to form a smooth paste. Leave to cool.

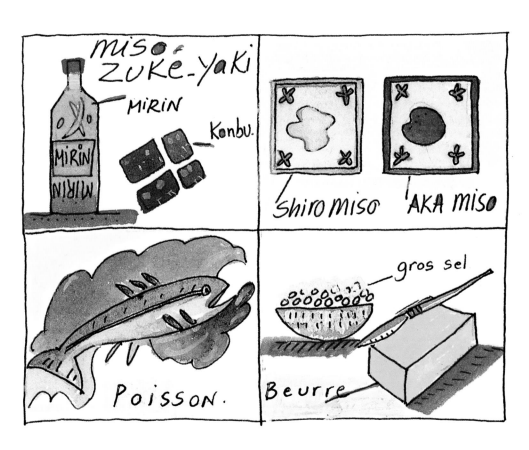

✳ **RESTAURANT**

AZABU

3, rue André Mazet 75006 Paris

tel: 01 46 33 72 05

métro: Odéon ✳

3 Pour the marinade into a large resealable plastic bag. Sprinkle the fish fillets with a bit of sea salt, and add to the marinade. Seal the bag, squeezing out the air. Turn the bag over several times so that the fish fillets are completely coated in the marinade, and refrigerate for 24 hours.

4 When ready to cook, remove the fish from the bag and gently scrape away the miso paste.

5 Heat the butter in a large sauté pan until hot. Cook the fillets, in batches if necessary, turning once, until golden brown. Serve immediately.

CHICKEN BRAISED WITH VEGETABLES
Chikuzen-ni

When the Japanese lycée (high school) in St. Cyr-sur-Oise needed a chef who could cook Japanese dishes for the students, they contacted Le Cordon Bleu. Sayuri Kigure was chosen from many talented Japanese chefs graduating at that time. She prepared meals at the lycee for several years before moving on to cook under 3-star chef Alain Ducasse at his Paris restaurant, Spoon. The following dish is typical of what Sayuri would prepare for the homesick lycee students: chicken and vegetables, stir-fried then braised in a flavorful broth. Japanese cooks cut their vegetables into asymmetrical shapes for visual appeal. Experiment with slicing vegetables on a diagonal or into triangles while keeping all the pieces an equal size for even cooking.

SERVES 4

- - - - - - - - - - - - - - - - - - - -

1	tablespoon cornstarch
2	tablespoons sake
4	boneless, skinless chicken thighs, cut into ½-inch (1½ cm) cubes
4	medium potatoes, peeled
2	carrots, peeled
2	medium leeks, trimmed and well washed
1	cup canned bamboo shoots, drained
5	shiitake mushrooms, stemmed
2	ounces (60 g) snow peas
1	tablespoon canola or vegetable oil
1	cup dashi
1	tablespoon sugar
3	tablespoons soy sauce

1 Stir the cornstarch and sake together in a medium bowl until the cornstarch dissolves. Add the chicken pieces and toss to coat. Marinate for 30 minutes

2 Meanwhile, cut the potatoes, carrots, leeks, and bamboo shoots into asymmetrical shapes of the same size. Quarter the mushrooms.

3 Cut the snow peas lengthwise in half at a diagonal. Blanch in boiling water for 30 seconds. Drain and set aside.

4 Heat the oil in a large skillet over high heat. Add the chicken and cook, shaking the pan occasionally to turn the pieces, until browned evenly.

5 Add all the cut vegetables except for the snow peas and stir-fry 3 minutes.

6 Add the dashi and sugar. Adjust the heat to a steady simmer and place a round of parchment paper cut to a diameter 1 inch (2.5 cm) smaller than the pan directly on the ingredients. (The paper keeps the ingredients moist while allowing the liquid to reduce. The vegetables will also retain their colors better than they would with a tight-fitting lid.) Cook 10–12 minutes, until the liquid has almost completely evaporated and the vegetables are tender.

7 Add the soy sauce and snow peas, cover, and continue cooking 1 minute. Remove from heat and let rest for several minutes for the flavors to blend before serving.

DEEP-FRIED PORK CUTLETS
Tonkatsu

Tonkatsu, deep-fried pork cutlets, are very popular in Japan. This familiar comfort food often turns up in Paris on menus in Japanese restaurants that offer quick lunch deals. The cutlets are coated in panko—crispy, airy bread crumbs that, when fried, produce a very crunchy coating. Tonkatsu is served with a condiment of the same name, which is similar to Worcestershire sauce.

SERVES 4

4   slices boneless pork loin or tenderloin, 4–6 ounces (100–170 g) each

salt and freshly ground black pepper

2   eggs, lightly beaten

2   cups panko bread crumbs (see Glossary)

1   cup all-purpose flour

vegetable oil for deep-frying

1   lemon, cut into wedges

½   head green cabbage, shredded

tonkatsu sauce

1   If necessary, score the fat that rims the cutlets to keep the meat from curling during cooking. Season with salt and pepper. Spread the flour and panko on separate plates. Dredge the cutlets in the flour, shaking off the excess, then dip in the beaten egg and finally press into the panko, turning to coat both sides evenly. Place the breaded meat on a wire rack set over a baking sheet to allow the coating to dry a little before frying, about 5 minutes.

2   Fill a heavy bottomed pot with about 3 inches (7½ cm) of oil and heat to 350°F (180°C). Deep-fry the cutlets, turning once or twice to brown evenly, until golden brown. Drain on paper towels, then slice crosswise in half. Serve warm on a bed of the shredded cabbage accompanied by tonkatsu sauce and lemon wedges.

MEAT-EATING TABOO

The Japanese began officially eating meat only about 130 years ago. When Buddhism (which strives to maintain a harmonious relationship with nature) was introduced to Japan in the 6th century, hunting and fishing became taboo. Over the centuries, fish was reintroduced into the Japanese diet, but other animal flesh remained prohibited.

At the end of the 17th century, Japan formally closed itself off from the rest of the world, fearing trade wars and Christianity. For the next 250 years, Japan developed in isolation, and *washoku*, Japanese home-style cooking, took on many of the characteristics that are still reflected in the way food is chosen and prepared today. Great emphasis is placed on eating seasonal foods at the peak of their freshness. Dishes are prepared to maintain the integrity of each ingredient's flavor. There are no heavy sauces or long, complicated cooking procedures.

When Japan reopened to trade with the rest of the world in the 19th century, the Japanese emperor gave a banquet at which meat was served, ending the taboo and indicating his desire to align himself with the rest of the world.

The fascination the Japanese and French have for each other's cooking may very well be because the cuisines are so different.

SOBA NOODLES WITH SMOKED DUCK BREAST
Novilles de Soba aux Tranches de Magret de Canard Fumé

When Akiko Ida and Pierre Javelle, both food photographers and gourmands, set up house together, it was a given that Akiko would indulge her passion for cooking and take over the kitchen. Luckily for Pierre, he enjoys Japanese dishes, although he will occasionally make a chocolate mousse just to tip the scales slightly. Akiko gave us the following recipe, in which she uses French smoked magret de canard. She finds its taste more similar to Japanese duck than the fresh duck available in Paris. Soba noodles are made from buckwheat flour, which gives them a distinct brown-gray color. Many Japanese rinse their noodles after cooking, but Akiko thinks this washes away much of the rich, hearty flavor of the grain.

SERVES 4

. . . .

2   leeks, trimmed

7   cups dashi

½   cup soy sauce

1   tablespoon sugar

2   tablespoons mirin

8   ounces (250 g) dried
    soba noodles

8   ounces (250 g) smoked
    duck breast, sliced

1   tablespoon shichimi
    (see Glossary)

1 Slice the leeks lengthwise in half, then cut each half on a diagonal into 1½-inch (4 cm) pieces. Rinse well.

2 Pour the dashi into a large saucepan and bring to a boil. Add the soy sauce, sugar, mirin, and leeks. Reduce the heat to a simmer, cover, and cook 5 minutes, or until the leeks are tender.

3 Meanwhile, cook the soba noodles in a pot of unsalted boiling water, about 3–4 minutes. Drain and place in a bowl. Pour a ladle of the simmering broth over the noodles to keep them from sticking together, and set aside.

4 To serve, divide the noodles evenly among 4 individual bowls and lay 3 slices of duck breast over each portion. Ladle the steaming broth and leeks over the noodles and sprinkle with the shichimi. Serve any remaining slices of duck breast separately.

"THE PLACE I LIKE BEST IN THIS WORLD IS THE KITCHEN. NO MATTER WHERE IT IS, NO MATTER WHAT KIND, IF IT'S A KITCHEN, IF IT'S A PLACE WHERE THEY MAKE FOOD, IT'S FINE WITH ME. IDEALLY IT SHOULD BE WELL BROKEN IN. LOTS OF DISH TOWELS, DRY AND IMMACULATE. WHITE TILE CATCHING THE LIGHT (TING! TING!)." —Banana Yoshimoto, "Kitchen"

JAPANESE GROCERY STORES IN PARIS

The two grocery stores at which Japanese shop in the Opéra neighborhood are Juji-Ya, a take-out snack bar/video rental with shelves piled higgledy-piggledy with Japanese products, and Kioko, a more upscale shop that carries all the basics, including red-bean ice cream.

Near the former Nikko Hotel (now Novotel) and the Japanese Cultural Center, Kanae has most of the ingredients necessary for a Japanese meal. Because these grocery stores are quite expensive, however, many Japanese now shop at Korean grocers in the Opéra neighborhood or in the Japanese section of Chinatown supermarkets.

JUJI-YA
46, rue Sainte-Anne
75001 Paris
tel: 01 42 86 02 22
métro: Pyramides

KIOKO
46, rue des Petits-Champs
75001 Paris
tel: 01 42 61 33 65
métro: Pyramides

KANAE
11, rue Linois
75015 Paris
tel: 01 40 59 98 03
métro: Charles-Michels

DESSERTS

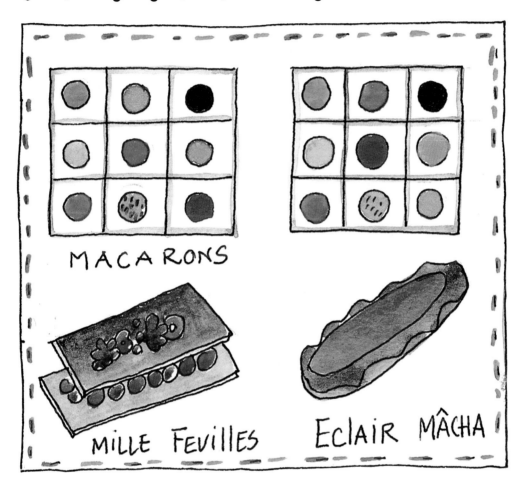

MACARONS

MILLE FEVILLES

ECLAIR MÂCHA

GREEN TEA MADELEINES
Madeleines au Thé Matcha

Go into any upscale tea salon these days and you will be just as likely to be offered green tea madeleines as the lemon-flavored version made famous by Proust.

MAKES 12

- ¾ cup plus 1 tablespoon all-purpose flour
- 1 teaspoon baking soda
  pinch of salt
- 1 teaspoon green tea powder (matcha)
- 2 large eggs
- ⅓ cup plus 1 tablespoon sugar
- 1 tablespoon honey
- 8 tablespoons butter, melted and cooled

1 Sift the flour, baking soda, salt, and tea powder together twice to mix thoroughly.

2 Place the eggs in the bowl of a heavy-duty mixer and beat 30 seconds. Add the sugar and honey and beat on medium speed 5–8 minutes, or until pale and thick. This is an important step—do not underbeat.

3 Add the dry ingredients to the egg mixture and beat just until incorporated. With the mixer running, slowly add the butter and beat until smooth. Cover the bowl with plastic wrap and refrigerate for at least 3 hours, or overnight.

4 Preheat the oven to 450°F (230°C). Grease and lightly flour a madeleine tin. Fill each cavity two-thirds full with batter. Place in the oven. After 5–8 minutes, or as soon as the madeleines have risen and become plump, reduce the heat to 350°F (180°C), and continue baking another 5 minutes.

5 Invert the madeleines onto a wire rack and serve warm or at room temperature.

pâtisseries de Sadaharu Aoki

ECLAIR MÂCHA
pâte à choux crémeux de thé vert

figues — — abricots

DUOMO Chocolat

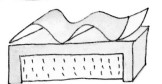

Côte d'ivoire
biscuit de coco

Chocolat et zucchini

WAGASHI—TOO BEAUTIFUL TO EAT?

Almost too beautiful to eat, *wagashi* are traditional Japanese confections that have developed into an edible art form. Originally created as religious offerings, they play an important role in tea ceremonies—and are also given as gifts and enjoyed as snacks. Designed to appeal to the five senses and, above all, to be appreciated for their beauty and texture, *wagashi* are made with very little sugar and are subtly flavored. The humble ingredients used to make *wagashi*—beans, grains, sesame seeds, potatoes, and sugar—turn into sophisticated creations in the hands of *wagashi* pastry chefs. There are more than 3,000 different types of *wagashi* pastries.

The Toraya firm has specialized in *wagashi* since the 17th century. In 2005, Toraya celebrated the 25th anniversary of its presence in Paris. Toraya was ranked by *Le Figaro* as the second-best tearoom in Paris, and 70 percent of its clientele is French.

The pastry chefs there have adapted their *wagashi* slightly to suit Gallic tastes, as well as inventing names and shapes for their confections such as "Sunset on Mont St. Michel" and "Louvre Lights."

Minamoto Kitchoan, another *wagashi* specialist, recently moved to the Place de la Madeleine, becoming the neighbor of the quintessential French gourmet store, Fauchon.

MINAMOTO KITCHOAN
17, place de la Madeleine
75008 Paris
tel: 01 40 06 91 28
métro: Madeleine

TORAYA
10, rue Saint-Florentin
75001 Paris
tel: 01 42 60 13 00
métro: Concorde

BLACK SESAME MACAROONS
Macarons au Sésame Noir

Paris has been macaroon-mad for quite some time now, and it is almost de rigueur that master pastry chefs produce their personalized macaroon. Pierre Hermé launches his new collection each season in the same way designers present their clothing. The celebrated macaroon company Ladurée even sells a room freshener inspired by their violet-scented macaroons. The round pastel-colored cookies are light and slightly chewy, encased in a superfine crunchy outer layer. The fillings can range from classical—chocolate or praline—to the most unexpected, such as chestnut, green tea, or sesame, as in Sadaharu Aoki's (see page 158) recipe.

MAKES 16

- 2 cups confectioners' sugar
- 2¼ cups ground almonds
- 1 tablespoon black sesame seeds
- 4 egg whites
- 2 tablespoons granulated sugar

- 1 pastry bag fitted with a large plain tip

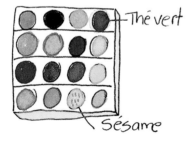

Thé vert

Sésame

1 Preheat the oven to 350°F (180°C). Line 2 baking sheets with parchment paper.

2 Sift together the confectioners' sugar and ground almonds into a bowl. Add the sesame seeds and stir with a fork to distribute them evenly.

3 Using an electric mixer, whip the egg whites in a bowl until almost stiff. Gradually add the granulated sugar, and beat to firm peaks.

4 Using a large spatula, gradually fold the ground almonds into the egg whites until smooth. Spoon the meringue into the pastry bag.

5 Pipe out the meringue into small even rounds, 1½ inches (4 cm) in diameter onto the lined baking sheets, spacing them 1½-inches (4 cm)

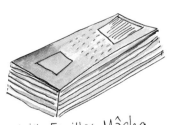

Mille Feuilles Mâcha.
Pâte Feuilletée caramélisée
Crémaux de thé vert japonais

apart. Let the macaroons sit at room temperature for 10–15 minutes, or until a light crust forms on the surface. Bake for 10–12 minutes with the oven door propped slightly ajar.

6 Remove the macaroons from the oven, lift up a corner of the parchment paper on each sheet, and run about 1 teaspoon of cold water between the paper and the baking sheet. Let stand for 2–3 minutes, then gently lift the macaroons off the paper and place on a wire rack to cool.

SESAME BUTTERCREAM

. . . .

6   large egg yolks
1   cup sugar
½   cup water
1   pound (450 g) butter, softened
2   heaping teaspoons black
    sesame paste
1   teaspoon vanilla

1 Grease a 1-cup, heatproof glass measuring cup with a little butter; place near stovetop. Put the sugar and water in a small saucepan and stir to dissolve. Heat the mixture until it reaches 240°F (115°C) on a candy thermometer. Then remove from heat and pour into the prepared measuring cup to stop the cooking.

2 Meanwhile, place the egg yolks in the bowl of a heavy-duty mixer and beat until pale and thick. With the mixer running, slowly pour the sugar syrup onto the egg yolks without allowing it to fall onto the beaters. Continue beating until mixture cools to room temperature.

3 Gradually add butter to the cooled egg mixture, mixing constantly. Once the butter has been completely incorporated, add the sesame paste and vanilla; beat until smooth.

4 To assemble: Pipe a little buttercream onto the flat side of a macaroon, and press together with another to make a sandwich. Repeat with the remaining buttercream and macaroons.

Millefeuilles FruitsRouges
Pâte Feuilletée caramélisée.

SADAHARU AOKI

"I've always done the opposite of everyone else. Then what I do becomes fashionable," says Sadaharu Aoki, the *enfant terrible* of the Parisian pastry scene. Aoki, who goes by the nickname Sada, is invariably included in the litany of Paris "it" chefs, along with Alain Passard, Hélène Darroze, and of course, Pierre Hermé.

Sada arrived in Paris 18 years ago, when he was in his early 20s, having completed cooking school and an apprenticeship at a well-known pâtisserie in Tokyo. In Paris he worked with top pastry chefs such as Jean Millet and then struck out on his own in 1998 with the help of a Japanese financier. From the start, his sleek, luscious French pastries with a Japanese twist caught people's imagination. The press initially described his green tea madeleines as "strange and subtle," but then came a universal swooning over the black sesame seed éclairs, along with his perfectly executed French classics such as *millefeuilles*—Sada's are lighter and flakier than most others. His atelier now churns out no less than five tons of macaroons a year.

Sada has absolute confidence in his taste. "I like doing things my way in order to show people what I like." And they do like what he likes—Louis Vuitton, Baccarat, and Hermès have all had Sada make special-order VIP presents for their customers, his pastries are served in high-end Parisian restaurants and brasseries, and ANA, the Japanese airline, uses his creations for their first-class service. He says he has always been lucky, but he doesn't mention all the hard work involved.

With three pastry shops in Paris, three in Tokyo, and one about to open in London, Sada has a lot on his plate. He also has several more dreams—he'd like to open a

pastry shop in New York and then, perhaps, a restaurant in Paris, which he considers a paradise for food lovers. His restaurant would be "a mix of France and Japan but something special, something rare."

35, rue de Vaugirard 75006 Paris
tel: 01 45 44 48 90
métro: St-Sulpice

56, boulevard Port Royal 75005 Paris
tel: 01 45 35 36 80
métro: Port Royal

GALERIES LAFAYETTE GOURMET
40, boulevard Haussmann 75009 Paris
métro: St. Lazare

SALTED CARAMEL TART
Tarte au Caramel Salé

The first time we tasted Sadaharu Aoki's salted caramel tart was in an upscale Parisian bistro. It was no surprise when we found out that it was the work of the avant-garde Japanese pastry chef. His updated and innovative approach to traditional French pastries and desserts results in sublime creations that have taken Paris by storm.

SERVES 6–8

SWEET PASTRY SHELL

1   cup all-purpose flour
¼   cup ground almonds
⅓   cup confectioners' sugar
½   teaspoon salt
4   tablespoons cold butter,
     cut into pieces
2   large egg yolks, lightly beaten

CARAMEL FILLING

1   cup corn syrup
1   cup heavy cream
1   vanilla bean, split lengthwise
¾   teaspoon coarse sea salt
1⅓ cups sugar
4   tablespoons unsalted butter

1 To make the pastry, place the flour, ground almonds, confectioners' sugar, and salt in a medium bowl. Make a well in the center of the dry ingredients and add the butter and egg yolks. Use your fingers to mix the ingredients together, adding a tablespoon of cold water if the dough seems dry. Shape the dough into a ball and flatten it into a disk with the palm of your hand. Cover it in plastic wrap and refrigerate for at least 1 hour.

2 Preheat the oven to 350°F (180°C). Roll the dough out to a ¼-inch (5 mm) thickness. Press into the bottom and up the sides of a 9-inch (23 cm) round tart pan with a removable bottom. (This pastry is very soft; if it tears while lining the tart pan, patch it up with pieces of unused dough.) Bake for 20 minutes, or until lightly golden. Remove from the oven and cool on a rack.

3 To make the filling, combine corn syrup, heavy cream, vanilla bean, and salt in a medium saucepan over low heat.

4 Meanwhile, place the sugar and butter in a large heavy saucepan and cook over medium heat, stirring, until the mixture turns a dark amber.

5 When the caramel is almost ready, raise the heat and bring the syrup to a boil. Carefully pour the hot syrup onto the caramel. (The mixture might splatter and rise rapidly; remove from heat if necessary, then return to heat.) Using a wooden spoon, stir over low heat until smooth and the temperature measures 240°F (114°C) on a candy thermometer. Remove the vanilla bean from the caramel, then pour it into the cooked tart shell. Let cool completely, then refrigerate until you are ready to add the ganache topping (see below).

GANACHE

- - - - - - - - - - - - - - - - - - -

4   ounces (110 g) milk chocolate, grated or finely chopped
4   tablespoons butter, chopped into small pieces
½   cup heavy cream
2   large egg whites
2   teaspoons sugar
    cocoa powder for dusting

1 Combine the chocolate and butter in a heatproof bowl.

2 Put the cream into a small saucepan and bring to a boil. Pour the hot cream over the chocolate and butter and let stand, without stirring, for 4 minutes, then stir gently until smooth. Let cool to room temperature. (If the chocolate and butter are not completely melted, place the bowl briefly over a pot of hot water.)

3 Beat the egg whites in a medium bowl and, as peaks begin to form, sprinkle in the sugar. Continue beating until stiff and glossy. Fold into the cool chocolate.

4 Remove the tart from the refrigerator. Spread the ganache (in a spiral pattern) over the cooled caramel filling and dust with cocoa powder. Refrigerate for at least 1 hour before serving.

MADAME HISADA

When one steps into Madame Hisada's cheese shop in a quiet area of the prosperous 16th *arrondissement*, it smells like most other fromageries, but something is decidedly different. The design is streamlined, the walls a pale gray color. The atmosphere is open and airy, the cheese neatly lined up and accessible to customers. Small details are a giveaway: Amid bottles of apple cider and creamy butter from Normandy, there are pretty ceramic dishes. Next to biscuits from Brittany there are small packets of rice crackers and tubes of wasabi paste in baskets. It's a Japanese-owned French cheese shop.

Sanae Hisada bought an existing cheese shop in 2004 and entirely transformed the interior. On weekends she also offers sushi made to order that she puts together in a kitchen in the back of the shop.

Hisada owns 18 specialty cheese shops back home in Japan; this shop is the icing on the cake after 20 years of hard work introducing European cheeses to the Japanese market. When Hisada first opened a small dairy shop in Japan 20 years ago, she says it wasn't successful at all. Imported, unprocessed cheese was not yet a hot item in Japan, and it took her several trips to France, an increase in the variety of her cheeses, and a market boom in French and Italian wines before her business took off. Imports of cheese into Japan have quadrupled since 1975 and were up to 260,000 tons in 2002.

Her husband, a former chef specializing in *kaiseki*, a sort of seasonal tasting menu, is now president of the company. He takes care of the business in Japan while Madame Hisada, who already holds the title of *Prud'homme*, the eminent second-level rank in the French Cheese Guild, tries to charm the French into accepting the fact that a Japanese woman might know everything there is to know about French cheese.

AFRICA SUR SEINE:
CAMEROON, SENEGAL, THE WEST INDIES, AND THE CARIBBEAN

"Only here in Africa can you see five grown-up men eating with one spoon—not because they are poor but because of their togetherness."—Anthony Charles Aondana, "Guinea" (from Harper's magazine)

AFRICA ON THE SEINE

Getting out of the metro at the Château Rouge station is a little like changing worlds. Young men hand out flyers advertising miraculous results obtained by *marabouts* (shamans or healers); women wearing brightly colored *boubous*, with children strapped to their backs, deftly negotiate prices for mammoth fish. Plantains, manioc, ginger, mounds of herbs, and red-hot Scotch bonnet chilies are piled up in market stalls. The acrid smells of dried fish and palm oil waft out of shops lined with shelves stacked with Jumbo bouillon cubes, peanut butter, and hibiscus tea. Live chickens squawk in their cages in the rue Myrha. The metro stop at Château d'Eau offers a similar experience; dozens of men and women compete with each other to lure passengers coming up the steps into the Afro-Caribbean beauty salons along the boulevard.

Immigration to France from its former colonies in sub-Saharan Africa is fairly recent and came in several waves. The first arrived in the early 1960s, made up primarily of men from Senegal, Cameroon, and Mali; the second wave came in the 1980s when their families joined them. This immigrant group continues its steady influx, and as a result, the African communities in Paris are vibrant and in constant evolution.

In the 1600s, France had already acquired the colonies of Martinique, Guadeloupe (in the Caribbean), French Guyana (on the Atlantic), and Réunion in the Indian Ocean. These islands are still French "overseas departments" and a large proportion of blacks in France are French nationals from the Caribbean and the Indian Ocean. The Île de France (the greater Paris area) has been nicknamed as the "third island," referring to the fact that there are as many people from Guadeloupe and Martinique—400,000 or so—living in the Paris area as in the Caribbean islands.

Throughout the 18th and 19th centuries, France became a major colonial power in West and Central Africa, but African influence in France was minimal. Very few Africans came to France and it was only after the First World War, when 134,000 West Africans, mainly Senegalese, fought for the French, that some settled in Paris.

ALL THAT WAS AFRICAN

Between the two world wars, all that was African was in vogue in the capital. Cubist and Fauvist artists were influenced by African art. Josephine Baker and other expatriate African-American musicians and writers were welcomed to the city. A few gifted African students came to Paris to attend college; some later became political leaders when their countries gained independence from France. Léopold Sédar Senghor, Senegal's much-loved president and poet, was the first African to become a member of the Académie Française. His close friend the West Indian poet Aimé Césaire held several government positions and was mayor of Fort-de-France, in Martinique.

African, Caribbean, and West Indian influence on French culture has been considerable in many areas, such as poetry, literature, fashion design, film—one of the earliest documentary-style films about the African presence in Paris was Paulin Vieyra's 1955 *Afrique-sur-Seine*—and last but not least, music. It's hard to imagine the Paris music scene over the past 25 years without Touré Kunda, Youssou N'Dour, Salif Keita, MC Solaar, Alpha Blondy, or Angelique Kidjo.

AFRICAN INGREDIENTS

As far as cuisine is concerned, African restaurants in Paris abound, but until a decade ago they remained mostly insular, catering to an African clientele and the odd French client who was being introduced to the restaurant by an African friend. In a multicultural turn of affairs, there was initially far more interaction between the African and Asian communities in Paris, because Asian merchants recognized the need to import the proper ingredients required for African dishes. As a result, most of the food markets in the Château Rouge neighborhood are run by Asians of Chinese origin, while the employees and customers are African or from the Antilles and the Indian Ocean.

However, African cooking is creeping into the consciousness of Parisians, with the emergence of restaurants intent on serving both French and African customers. A great number of Parisians have tasted the Senegalese specialty, fish or chicken *yassa*, and meat *mafé* made with peanut butter, because most restaurants, whether the owners are from Senegal, Cameroon, or the Ivory Coast, will serve these popular dishes.

The same ingredients are used in all sub-Saharan African cooking—the basics include peanuts, onions, okra, eggplant, and the all-important starches: rice, plantains, manioc, yams, and millet. Depending on the climate and geography of the individual countries, such as coastal Senegal or land-bound Mali, interpretations of these staple ingredients will differ in the choice of accompanying vegetables, and fresh fish or meat, and often a combination of the two.

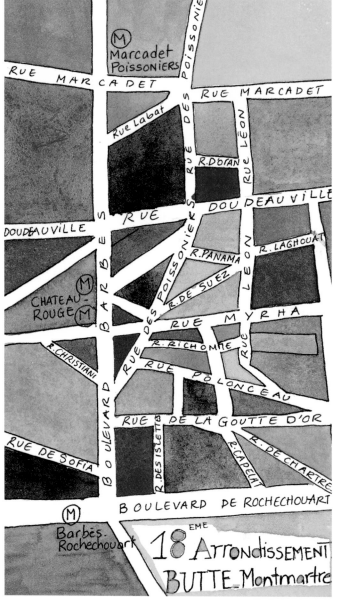

West Africans and the island populations from the Caribbean and the Indian Ocean use similar ingredients in their cooking because of the busy trade route that began in the 15th century between Africa, Europe, and the New World. For almost 400 years, this triangular shipping route created exchanges that fostered hybrid cultures and cuisines with a strong African influence. African slaves brought okra and yams to the islands, along with many types of greens, beans, and roots. At the same time, following the abolition of slavery, a number of freed slaves returned to Africa, bringing back with them adaptations of culinary practices that had come from Africa in the first place.

FINDING COOKBOOKS

In an era in which ethnic cookbooks abound in Paris, African cookbooks are rare. This can partly be explained by the fact that until recently, says Ibrahima Ba, the chef at Le Village, a friendly, bustling Senegalese restaurant in Belleville, African cooking wasn't organized in any manner—recipes were just passed down from one generation to the next. All this is changing, though, with the appearance of several glossy cookbooks, such as *La Cuisine de Ma Mère (My Mother's Cooking),* touted as the first Senegalese cookbook, written by the musician Youssou N'Dour and his mother to celebrate the meals he ate as a child in Dakar. Chef and restaurant owner Alexandre Bella Ola's cookbook, *Cuisine Actuelle de l'Afrique Noire (Cuisine from Today's Black Africa),* is already being reprinted. It maps out recipes from Western and Central Africa, organizing them according to the staples used in the region, such as peanuts, bananas, and okra.

West Indian cookbooks are easier to find, and the French Antilles are sometimes included in cookbook series on French regional cuisines. Babette de Rozières, a well-known cook from Guadeloupe, has done much to introduce cuisine from the French Antilles to the French through her restaurants, books, and television shows.

DEMYSTIFYING FOOD

For the moment, Parisians are more familiar with Creole cuisine (a term loosely used in France to designate cooking from the Caribbean and Indian Ocean). There are often stalls in local markets selling cooked food such as *samosas* or *accras*, and there are numerous Creole restaurants in Paris, as well as hip bars and clubs specializing in rum-based drinks from the Antilles.

Some Africans have begun to make it their mission to introduce their cuisine to the French. Malian businessman Moriba Ouendeno made a vow as a student years ago to make African food accessible to Westerners—and his successful company now ships natural fruit juices from Africa and vacuum-packed African dishes prepared in France all over Europe. Alexandre Bella Ola, from Cameroon, opened his spacious and upscale restaurant Moussa l'Africain last year, determined to "demystify" African cooking. Now that Parisians can easily find Colombo sauces, *achards* (vegetables preserved in oil), African sauces, and exotic herbal teas in their local supermarkets, African and Creole cuisines have finally become a reality in French kitchens.

APPETIZERS

THE BUSHMAN COCKTAIL

Georges Taffou Happy's two venues, La Jungle, which opened in 1997, and La Jungle Transafric, opened in 2001, are the only bars in Paris where you can find over 100 mixed drinks with names like the Panther's Milk (a secret recipe), the Masai Warrior (rum, gin, vodka, and ginger syrup), and the Sorcerer's Nest (gin and Bailey's with lemon). Georges came to Paris from Cameroon in 1985 as a student. He bartended on the side and soon found that the drinks he invented were a great success. When he brought in tapes of African music and his Parisian clientele began to dance on the tables, he decided that owning a bar and restaurant was perhaps his destiny.

✳ RESTAURANT

LA JUNGLE

56, rue d'Argout 75002 Paris

tel: 01 40 41 03 45

métro: Sentier/Les Halles

LA JUNGLE TRANSAFRIC

15, rue d'Aboukir 75002 Paris

tel: 01 45 08 54 17

métro: Sentier/Les Halles

MAKES 1

2   tablespoons (1 shot) Cognac
     dash (3 drops) of Cointreau

4   tablespoons ginger juice (see
     page 170)

4   tablespoons chilled champagne

1 Pour the Cognac and Cointreau into a cocktail shaker half filled with ice. Shake then strain into a champagne flute. Add the ginger juice and champagne. Stir once and serve.

FRESH GINGER JUICE
Jus de Gingembre

Zesty, spicy ginger juice is the perfect drink to accompany plantain chips. This juice is a refreshing apéritif with or without alcohol.

MAKES 4 CUPS

- 7 ounces (200 g) fresh ginger
- 4 cups water
- 1 cup lemon juice
- 2 cups pineapple juice
  sugar

1 Peel the ginger. Place in the bowl of a food processor and process until finely chopped. Transfer to a large pitcher or bowl and add the water. Let macerate for 48 hours in the refrigerator.

2 Strain the ginger juice; discard the ginger. Add the lemon juice, pineapple juice, and sugar to taste. This will keep up to 2 weeks in the refrigerator.

MORIBA OUENDENO

When Moriba Ouendeno arrived in Strasbourg, France, from Mali to study biochemistry, he was one of three African students in that discipline. "When everyone got together for parties, people always asked, 'What do you eat in Africa?'" he says.

Moriba would take a five-hour train ride to Paris to buy African ingredients, then go back to his dorm and cook for his fellow students. He vowed one day to bring Africa to Europe. After Moriba graduated, he worked in laboratory research for a time until he felt ready to start his own company in 1996. He began by packaging exotic fruit juices, with the underlying idea that they be 100 percent natural and operate on the basis of fair trade. With next to nothing as a budget, Moriba set up cooperatives in Africa for the juice extraction and packaged and distributed the juices in France. For his market research, Moriba handed out free samples of his hibiscus, ginger, tamarind, mango, baobab, and litchi juices in a supermarket in northeastern Alsace, placing his faith in the owner's comment, "If you can sell your juices here, you can sell them anywhere."

Now, ten years later, Moriba's juices can be found at most major retailers throughout northern Europe and at Fairway markets in New York. He has widened his product line to include natural herbal teas and vacuum-packed meals from Africa, including ever-popular dishes such as beef *mafé*, fish *tieb bou dienn*, and chicken *yassa*. Moriba will soon package vegetarian dishes for the U.S. market, and produce condiments and spices to be used by chefs. He also makes a ginger-flavored digestif, which is distilled in one of Alsace's premier eau-de-vie houses. "Twenty years in Alsace have left their mark on me!" he says.

"LIFE IS LIKE AN OKRA.
YOU SLIP, YOU FALL, YOU FALL, YOU SLIP."
—African proverb

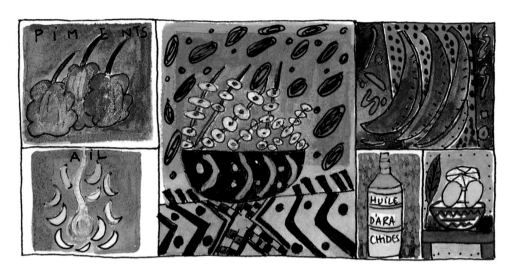

PLANTAIN CHIPS WITH CHILI-TOMATO DIP
Chips de Bananes Vertes

These chips are a perfect fit with a rum punch or an ice-cold beer. The fiery dip, made with the king of chilies—Scotch bonnets—is a great foil for the starchy, slightly sweet plantains.

SERVES 4

2   large, very firm greenish-yellow plantains
    vegetable oil for deep-frying
    sea salt

1 Wash the plantains with warm water. Cut off the ends, then make three lengthwise incisions in the skin of each. Remove the strips of peel by pulling slightly crosswise rather than straight down. Use a sharp knife to remove any tough fibers that remain. Slice the fruit on a diagonal into thin slices and place in a bowl of ice water for 30 minutes.

2 Heat the oil in a deep heavy saucepan to 370°F (190°C). Drain the plantains and pat thoroughly dry. Fry in batches until golden brown. Drain on paper towels. While still warm, sprinkle with sea salt and toss. Serve with the dip.

CHILI AND TOMATO DIP

MAKES 1¼ CUPS

1	Scotch bonnet chili
2	shallots
6	cloves garlic
8	ounces (225 g) ripe tomatoes
2	tablespoons lime juice
½	cup chopped fresh cilantro
	salt

1 Heat a large heavy skillet over high heat. Add the chili and dry-roast, pressing down occasionally with a wooden spoon, until the skin blackens. Transfer to a cutting board; set the pan aside. Wearing rubber gloves, cut the chili in half, then place in the bowl of a food processor.

2 Using the same skillet, dry-roast the shallots and garlic cloves 5 minutes, shaking the pan for even cooking. Transfer to the food processor.

3 Put the tomatoes into the hot skillet and roast, turning with the wooden spoon, until the skin blackens on all sides. Transfer to a cutting board. When cool enough to handle, slice the tomatoes in half, remove the cores, and discard. Add to the chili mixture.

4 Using the pulse button, process the ingredients until coarsely chopped; do not puree. Transfer to a bowl and add the lime juice and chopped cilantro. Season with salt and serve with warm fried plantains.

PLANTAINS

Plantains are the pasta and potatoes of Africa and the tropics. A type of banana, plantains must be cooked before they are eaten. There is no end to the variety of dishes or even alcoholic drinks that can be made with plantains. Most often, they are boiled and served as a side dish to a main meal, but they can also be fried, mashed, baked, or steamed and, depending on the seasoning, made into a savory or sweet dish. Plantains are eaten at all stages of ripeness. When green and unripe, they are starchy and bland and are often boiled or sliced and fried into chips. As they ripen, they turn yellow, their flesh becomes creamier, and they are good mashed and added to soups. When brown or black, they are ripe and turn sweet and are delicious when baked in their skins.

MANGO PUREE ON TOAST
Purée de Mangues sur Toasts

This recipe calls for small green mangoes with hard pale flesh. These mangoes are picked intentionally when they're immature. They never ripen and are sour and crisp. The entire fruit—skin, flesh, and pit—is used for making pickles or chutneys. Larger mature mangoes can also be green, but they have tougher skin and a hard pit. If left in a warm place, they will take on red, yellow, or orange hues and the flesh will soften and sweeten.

MAKES 2 CUPS

6   green mangoes
2   teaspoons olive oil
     juice of 3 limes
½   shallot, minced
1   bird's-eye chili, minced
     salt and freshly ground
     black pepper

1 Place the unpeeled mangoes in a large saucepan, cover with cold water, and bring to a boil. Cook 15 minutes; drain.

2 When the mangoes are cool enough to handle, peel with a sharp knife. Remove the flesh from the pits and put into the bowl of a food processor. Process until finely pureed. With the motor running, add the lime juice and olive oil. Transfer to a bowl.

3 Add the shallot and chili, and stir to combine. Season to taste with salt and pepper.

4 Serve on toasted bread points or as a dip with plantain chips.

CALIXTHE BEYALA

"That evening, the fragrance of crocodile stewed in tchobi sauce and mashed mangoes on toast were the heady stuff of which African legends are made. It was like a wind passing through forests, when spirits fly from branch to branch, disturbing the sleep of men. It was the odor of guava trees heavy with juicy fruit . . ." —Calixthe Beyala, *How to Grill Your Husband the African Way*

Novelist Calixthe Beyala was born in Cameroon and now lives in Paris. She is one of the most prolific and controversial authors on the African literary scene today. In *How to Grill your Husband...*, the main character, Mademoiselle Aissatou, lives in Paris and is in love with a Malian man, Souleymane Bolobolo, who still lives with his mother. Aissatou decides to seduce Souleymane by making him mouthwatering African dishes. At the end of each chapter, Beyala provides an authentic recipe, which refers to what Aissatou has made for Souleymane that day.

CODFISH FRITTERS
Accras

These bite-sized codfish fritters are found throughout the Caribbean. They are originally from West Africa, where they are known as accras and made with black-eyed peas. In Paris, it is the Caribbean version, made from salt cod, that is well known, but accras can be made with almost anything from sea urchins to shrimp or vegetables. This recipe was inspired by the accras served at the Otis Club, a restaurant specializing in food from the French Antilles.

MAKES 20

4   ounces (110 g) skinless, boneless salt cod
1   branch fresh thyme
1   cup chopped fresh parsley, plus 4 parsley stems
1   bay leaf
1   bunch fresh chives, chopped
1   onion, minced
2   cloves garlic, minced
1   bird's-eye chili, minced
2   cups all-purpose flour
2   large eggs
2   tablespoons water
½   teaspoon cayenne pepper
    salt and freshly ground black pepper
½   teaspoon baking powder
    oil for deep-frying

1 Soak the cod in plenty of cold water for at least 12 hours, or up to 2 days, changing the water frequently. Drain and rinse.

2 Place the cod in a saucepan with water to cover and add the thyme, parsley stems, and bay leaf. Bring to a boil over high heat, then reduce to a simmer and cook 30 minutes; drain.

3 When the cod is cool enough to handle, shred it with your fingers, discarding any remaining skin or bones. Mix with the chopped parsley, chives, onions, garlic, and chili in a bowl and set aside.

4 Put the flour in a large bowl and make a well in the center. Break the eggs into the well and add water, cayenne pepper, salt, and black pepper. Mix to combine and set aside for 1 hour. When ready to use, stir the baking powder and shredded salt cod into the batter.

RESTAURANT

RESTAURANT OTIS CLUB
61, rue Rodier 75009 Paris
tel: 01 42 81 25 91
métro: Anvers

5 Heat the oil in a deep heavy saucepan. Drop spoonfuls of batter into the oil, scooping up the mixture with one spoon and pushing it into the hot oil with another one, working in small batches. Cook the fritters until golden, about 2 minutes. Remove and drain on paper towels. The fritters can be made up to 2 hours ahead and reheated on a baking sheet in a 350°F (180°C) oven for 5 minutes.

MAURITIAN-STYLE BEGGAR'S PURSES
Paniers à la Mauricienne

Mauritius has one of the most multiethnic cuisines in the world. Creole, Indian, Chinese, and French influences come together harmoniously, and the menu at Rafiq Hamjah's restaurant, Comme sur une Ile, reflects this diversity: The plat du jour can be a spicy French daube one day, and the next, shrimp in a Creole rougaille sauce. Rafiq Hamjah created his paniers à la mauricienne by putting the warm flavors of India into a crunchy Chinese wonton skin. These paniers (baskets) are perfect as hors d'oeuvres or can be served 3 per person on a bed of crisp lettuce as a starter.

MAKES 30

- 4 medium new potatoes, peeled
- 1 6-ounce (170 g) can tuna in water, drained, or 7 ounces (200 g) cooked fresh tuna
- 1 shallot, minced
- 1 cup chopped fresh coriander
- 6 scallions, white bulb and green top finely sliced
- 1½ teaspoons ground cumin
- 1 teaspoon cumin seeds
- 1 tablespoon curry powder
- salt and freshly ground black pepper
- 30 wonton skins
- oil for deep-frying
- Tomato-Chili Dip (page 173)

✳ RESTAURANT

COMME SUR UNE ILE

83, rue Orfila 75020 Paris

tel: 01 46 36 03 24

métro: Gambetta/Pelleport ✳

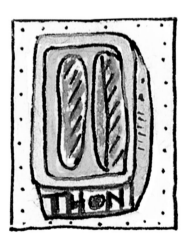

1 Place the potatoes in a pot of cold water and bring to a boil over high heat, then reduce to a simmer and cook uncovered until tender. Drain and place in a large bowl. Crush the potatoes while still warm. Add the tuna, shallot, coriander, scallions, cumin, cumin seeds, and curry powder; mix well. Season with salt and pepper.

2 Line a baking sheet with parchment paper. Lay a wonton skin on a work surface and place a tablespoon of the potato mixture in the center. Moisten the edges with water, then bring up the corners to create a small pouch. Pinch the top of the purse together, giving it a twist to seal. Repeat with the remaining wonton skins and filling.

3 Heat the oil in a deep heavy saucepan. Deep-fry the pouches 6–8 at a time, until golden brown. Drain on paper towels and serve hot with the tomato-chili dip.

OCTOPUS SALAD WITH KAFFIR LIME
Salade de Poulpe avec Combava

Rafiq Hamjah catered Mauritian food for years before he decided to open his restaurant on the hilly northern side of Paris. His restaurant is small and immaculate, his cooking clean-tasting and spice-laden. It's the simple addition of the zest of kaffir limes that makes the following recipe so special. In order for the octopus to be tender, it must be simmered slowly for a long time, much like a tough piece of meat. Freezing octopus before it is cooked may speed up the time it takes for the octopus to become tender. The flavor improves if left to marinate for several hours, or overnight.

SALADE DE POULPE AVEC COMBAVA.

SERVES 4

1 pound (500 g) cleaned octopus
1 teaspoon salt
3 large tomatoes, diced

VINAIGRETTE

1 tablespoon lime juice
1 teaspoon salt
1 teaspoon of freshly ground black pepper
3 tablespoons olive oil

2 large shallots, minced
grated zest of 1 kaffir lime or 2 kaffir lime leaves, shredded

1 Place the octopus in a saucepan, add cold water to cover and 1 teaspoon salt, cover, and bring to a boil. Reduce heat and simmer until tender, 30–45 minutes, or until the sharp point of a knife enters easily into the thickest part of the octopus.

2 Remove from heat and let the octopus cool in the cooking liquid without removing the lid. Drain into a colander, scrape away any loose skin and suckers, and slice into bite-sized pieces.

3 To prepare the vinaigrette, combine the lime juice, salt, and pepper in a medium bowl, then whisk in the olive oil. Add the cooked octopus and toss with the vinaigrette. Marinate in the refrigerator for at least several hours, or overnight.

4 When ready to serve, add the tomatoes, shallots, and zest to the octopus and toss.

"TAKE THE SMELL BUT LEAVE THE FLOWER."
—Creole proverb

PINEAPPLE SALAD WITH CHILI
Ananas au Piment

Native to the Caribbean, Scotch bonnet chilies are the hot pepper of choice for West African and Creole dishes. Twice as hot as jalapeños, they are not for the faint of heart! At Moussa l'Africain, Alexander Bella Ola adds some fire to a cool tropical fruit salad with a sprinkling of this red-hot chili. Serve with grilled meats.

SERVES 4

1   Scotch bonnet chili, seeded and finely minced

   juice of 1 lime

   salt to taste

1   pineapple, peeled, cored, and cut into bite-sized pieces

1   papaya, peeled, seeded, and cut into bite-sized cubes

✱ RESTAURANT
MOUSSA L'AFRICAN
25-26, avenue Corentin Cariou
75019 Paris
tel: 01 40 36 13 00
métro: Porte de la Villette ✱

1   Combine the chili, lime juice, and salt to taste in a small bowl.

2   Put the fruit in a serving bowl; pour over the chili sauce and toss. Refrigerate for at least 1 hour before serving.

PIMENTS ANANAS

PAPAYE CITRONS VERTS

MAIN COURSES

FISH WITH RICE
Tieb bou Dienn

The national dish of Senegal is based on rice and fish cooked in a tomato broth. Chef Ibrahima Ba of Au Village restaurant makes a an authentic version using yet, a fermented dried mollusk, and riz-cassé-deux-fois, or "twice-broken rice." In Senegal, broken rice is preferred over regular rice, but long-grain rice can be used.

★ RESTAURANT

RESTAURANT AU VILLAGE
86, avenue Parmentier
75011 Paris
tel: 01 43 57 18 95
métro: Parmentier

1 Rinse the rice, cover with cold water, and soak for at least 1 hour. Drain.

2 To make the stuffing, place the parsley, garlic, chili, and bouillon cube in a blender or food processor. Pulse to form a thick paste.

3 Slice deep slits into one side of each fish fillet to form a pocket. Stuff the pockets with the paste, reserving any extra.

4 Pour 2 inches (5 cm) of oil into a large heavy saucepan and heat until hot. Brown the fish on both sides. Drain on paper towels.

SERVES 6–8

3   cups broken rice

FISH AND AROMATIC STUFFING

1   bunch fresh parsley

3   cloves garlic

1   bird's-eye chili

2   bouillon cubes (Knorr, Maggi, or Jumbo brand)

4   pounds (2 kg) 1-inch (2.5 cm) thick cod, mako shark, or bluefish fillets or steaks

    oil for deep-frying

RICE AND VEGETABLES

2   onions, minced

1   6-ounce (170 g) can tomato paste

2   ounces (50 g) *yet* (dried stockfish), washed and diced (optional)

5   cups water

½   teaspoon salt

1   pound (450 g) green cabbage, hard leaves removed and cut into thin wedges

2   medium carrots, peeled and cut into 1-inch (2.5 cm) pieces

2   medium turnips, peeled quartered

1   small eggplant, cut into 1-inch (2.5 cm) cubes

½   pound (225 g) manioc, peeled and cut into 1-inch (2.5 cm) chunks

1   bird's eye chili

2   tablespoons vegetable oil

5 To cook the vegetables, pour off all but a few tablespoons of the oil from the saucepan and add the onions. Cook over medium heat until soft and slightly brown. Add two-thirds of the tomato paste, any leftover stuffing, the *yet*, ½ teaspoon salt, and 1 cup water. Cook at a low simmer for 10 minutes, stirring often until mixture has reduced and thickened. Add the remaining 4 cups water and the cabbage. Bring to a simmer and cook, covered, 10 minutes. Add the rest of the vegetables and the chili and cook 20 minutes. Place the browned fish fillets on top of the vegetables and return the cover, lower the heat, and simmer until the fish is opaque and cooked through, about 7–10 minutes.

6 Remove the fish, cover and keep warm. Continue cooking the vegetables until tender, remove, cover, and keep warm.

7 Strain the sauce into a large bowl. You should have 5 cups. Add water if necessary, and pour back into the saucepan. Bring the measured liquid to a boil, stir in the remaining tomato paste and the oil. Taste for seasoning, adding salt if necessary. Add the drained rice to the saucepan. The liquid should cover the rice by ½ inch (1 cm); add more cooking liquid or water if necessary. Bring to a boil, reduce the heat, cover, and simmer 18-20 minutes, or until liquid is absorbed and rice is tender.

8 While the rice is cooking, pour any extra cooking liquid into a small saucepan and simmer to reduce.

9 To serve, spoon the rice onto a large serving platter and arrange the fish and vegetables on top. Pour the reduced cooking liquid into a bowl and serve alongside as a sauce.

MANIOC

Manioc is also known as yuca, manidioca, sweet potato tree, tapioca, and cassava. The big, hardy, tuberous roots constitute one of the world's largest stock crops for starch. Because of its high starch content, manioc is a primary source of calories in poor countries. It requires a minimum amount of maintenance, thriving even in poor soil. Manioc originated in South America and was brought to Africa in the mid-1600s by Portuguese traders. It soon spread throughout the tropics and beyond, following slave routes and commercial trading. It is now grown in three regions of the world, including West Africa and the Congo Basin.

Because it contains cyanogenic glucosides, which can be poisonous, manioc must always be cooked before it is eaten. The bark is peeled or scraped away from the roots, which are then boiled, steamed, fried, or roasted. Cooked manioc is very versatile: it can be eaten like potatoes or pounded into a paste that is steamed or stirred into stews. It can also be grated, dried, and milled into a flour to make breads, pastas, and cookies. Tapioca is the starch extracted from the manioc root—tapioca pearls are used to make thick, sweet desserts, while the flour and flakes are used as a binder for everything from toothpaste to soups. In Africa, people also eat manioc leaves as a green vegetable, an inexpensive source of protein and vitamins A and B.

CHICKEN CURRY
Poulet au Cari

Marie Thérèse Huguet de Bernardi de Sigoyer and her son, François, have been running Le Bernica for almost 30 years. They shared a few of their recipes with us, including this favorite, a chicken cari. Cari is a Tamil word used on the island of Réunion to signify a ragout. A true cari contains only a single spice: turmeric, which gives it a rich yellow color. It's important not to rush this dish; the simmering period releases the flavors of the ingredients.

SERVES 6

- 4   cloves garlic
- 4   whole cloves
- 2   tablespoons canola oil
- 6   whole chicken thighs, cut into 3 pieces each
- 2   medium onions, finely minced
- 1½ tablespoons turmeric
- 4   medium, ripe tomatoes, diced, or 2 cups canned tomatoes, diced, with their juice
- 1   teaspoon fresh thyme
- 1   cup water
     salt and freshly ground black pepper
- ½   cup fresh parsley, chopped

RESTAURANT

LA BERNICA
4, impasse de la Gaité
75014 Paris
tel: 01 43 20 39 02
métro: Edgar Quinet

1 Using a mortar and pestle, or the side of a heavy knife, crush the garlic and cloves.

2 Heat the oil in a large heavy saucepan over high heat. Add the chicken and brown on all sides. Add the onions and cook until translucent, about 10 minutes. Sprinkle the turmeric and the garlic mixture over the meat, stir, and cook until the garlic is soft, about 3 minutes. Add the tomatoes and thyme, lower the heat, and simmer 15 minutes, or until chicken is half done.

3 Pour the water into the pot, and simmer 30 minutes, or until the chicken is tender.

4 Taste the sauce for seasoning. If the flavors need to be more concentrated, remove the chicken pieces to a serving dish, cover, and keep warm. Bring the sauce back to a boil and reduce.

5 Sprinkle with the chopped parsley, and serve accompanied by steamed rice.

PORK COLOMBO
Colombo de Porc

Colombo is the curry powder of the French West Indies. Similar to curry, it arrived in the Caribbean when workers from the Far East were recruited to replace the newly emancipated slaves in 1845. The dish is named after the capital of Sri Lanka, but that's all that remains of the original seasoning. Henry Durimelle is originally from Guadeloupe. A passionate cook, he often makes dishes he ate as a child. This is his version of a colombo made with pork.

SERVES 6

- 3 pounds (1.5 kg) pork loin (shoulder chop end if possible), cubed into bite-sized pieces
- 3 tablespoons white-wine vinegar
- 4 cloves garlic, finely minced
- 3 whole cloves, crushed
- 1 bird's-eye chili, minced
- 1 teaspoon salt, or to taste
- 1 teaspoon freshly ground black pepper, or to taste
- 3 tablespoons vegetable oil
- 1 onion, finely minced
- 6 sprigs fresh parsley, chopped
- 1 large green (unripe) mango, peeled, seeded, and cubed
- 4 potatoes, peeled and cut in half
- 1 large eggplant, cubed
- 2 zucchini, halved lengthwise, then cut into 3-inch (7.5 cm) pieces
- 2 tablespoons colombo powder (see Glossary)
- 1 branch fresh thyme
  juice of 1 lime

1 Place the pork in a bowl and add the vinegar, garlic, cloves, chili, salt, and pepper. Let marinate for 1 hour in the refrigerator.

2 Heat the oil in a large heavy saucepan over medium-high heat. Add the minced onion and parsley and cook until the onion is soft. Add the pork and green mango cubes and brown the pork, stirring occasionally, 10–15 minutes.

3 Add the potatoes, eggplant, and zucchini to the pot, sprinkle with the colombo powder, and stir to coat. Pour in enough water to barely cover the ingredients. Add the thyme, cover, and bring to a boil. Reduce heat to maintain a simmer and cook 50–60 minutes, or until the meat is tender.

4 Check the seasoning, and stir in the lime juice. Serve accompanied by steamed rice.

SHRIMP ROUGAIL
Rougail de Crevette

On the Indian Ocean islands of Réunion and Mauritius, rougail can be a fiery hot condiment or, as in the following recipe, a simple but spicy tomato-based sauce. Rafiq Hamjah, chef and owner of the restaurant Comme Sur une Île, gave us this easy-to-prepare recipe; he stresses the importance of using unpeeled shrimp. Make sure to put out a lot of finger bowls.

SERVES 6

- 6   cloves garlic, crushed
-     2-inch (5 cm) piece of fresh ginger, peeled and chopped
- 1   28-ounce (875 g) can whole tomatoes, drained
- 2   tablespoons canola oil
- 2   small onions, minced
- 1   bird's-eye chili, finely minced
- 1   tablespoon ground cumin
-     salt and freshly ground black pepper
- 2   pounds (1 kg) medium shrimp, in the shell
- ½   cup chopped fresh coriander

1 Using a mortar and pestle, or the side of a heavy knife, crush the garlic and ginger. Puree the tomatoes in a blender.

2 Heat the oil in a large heavy saucepan over medium-high heat. Add the onions, garlic, ginger, and chili and cook until the onions are soft. Sprinkle with the cumin and salt and pepper to taste and cook 2 minutes. Stir in pureed tomatoes, cover, and simmer for 15 minutes.

3 Remove the cover and add the unpeeled shrimp, stirring to coat. Cook until just done, about 3-5 minutes. Do not overcook, or the shrimp will be tough and hard to peel.

4 Stir in the fresh coriander and serve immediately, with steamed rice.

BEEF AND OKRA STEW
Boeuf aux Gombos

Okra and red palm oil make this simple West African stew tasty and healthful. Okra, or gombos, is eaten throughout Africa. Filled with vitamins, minerals, calcium, and fiber, the okra pods release a viscous liquid when cut that expands as they cook, making them a great thickening agent for soups and stews. Okra should be picked young, so when buying, look for small, tender pieces, 2 to 3 inches in length. Red palm oil, not to be confused with palm kernel oil, is produced from palm fruit and contains both carotenoids and super-antioxidants. You will know you are buying palm oil and not palm kernel oil by its bright red color. This is our adaptation of several recipes.

SERVES 6

- 3 tablespoons red palm oil (or substitute vegetable oil)
- 2 pounds (1 kg) stewing beef
- 1 onion, finely minced
- 6 cloves garlic
  3-inch (7 cm) piece of fresh ginger, peeled
- 6 scallions, trimmed
- 3 tomatoes, quartered
- 3 bay leaves
- 2 bouillon cubes (Maggi, Knorr, or Jumbo brand)
- 1 Scotch bonnet chili (optional)
  20–30 small okra, finely diced

1 Heat the oil in a large saucepan over medium-high heat. Add the meat and brown, stirring occasionally, about 10 minutes. Add the onion and continue cooking another 5–7 minutes, or until soft.

2 Meanwhile, puree the garlic, ginger, scallions, and tomatoes in the bowl of a food processor. Stir the puree into the meat and simmer 10 minutes.

3 Add the bay leaves, bouillon, and water to cover the ingredients. Cover and simmer 35–45 minutes, or until the beef is fork-tender.

4 For a very spicy dish, mince the Scotch bonnet and add to the stew. For more moderate heat, add the chili whole.

5 Add the okra to the pot and cook, uncovered, for 10 minutes. Remove the Scotch bonnet chili if you added it whole. Serve accompanied by steamed rice.

ALEXANDRE BELLA OLA

The opening of chef Alexandre Bella Ola's restaurant Moussa l'Africain, just opposite the vast science and arts complex of La Villette, was a novel event. One of the first large (seating capacity: 250) upscale African restaurants in Paris, Bella Ola's intention was to "demystify African cuisine" and make it accessible to all. African dishes are presented within a European framework that he thinks people will find reassuring.

Armed with the experience he acquired with his first restaurant, Rio dos Camaraõs (the name the Portuguese gave to the country of Cameroon), and an African cookbook to his name, Bella Ola went all out. Moussa l'Africain serves mouthwatering dishes from West Africa and hosts live African music on the weekends. Bella Ola, who was raised in Yaoundé, Cameroon, didn't limit himself to specialties from his country. "In most areas of Africa where the geography is similar, the ingredients and sauces are the same. African cuisine is simple, rustic food. Either you know how to deal with a tomato or you don't!"

This former theater actor who came to Paris 26 years ago to attend a conservatory for dramatic arts fell into the restaurant business by going back to what he did as a child—cooking. Growing up, he spent hours in the kitchen with his father, who had worked as a cook for the French administration during colonial times.

Ethnic cuisine is big in Paris, says Bella Ola, who also teaches African cooking classes.

THE CEO'S CHICKEN
Poulet DG "Directeur Général"

This very popular dish from Cameroon is considered luxurious and only for movers and shakers, hence the name DG, short for Directeur Général (or CEO). It's also a favorite in Paris at Moussa l'Africain, where the chef, Alexandre Bella Ola, comes from Cameroon. Pepe and djansan, both native to Cameroon, are two ingredients you will not find in your local grocery store, but they are available by mail-order and in shops specializing in African ingredients. Pepe is a dark brown, smooth nut. Like a peanut, the shell is removed to get to the soft interior flesh, which has a peppery taste. Djansan, which resemble dried chickpeas, are the aromatic seed kernels of the Ndjansan tree, native to tropical Africa.

SERVES 6

- 4   pepe nuts
- 30   djansan seeds
- 1   onion, minced
- 3   cloves garlic, minced
-      1-inch (2.5 cm) piece of fresh ginger, peeled and minced
- ½   cup fresh parsley leaves
- 3   cups water
- 4   green plantains
-      vegetable oil for deep-frying
- 2   tablespoons peanut oil
- 6   whole chicken thighs, cut into 3 pieces each
- 3   carrots, peeled and cut into ½-inch (1 cm) slices
- 1   leek, washed and cut into ½-inch (1 cm) slices
- ½   red bell pepper, diced
- ½   yellow bell pepper, diced
- 1   bouillon cube (Maggi, Knorr, or Jumbo brand)
- 2   tablespoons curry powder

✳ RESTAURANT

MOUSSA L'AFRICAIN
25-27, avenue Corentin Cariou
75019 Paris
tel: 01 40 36 13 00
métro: Porte de la Villette ✳

1 Put the pepe and djansan in separate bowls, cover with boiling water, and soak 10 minutes. Drain the pepe, cut in half, and remove the soft interior. Drain the djansan.

2 Combine the onion, garlic, ginger, parsley, pepe, and djansan in the bowl of a food processor and pulse until finely chopped. With the motor running, add 1 cup of the water and process until smooth. Set aside.

3 Wash the plantains with warm water. Remove the ends, then make three incisions lengthwise into the skin of each. Peel off the tough skin with a sharp knife, which is easier if you pull the skin slightly crosswise rather than straight down. Slice the plantains on a diagonal into ½-inch (1 cm) slices. Heat ½ inch (1 cm) of oil in a medium heavy sauté pan and fry the plantain slices, in batches, until they are lightly browned. Drain on paper towels.

4 Heat the peanut oil in a large saucepan over high heat. Brown the chicken pieces, in batches, then remove and set aside. Drain the oil from the saucepan and add the remaining 2 cups of water. Return the chicken to the pan, along with the onion mixture, carrots, leek, and diced peppers. Crumble the bouillon cube into the pot and sprinkle over the ingredients, along with the curry powder. Simmer 30 minutes, or until the chicken is tender. Add the fried plantains and cook 10 minutes to warm through. Serve accompanied by steamed rice.

LAMB MAFE
Mafé d'Agneau

Mafé is a well-known West African dish likely to be found in any African restaurant in Paris. Made with peanuts, tomatoes, ginger, and garlic, it's rich and savory. It can be prepared with any meat, fish, or vegetables. This lamb version is made with the French brand of unsweetened peanut butter, Dakatine, which is primarily used by the African community in France. Mafé is made differently in each region of Africa. Thérèse Fischer-Djimbong, who grew up in Cameroon, showed us how to prepare her version.

SERVES 6–8

10 cloves garlic
    3-inch (7.5 cm) piece of fresh
    ginger, peeled and chopped
1   large tomato, quartered
½   cup water
1¼ cups peanut oil
2   onions, finely minced
4   pounds (1.8 kg) lamb, cubed

1 Put the garlic, ginger, and tomato in the bowl of a food processor and blend to a smooth puree. Add the water and blend until mixed thoroughly.

2 Heat ¾ cup of the oil in a large casserole over high heat. Add the onions and cook until translucent. Add the meat all at once and brown well, turning occasionally, about 15 minutes.

2½ cups smooth natural peanut butter

6 carrots, peeled and cut lengthwise in half, then into 3-inch (7 cm) lengths

1 Scotch bonnet chili

2 bouillon cubes (Maggi, Knorr, or Jumbo brand)

3 bay leaves

salt and freshly ground black pepper

3 zucchini, cut lengthwise in half, then into 3-inch (7 cm) lengths

3 Pour the pureed mixture over the meat and stir to coat, lower the heat, and cook for 5 minutes. Add water to barely cover, bring to a low boil, and cook 10 minutes, or until slightly reduced. Stir in the peanut butter, mixing until blended. Add the carrots, whole chili, bouillon cubes, bay leaves, and salt and pepper to taste. Partially cover, reduce heat to low, and simmer for 25–35 minutes, or until meat is tender. Add the zucchini and simmer until tender, about 10–12 minutes.

4 Before serving remove the Scotch bonnet chili from the pot and place in a small bowl, mash with the back of a fork, and stir in ½ cup of peanut oil.

5 Taste the sauce and adjust the seasoning. Serve with steamed rice and chili sauce.

THERESE'S ZEBRUR

Hibiscus blossom tea, Ethiopian coffee, Mexican honey, cocoa from Ghana, and jam from Swaziland line the shelves of Thérèse Fischer-Djimbong's shop. Next to the packages of quinoa, there are stacks of jars of lemon verbena and almond soaps, pillowcases from Mali, Touareg jewelry, and brightly colored clothing. The items Thérèse sells in her shop, Zébrur, in Montparnasse, are via a system of fair trade.

Originally from Cameroon, Thérèse came to Paris in 1976 with a degree in dress design. After working in ready-to-wear, Thérèse opened Zébrur in 2005, with the idea that it would celebrate cross-cultural exchanges. When there are neighborhood parties, Thérèse cooks an enormous vat of the Cameroonian national dish, *ndole*, (meat or fish in a sauce made with the bitter leaf

ndole), or a lamb *mafé*, which is then served at the community center. She can now readily find any ingredient necessary for African dishes, which was not the case when she first arrived in Paris 30 years ago: "We used to have to wait until someone came from Cameroon to bring us ingredients."

GEORGES' FISH YASSA
Yassa au Poisson Façon Georges

Ask a Parisian to name an African dish, and he will say yassa. As with all African dishes, there are many variations. This one is from Georges Turpin, one of the Senegalese owners of Parivic, a specialty fish store in the Château Rouge neighborhood. The lime, onion, and mustard marinade can also be used for beef or chicken.

SERVES 6

- 2 bouillon cubes (Maggi, Knorr, or Jumbo brand)
- 2 cloves garlic, finely minced
- 3 tablespoons Dijon mustard
- ½ teaspoon red pepper flakes
- 2 1 pound, 12-ounce (700 g) fish steaks
- 3 large onions, thinly sliced
- ½ cup lime juice
- 1 teaspoon salt
- 2 carrots, peeled and cut into ½-inch (1 cm) slices
- ¼ cup vegetable oil
- 5 ounces (150 g) pitted green olives
- 3 bay leaves
- 1 bird's-eye chili
- 1 cup water
- ½ cup chopped fresh parsley

1 Crumble the bouillon into a small bowl, then add the garlic, 2 tablespoons mustard, and red pepper flakes, stirring to make a paste. Rub the fish steaks with the paste. Place in a shallow dish, cover with plastic wrap, and marinate 1 hour.

2 Meanwhile, place the onions in a large bowl and add the remaining tablespoon mustard, the lime juice, and salt. Cover with plastic wrap and marinate 1 hour.

3 Put the carrots in a pot of salted cold water, bring to a boil, and cook until tender, about 10 minutes. Drain and set aside.

4 Drain the onions in a colander, reserving the marinade. Heat the oil in a saucepan large enough to hold the fish. Add the onions and cook until soft. Add the reserved marinade and water, cooked carrots, olives, bay leaves, and chili. Simmer on medium heat for 15 minutes. Place the fish on top of the other ingredients, partially cover the pan, lower the heat, and cook 10–15 minutes, or until the fish is cooked through. Serve warm accompanied by steamed rice.

PARIVIC

The Goutte d'Or in northern Paris is a bustling, crowded neighborhood, home to many North and West African immigrants. It is also the place to go to buy African fish. For most West Africans, fish, whether saltwater or freshwater, is a way of life. In Georges Turpin's Parivic, a spacious store painted blue and white, specializing in African frozen fish, clients behave like professional fishmongers. They grab enormous grouper by the tail and examine them carefully; they rummage in the freezer searching for the perfect tilapia.

Georges was born in Dakar and came to France at the age of six. His father began the business in 1992, and Georges joined him in 2000. The Turpins import fish from many countries, including Oman, Thailand, and Indonesia, but their main supplier is Senegal.

Georges can usually tell where his clients come from by what sort of fish they buy. "The Senegalese buy *mérou* [grouper], tilapia, and sea bream. People from the Congo buy *chinchard* [mackerel], *capitaine* [giant African threadfin], and *bar* [sea bass]. Cameroonians buy sole, they like it to be very big. The Ivory Coast community likes *tassergal* [bluefish]."

Parivic sells fish both retail and wholesale and supplies most of the major African restaurants in Paris. Even Africans with shops in other cities in France drive to Paris for the day (with coolers) to buy a supply of fish.

Georges also sells anything you might need to cook with the fish: peanut butter, oil, Jumbo bouillon cubes, herbs, and bags of broken rice are all neatly stacked on shelves above the large freezers.

Poissonerie Parivic 1, Rue de Panama 18ème

DESSERTS

MILLET COUSCOUS WITH FRESH FRUIT
Thiacri

Little pearls of millet couscous mixed with sweetened yogurt and topped with fresh fruit is one of the few true African desserts.

SERVES 6

1   cup *thiacri* (millet couscous)
2   tablespoons sugar
½   teaspoon vanilla
2   cups plain yogurt
1   cup cut-up or sliced fresh fruit

1 Pour 3 cups of boiling water over the millet couscous in a bowl. Cover and let sit 15 minutes, or until the water is completely absorbed.

2 Stir the sugar and vanilla into the yogurt.

3 Divide the millet between six bowls, spoon the yogurt on top, and cover with the fruit.

BANANA TART
Tarte aux Bananes

This is an easy banana tart from the Island of Reunion, similar to the one Marie Thérèse Huguet de Bernardi de Sigoyer makes at Le Bernica restaurant (see page 187).

SERVES 6

2½ cups all-purpose flour
½ teaspoon salt
2 sticks cold unsalted butter, cut into pieces
5-6 tablespoons ice water

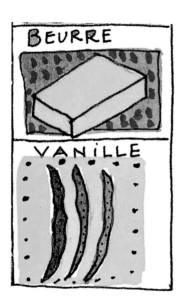

1 Put the flour and salt in the bowl of a food processor and pulse once to blend. Add the butter and pulse until the mixture resembles coarse meal, about 10 seconds.

2 With the motor running, add the ice water 1 tablespoon at a time until the dough holds together. Add only as much water as necessary, and do not process for more than 30 seconds total.

3 Turn the dough out onto a work surface and gather into a loose ball. Place the dough on a piece of plastic wrap and flatten with the palm of your hand into a disk. Wrap and chill in the refrigerator for 1 hour.

4 Preheat the oven to 375°F (180°C). Roll the dough out on a lightly floured work surface to a thickness of ¼ inch (7 mm). Place the pastry in a 9-inch (23 cm) tart pan with a removable bottom and press it into the bottom and up the sides. Cover with a sheet of aluminum foil large enough for the edges to extend beyond the rim of the tart pan, and bake for 10–12 minutes. Near the end of baking, remove the foil to allow the pastry to dry out and brown slightly. Remove the pastry from the oven and cool on a wire rack. Leave the oven on.

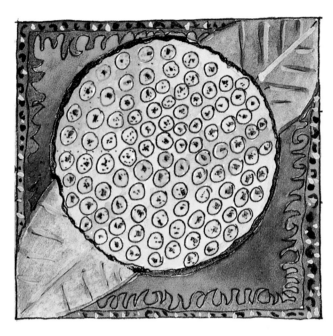

CITRONS VERTS

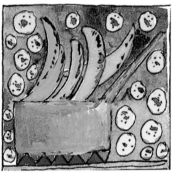

FILLING

- -

7 ripe bananas

½ cup water

½ vanilla bean, split lengthwise

1 tablespoon sugar

⅛ teaspoon ground cinnamon

6 tablespoons unsalted butter, cut into pieces

juice of 1 lime

brown sugar for sprinkling

1 Peel and slice 4 of the bananas. Combine the water, vanilla bean, sugar, cinnamon, and lime juice in a medium saucepan and heat, stirring, until the sugar has dissolved. Add the banana slices and butter and simmer until the banana slices soften. Remove from the heat.

2 Peel the remaining bananas and cut on a diagonal into ¼-inch (7 mm) slices.

3 Spread the banana mixture evenly on the bottom of the cooled tart shell and cover in overlapping circles with the uncooked banana slices. Sprinkle with brown sugar and bake for 15 minutes.

A SENEGALESE STREET IN PARIS

The quiet rue Elzévir in the uber-chic Marais neighborhood, lined with 17th-century *hôtels particuliers* (townhouses), is decidedly African in spirit, thanks to Valérie Schlumberger. This pioneering Parisian discovered Senegal in 1969, when she moved to Dakar with her husband, an ethnologist. "I liked it the minute I stepped off the plane," says Valérie. She remained in the country for seven years, learning Wolof along the way and exporting African clothing to France. Back in Paris seven years later, and the mother of three children, she wrote a novel, modeled, did costume design, and acted in and produced films, returning to Senegal as often as possible. In 1995, 26 years after her initial visit to Senegal, Valérie realized an ambitious plan: the CSAO (Compagnie du Senegal et de l'Afrique de l'Ouest) was Paris's first large-scale shop selling African arts and crafts. "It was the outcome of years of work experience and contacts I made in Senegal," she says.

Valérie established a system of cooperatives in Senegal; the CSAO serves as a distributor for their products, which range from toys made with recycled cans to elegant armchairs woven with fishing net. She also founded an association, ASAO (Association du Sènègal et de l'Afrique de l'Ouest), that helps street children in Senegal. Riding on the tremendous success of the CSAO, Valérie opened a Senegalese restaurant, Le Petit Dakar, on the same street a few years later. In 2003 she formed a partnership with Senegalese musician Youssou N'Dour and opened Jokko, a bar and gallery across the street from Le Petit Dakar. Ever passionate about Senegal, Valérie is now considering opening an African grocery store and expanding her restaurant.

CSAO
9, rue Elzévir 75003 Paris

LE PETIT DAKAR
6, rue Elzévir 75003 Paris

JOKKO
5, rue Elzévir 75003 Paris

ASAO
15, rue Elzévir 75003 Paris

COCONUT AND LIME FLAN
Flan à la Noix de Coco

Coconut milk and lime zest give this popular dessert its Caribbean flavor. Henry Durimelle, a gourmet from Guadeloupe, gave us the recipe for his version of coconut flan.

SERVES 6

CARAMEL

1 cup sugar
½ teaspoon butter

FLAN

6 large eggs
1½ cups sweetened condensed milk (one small can)
2 cups unsweetened coconut milk
½ teaspoon ground cinnamon
½ teaspoon ground nutmeg
   grated zest of 1 lime

1 Put a rack in the middle of the oven and preheat to 300°F (160°C). Place a 9-inch (23 cm) flan dish or nonstick round cake pan near the stove top.

2 To make the caramel, put a small heavy saucepan over low heat, add the sugar and butter, and increase heat to high. Cook, without stirring, occasionally swirling the pan, until the sugar melts and turns dark golden. Immediately pour the caramel into the prepared dish. Wearing oven mitts, tilt the pan to coat the bottom and ½ inch (1 cm) up the sides. Set aside.

3 To prepare the flan, put all the remaining ingredients into a bowl and whisk to combine. Pour the mixture into the caramel-lined dish. Place in the oven and cook for 35–40 minutes, or until a knife inserted 1 inch (2.5 cm) from the edge of the dish comes out clean. The center of the custard should still tremble. Cool completely, then refrigerate the flan for 4–6 hours.

4 To serve, dip the bottom of the dish into hot water to warm the caramel. Cover the flan with a rimmed platter, and invert the flan onto the platter. Gently remove the dish, allowing the caramel to spill out onto the flan.

MANGO TART WITH COULIS
Tarte Fine aux Mangues avec son Coulis

A single layer of thinly sliced mangoes topped by buttery puff pastry is all that's behind Rougia Dia's signature dessert. Pureed mango enhanced with lemon juice accompanies this sun-filled tart.

SERVES 6

MANGO COULIS

1   ripe mango, peeled, seeded, and chopped
2   tablespoons sugar
1   tablespoon lemon juice

2   ripe mangoes, peeled, seeded, and thinly sliced
1   teaspoon butter
1   tablespoon sugar
1   sheet puff pastry, defrosted according to package

1   To make the coulis, puree the mango in the bowl of a food processor until smooth. Strain through a sieve into a bowl. Stir in the sugar and lemon juice. Chill until ready to serve.

2   Preheat the oven to 350°F (170°C). Grease the bottom of a 9-inch (23 cm) pie pan with butter. Sprinkle with sugar, then tap to remove the excess. Place the mango slices in the pan in a single layer forming a neat, overlapping circular row.

3   To make the tart shell, roll the pastry out thinly on a lightly floured surface. Cut out a circle slightly larger than the pie pan. Lay the pastry on top of the mango slices, gently tucking in the sides to enclose the fruit. Place in the oven and bake 20–25 minutes, or until the crust is golden brown.

4   Remove the tart from the oven and allow to rest 2 minutes, then invert onto a serving plate. Serve accompanied by the mango coulis.

ROUGUI DIA

When Rougui Dia took over the reins in the kitchen of the restaurant belonging to the venerable Petrossian caviar empire, the press was agog. A woman! And with an African background, no less. Thirty years old, calm, and reserved, Rougui Dia grew up in the suburbs of Paris, born to Senegalese parents, with a mother who loved to cook. Her parents regularly got up at 5AM and drove to Rungis (the gargantuan Parisian wholesale market), taking whichever of the seven children wanted to go with them.

Rougui became interested in cooking professionally when she was in her teens, after her family noticed the fact that she could flawlessly execute certain complicated Senegalese dishes. She decided to get a degree in cooking in a state-run program and braved several apprenticeships in Parisian kitchens before landing at Petrossian in 2001. Rougui was already intimately familiar with fish due to her training at home, and this gave her a good starting point in a restaurant in which fish is all-important.

She blossomed under the watchful eye of chef Sébastien Faré, and when he left in 2005, Petrossian's owner, Armen Petrossian, decided to put Rougui in charge. The restaurant's menu has gently evolved to include certain exotic touches, such as scorpion fish with plantains; prawn ravioli with a dash of coconut; wild Iranian shrimp with a crunchy, curry-flavored exterior; and her signature dessert, *tarte fine aux mangues*.

While Rougui has delicately balanced Eastern European cooking with African influences, she occasionally takes time to cook Senegalese dishes for her large all-male kitchen staff. With a maternal smile she says, "They've tried and liked *mafé*, *yassa*, *pastels*, and sugar fritters."

PETROSSIAN
18, boulevard de La Tour-Maubourg
75007 Paris
tel: 01 44 11 32 32
métro: La Tour-Maubourg

THE BEST MEZZE WEST OF BEIRUT
LEBANON AND SYRIA

"Then she told us about the Syrian soldier who fell in love with her... 'He loved you for your stuffed zucchini in yogurt,' interrupted Ruhiyya."
—Hanan Al-Shaykh, "Beirut Blues"

BEIRUT IN PARIS

During the golden days of Lebanon in the 1960s, when Beirut was known as the Paris of the Middle East, few Lebanese could imagine that Paris, France, would become home to so many of them just a few years later. Although intellectuals and students from the Levant had been coming to Paris since the late 19th century, in 1975 there were fewer than 6,000 Lebanese living in France. From then and for the duration of the 15-year Lebanese civil war, more than 155,000 Lebanese arrived in France, with a majority settling in Paris. Many began businesses, and among these, restaurants flourished, bringing the flavors of rose water, cinnamon, mint, thyme, and sumac to the French capital, forever altering its culinary landscape. From a paltry three in 1975, there are now more than 130 Lebanese restaurants in Paris.

A CULINARY TRADITION

Lebanon and Syria share a great culinary tradition inherited from the different cultures that influenced their major cities: Saida (Sidon), Beirut, Tripoli, Damascus, and Aleppo. Egyptians, Babylonians, Assyrians, Persians, Greeks, Romans, and finally Ottoman Turks all left their mark on the local cuisine. "We know from cookbooks that by the 19th century, with the arrival of vegetables from the New World, Lebanese and Syrian cuisines were as we know them today," says Farouk Mardam-Bey, a culinary historian, editor, and writer.

The Lebanese adapted and refined Ottoman dishes, perfecting the presentation and making certain specialties lighter. The omnipresent *mezzé* table, or selection of appetizers, is a balance of cold and hot dishes, ranging from tabbouleh, a combination of finely chopped parsley, onions, tomatoes, and a hint of mint with bulgur (cooked cracked wheat); hummus, made with ground chickpeas, sesame

Sésame.

oil, garlic, and lemon juice; and *m'tabal* (or *baba ghanoush*), a smoky mixture of eggplant, sesame oil, lemon juice; to oval *kibbeh*—bulgar stuffed with ground lamb, pine nuts, and chopped onions, flavored with cinnamon. No meal is eaten without *khubz Arabi*, or Arabic bread, known as pocket or pita bread in the United States. Far thinner and flatter than the typical pita, it is round and easily split in order to make sandwiches, or used as a utensil for scooping food, or toasted then torn and sprinkled on salads and other dishes. In France it is called *pain Libanais* (Lebanese bread) or *pain Arabe*. Skewered grilled meats and dishes made with grains and lentils are served after the *mezzé*.

Lebanese and Syrian cooking is similar in the region of Damascus. Damascenes, however, have a particular talent for sweets, such as *maa'moul*, sugar-dusted semolina cookies stuffed with pistachios, and *atayef*, crepes filled with clotted cream or fresh goat cheese and covered with an orange-flower syrup or their world-famous apricot paste. In Aleppo, in the north, Persian influences are more apparent, with the use of fruit in dishes such as meats flavored with pomegranate syrup or grilled meatballs with black cherries. Aleppo is also said to be the capital of *kibbeh* with no less than 60 different recipes for the ground lamb and bulgar mix.

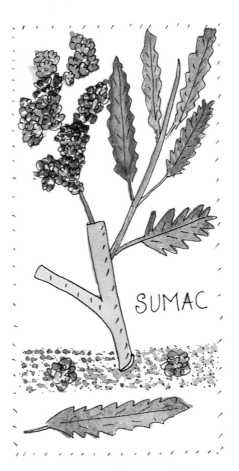

SUMAC

A FRENCH MANDATE

Modern Lebanon and Syria were established in 1920 under a French mandate, yet ties between France and the areas that became Lebanon and Syria go back to the times of the Crusaders, when contact was made between the Maronite Christians from Mount Lebanon and the Roman papacy. This led to France developing a long-standing relationship with the Maronites and other Christians in the Levant.

In the 19th century, French Romantic poets and writers such as René Chateaubriand, Alphonse de Lamartine, and Gérard de Nerval all traveled to the area and wrote at length about it. By the time Lebanon and Syria gained their independence from France in 1946, the French language, educational system (introduced by religious missions), and habits were so well ingrained in the Lebanese culture (far less in Syria) that to this day, while slowly losing out to English, French remains the most widely spoken language in Lebanon after Arabic and is still taught in 70 percent of private primary schools. French influence on the local cooking, however, was minimal, other than the introduction of baguettes, croissants, and French fries.

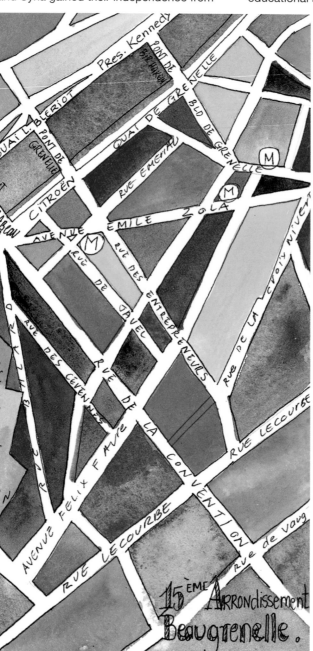

Paris is a nerve center for Lebanese—a great number of world-renowned writers, filmmakers, musicians, academics, and businesspeople have settled in the city, and politicians and military figures often took refuge in Paris at various times during the civil war. At first, a great number of Lebanese who were able to come to Paris were from privileged backgrounds, and most invested in real estate in the residential 15th and 16th *arrondissements* in the western part of the city. Many Lebanese restaurants are located in these neighborhoods.

Thym

Zaatar

ECHOES FROM PARIS

As the civil war was ending in 1990, Lebanese immigrants came to France for economic reasons. At the same time, a great number of the Lebanese Paris residents returned to Lebanon, many of them choosing to live between both countries, although the events last summer tipped the scales in favor of Paris once again. There is a small Syrian community in Paris, but the Syrians tend to be more discreet, or to blend in with the Lebanese community.

"The Lebanese in France feel so much at home here that they forget they're abroad," says Elias Masboungi, who writes a weekly gossip column about the community called *Les Echos de Paris* for the Beirut daily *L'Orient le Jour.*

Given the relatively small number of Lebanese living in Paris—estimates range from 25,000 to 50,000—the community nevertheless has had a far-reaching impact on the city. Besides cultural and culinary influences, the Lebanese's fun-loving reputation has rubbed off on the city: Johny Saadeh has been organizing Lebanese and Oriental Night parties beginning at 11PM every Monday for the past two years at a club on the Champs Elysées, and now another trendy club is sponsoring Lebanese theme nights on Fridays where a "Beirut nightlife ambiance" is guaranteed.

But the clubbers agree that one of the best things about dancing all night is looking forward to eating the *man'ouche*: the paper-thin pizza smothered with a thyme, sumac, sesame seed, and olive oil spread that is served for breakfast.

Note: In this chapter we have used phonetic spellings of the informal Arabic spoken in Lebanon and Syria.

APPETIZERS

ROASTED EGGPLANT PURÉE
M'tabal

Gina Diwan, a Lebanese fashion designer, moved to Paris knowing only how to make coffee. She has since become a top-notch cook, famous for her generous dinners. This is her version of baba ghanoush, or m'tabal, as it's called in Lebanon, a classic mezzé that always finds a place on her table. Variations of m'tabal include adding a few spoonfuls of pomegranate syrup to give it a flavorful tanginess or a dollop of yogurt for a smoother texture.

SERVES 4

1 large eggplant
  juice of 2 lemons
2 tablespoons tahini
1 teaspoon salt
  olive oil
  sumac

1 Preheat the oven to 350°F (180°C). Prick the eggplant all over with a fork. Place it in a baking dish and bake until soft. (Or cook it over a charcoal grill or an open fire for a smoky flavor.)

2 Remove the skin while the eggplant is still hot, place the flesh in a bowl, and drizzle with the lemon juice to keep it from darkening. Mash the eggplant with a fork to make a lumpy puree. (Do not use a food processor, since it would turn the cooked eggplant into soup.) Stir the tahini and salt into the eggplant. Transfer to a serving dish, drizzle with olive oil, and sprinkle with sumac.

TABBOULEH SORBET
Sorbet au Tabboulé

Salim Heleiwa, a Lebanese immigrant who set up his sorbet business, Sorbet & Co., on the outskirts of Paris, makes traditional French sorbets for restaurants. When Karim Haidar of Liza came to him with a request for tabbouleh sorbet, Salim balked at first, but then he set about the job, eventually coming up with exactly what Karim had in mind. Here is a version of his delicious and unusual recipe.

SERVES 6–8

1¼ cups strained lemon juice

½ cup plus 3 tablespoons milk

2 tablespoons water

1 tablespoon olive oil

4½ cups fresh parsley, chopped

2 cups fresh mint, finely chopped

½ cup chopped onions

¼ cup crushed tomatoes

¼ cup confectioners' sugar

1 rounded teaspoon salt

¼ teaspoon white pepper

¼ teaspoon freshly ground black pepper

1½ teaspoons powdered pectin

1 Combine the lemon juice, milk, water, and olive oil in a bowl.

2 Place the parsley, mint, onion, and tomatoes in the bowl of a food processor. Moisten with a small ladleful of the liquid ingredients, and process to a fine puree.

3 Stir the pureed ingredients into the remaining liquid ingredients. Add the sugar, salt, peppers, and pectin and mix well. Pour the sorbet mixture into a metal pan lined with plastic wrap (or ice trays). Cover with plastic wrap and place in the freezer for at least 6 hours, or overnight.

4 Remove the frozen sorbet from the freezer and allow to soften. Break into pieces and process in a food processor to an icy slush. Pour into a serving bowl and return to the freezer to set for at least 1 hour before serving. Alternatively, the sorbet can also be churned in an ice-cream maker according to the manufacturer's directions. Then freeze and allow it to soften for 15 minutes in the refrigerator before serving.

KARIM HAIDAR

LIZA

14, rue de la Banque 75002 Paris
tel: 01 55 35 00 66
métro: Bourse

There is a new kind of Lebanese restaurant in Paris, where you won't find hummus or tabbouleh. At Liza's, you might instead find a tabbouleh sorbet or calamari sautéed in garlic and topped with fresh coriander. The co-owners, Swiss-hotel-school graduate Liza Soughayar and executive chef Karim Haidar, see eye to eye on how they want to present Lebanon: contemporary, creative, and hip—no folklore allowed. The pair also owns the adjacent "L" bakery, where Lebanese bread is made each day, but reinterpreted club sandwiches and Lebanese *man'ouche* (sandwiches) are also sold.

Liza restaurant is the reflection of Beirut today in its look—innovative and impeccably furnished by young Lebanese designers. But the cuisine is pushing aside tradition as well, thanks to Karim, a former lawyer, now chef/ entrepreneur. "My philosophy is '*pourquoi pas*?'" he says. Karim spent much of his childhood in Beirut in his mother's kitchen. On his own with his elder brother in Paris while the civil war dragged on in Lebanon, Karim launched into cooking at 16.

Karim began his professional life when he opened his own restaurant in Paris in 1999. He then moved to London to take over the kitchen at Fakhreldine, one of the city's top Lebanese restaurants. He is still a partner there and is in the process of launching a series of mezzé bars in London.

But Paris is his base, and he supervises the kitchen and the French chef he trained for Liza, Jean Bataille. At Liza, the menu changes frequently, reflecting Karim's constant search for new ways to rework Lebanese recipes.

With a cookbook just out on Lebanese food that he co-wrote with Lebanese author Amin Maalouf's wife, Andrée, he still has enough energy left to start up an informal Lebanese "cafeteria" and to open a second bakery in Paris with Liza.

ROLLED FILO PASTRY STUFFED WITH CHEESE
Ra'at/Cigares au Fromage

Children love Lebanese mezzé; there is always something that pleases them among the numerous small dishes. Just a few blocks from the Eiffel Tower, the tiny restaurant Samaya offers a simple assortment of freshly made appetizers and grilled meats. Their version of ra'at, created with a mixture of haloumi, a cheese made from sheep's milk, and feta cheese is sure to be a hit with any child. If you find them too salty, slice the feta and haloumi and soak in several changes of cold water for about 15–20 minutes.

MAKES 30

- 14 ounces (400 g) haloumi
- 7 ounces (200 g) feta
- 1 medium onion, grated
- 1 large egg yolk
- ½ bunch fresh parsley, leaves finely minced
- 1 teaspoon white pepper
- 9 sheets frozen filo dough, thawed
- melted butter for brushing
- oil for deep-frying

1 Combine the haloumi, feta, and grated onion in the bowl of a food processor. Blend to a paste. Add the egg yolk, parsley, and pepper and blend until well combined. Remove to a bowl.

2 Lay the sheets of filo dough on a lightly floured work surface with a short end toward you. Cut the pastry into 5-inch-wide (13 cm) strips, slicing through all the sheets. Place a single strip on the work surface, with a short end facing you. Set the rest of the filo aside, covered with a lightly dampened kitchen towel. Fold the strip of pastry lengthwise in half. Spoon a heaping tablespoon of the cheese mixture onto the center of the bottom strip. Roll up the pastry, folding in the long sides as you go. Brush with butter to seal and place seam side down on a baking sheet. Continue with the rest of the pastry and filling.

 RESTAURANT

SAMAYA

31, boulevard de Grenelle
75015 Paris
tel: 01 45 77 44 44
métro: Bir-Hakeim

3 Refrigerate the cigars briefly (10–15 minutes) to allow the butter to harden so the seams are well sealed.

4 Heat 3 inches of oil in a deep heavy saucepan to 350°F (180°C). Fry the cigars in batches until golden brown. Drain on paper towels. Serve warm.

LENTILS WITH BULGAR
M'jaddara

"Fresh, healthy, and delicious" is how Anis Nacrour, a French diplomat with Syrian origins, describes this lentil dish, which can be eaten warm or cold and is often made with rice instead of bulgar. He advises against using the more expensive and sought-after Puy lentils—plain brown lentils work best here.

SERVES 6

- 1 cup coarse bulgar
- 1⅓ cups brown lentils
- ½ teaspoon 7-spice powder (see Glossary)
- 5 tablespoons olive oil
- 1 large white onion, chopped
- ½ bunch fresh mint, leaves chopped
- salt and freshly ground black pepper

1 Rinse the bulgar, then soak in warm water for 10 minutes; drain.

2 Rinse the lentils and combine in a medium saucepan with 4 cups cold salted water and the 7-spice powder. Bring to a boil, then lower the heat and simmer, uncovered, for 15 minutes. Skim off any foam that rises to the surface. Stir in the bulgar and cook for an additional 15 minutes, or until the bulgar and lentils are tender.

GARNISHES

yogurt

sliced cucumber

crushed garlic

chopped scallions

3 Meanwhile, heat 3 tablespoons olive oil in a large sauté pan. Add the onions and cook over medium-high heat until soft and beginning to color. Remove the onions with a slotted spoon and drain on paper towels.

4 When the lentil and bulgar mixture is cooked, drain any excess liquid, put into a large bowl, and toss with the remaining olive oil. Sprinkle with fried onions and serve with the garnishes on the side.

ANIS NACROUR

Abricots / Oranges / Figues de Barbarie / Figues

For Anis Nacrour, life is a delicate balancing act of two cultures—not only in his job as a French diplomat but also in his personal life. Anis was born in Syria but as a young child grew up in Chile, with his French mother and his Syrian father; he moved back to Syria at the age of 12. Anis lived in the large family compound, which meant that he could wander from his grandmother's house to his uncle's house and back into his own home, gathering delicious tidbits along the way; someone was always cooking something. He says, "It was a permanent state of culinary exaggeration, with constant gustatory fireworks going off."

Anis recalls the terrace being covered with fruit that had been laid out to dry in the sun to then become fruit confits, homemade jam, tomato paste, or cherry eau-de-vie.

He arrived in Paris 30 years ago as a student, armed with what he calls "an identity card of tastes and flavors." He began cooking to impress girls, and usually with Syrian influences because it was original. He would bring back ingredients from his visits home— the special 4-spice mix his aunt prepared, sumac, and cardamom, which he put in rice. He experimented, searching for the tastes of his childhood, and came up with an easy cuisine that, he says, won't satisfy purists but pleases him and his friends tremendously.

THREE SMALL DISHES
Mezzé

The following three recipes, all delicious small dishes, are adapted from culinary historian and gourmet Farouk Mardam-Bey's cookbooks. They can be served individually or as part of a selection of mezzé.

PUMPKIN PUREE WITH TAHINI
Purée de Potiron

When pumpkin arrived in the Middle East from the New World, it enriched the local cuisines. A welcome addition, it was used in stews, hollowed out and stuffed, or, as in this recipe, simply pureed with tahini into a dip for Arabic bread.

SERVES 6

- 2 pounds (1 kg) pumpkin, peeled, seeded, and cubed
- ½ cup tahini
- 3 cloves garlic
- 1 teaspoon salt
  juice of 2 lemons
- 1 teaspoon ground cumin
  chopped fresh parsley

1 Place the pumpkin with 1 cup water in a large saucepan and cook covered at a low boil for 30 minutes, until soft.

2 Drain and transfer the pumpkin to a food processor or blender and puree. Remove to a bowl and stir in the tahini.

3 Crush the garlic with the salt to a smooth paste in a mortar and pestle, or using the side of a heavy knife. Stir into the pumpkin puree along with lemon juice.

4 Sprinkle with the cumin and parsley and serve, with wedges of Arabic or pita bread.

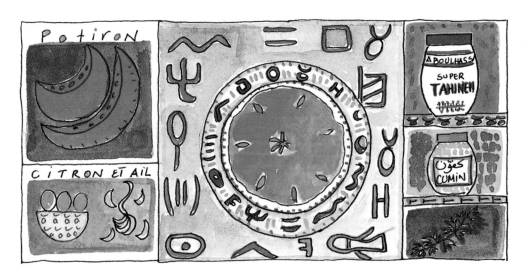

SPICY TOMATOES
Tomates Piquantes

These are simple ingredients made special by the sour lemony flavor of sumac, which can become addictive. Sumac is sometimes ground with salt, so taste before adding more seasoning.

SERVES 6

- ½ cup plus 1 tablespoon olive oil
- 4 cloves garlic, thinly sliced
- 2 pounds (1 kg) tomatoes, peeled, seeded, and diced
- 1 teaspoon ground cumin
- 1 teaspoon sumac
- 1 teaspoon red pepper flakes
- salt and freshly ground black pepper

1 Heat the oil in a medium saucepan over medium heat. Add the garlic and sauté 1 minute. Add the tomatoes and cook over low heat for 10 minutes. Season with the cumin, sumac, red pepper flakes, and salt and pepper to taste. Continue cooking 5 minutes, then remove from heat.

2 Let cool, and serve at room temperature.

CHICKPEA HUMMUS
Panade de Pois Chiches

This family-style dish is one variety in a group of dishes based on broken toasted Arabic bread, covered with assorted toppings and flavored yogurt. The addition of juicy, jewel-like pomegranate seeds gives a sweet-tart note as well as beautiful color to the dish.

SERVES 6

- 2½ cups dried chickpeas
- 1 tablespoon baking soda
- 3 Arabic (or pita) breads
- 2 cloves garlic
- 1 teaspoon salt
- 1 cup plus 2 tablespoons yogurt
- 2 tablespoons tahini
- 1 pomegranate
- 1 tablespoon butter
- ⅓ cup pine nuts
- ½ teaspoon ground cumin
- ½ teaspoon cayenne pepper

1 Soak the chickpeas in water to cover overnight; drain. Combine with 3 quarts (3 liters) water and the baking soda in a large saucepan and cook at a low simmer until tender, about 30 minutes. Drain, reserving the cooking liquid.

2 Preheat the broiler. Open the breads and separate the two halves. Place them smooth side down under the broiler and toast until lightly browned and crisp. Break into pieces and place in the bottom of a serving bowl.

3 Crush the garlic with the salt using a mortar and pestle, or the side of a heavy knife. Combine with the yogurt and tahini in a bowl.

4 Cut the pomegranate in half. Remove the juicy seeds and discard the bitter pith. Sauté the pine nuts in the butter until golden brown, and reserve with the pomegranate seeds.

5 Moisten the broken bread slightly with some of the reserved cooking liquid, then spread the chickpeas on top. Cover with the yogurt sauce and sprinkle with the cumin, cayenne pepper, pomegranate seeds, and pine nuts.

FAROUK MARDAM-BEY

You might think that Farouk Mardam-Bey spends his days behind a hot stove. Actually, the author of *Ziryab: Authentic Arab Cuisine* and *The Little Ziryab* (a cookbook for children), co-author of *The Treatise of the Chickpea*, and editor of a cookbook series called *L'Orient Gourmand* is also the director of Arabic-language fiction at the French publishing company Actes Sud and a literary advisor at the Arab World Institute in Paris.

As a child growing up in the gastronomical city of Damascus, Mardam-Bey was "a difficult eater. It was only as an adolescent that I became a gourmand." He arrived in Paris in 1965 as a university student. There were only a few Lebanese restaurants in Paris at the time, he recalls, ingredients were hard to get, and "when we made hummus, it was a great day." In 1995, he was asked to write a culinary column for *Qantara*, the Arab World Institute's journal. The articles that he wrote over five years became the basis for his first cookbook. As a food critic, Mardam-Bey used the pen name Ziryab, inspired by the 9th-century Iraqi erudite who lived in Cordoba, the cultural capital of Islamic Spain. Ziryab, a gifted musician, poet, and astronomer, was also an epicure. The order in which we eat our meals today is attributed to him.

Mardam-Bey is particularly interested in culinary history and speaks passionately about the hybrid aspect of Middle Eastern cuisine during the Ottoman period.

When he turns to the palpable aspect of cooking, Mardam-Bey shops at markets in Belleville or Ménilmontant and buys his spices from a merchant from the ancient Syrian city of Antioch, today Antakya, in Turkey. He cooks daily for his family, whipping up *kibbeh* and lamb with rice and vegetables, as well as mezzé dishes.

FISH WITH TAHINI SAUCE
Tagen de Poisson

One of our favorite small appetizers is fish tagen, fresh fish cooked in a creamy sauce made with tahini and onions. At the restaurant Feyrouz, it is served cold along with other salads, but it can also be eaten warm over rice.

SERVES 6

½   cup tahini
    juice of 3 lemons
1   teapoon salt
1   cup water
½   cup olive oil
3   large onions, cut in half,
    then thinly sliced
⅓   cup pine nuts
1½ pounds (675 g) cod fillet,
    cut into cubes

1 Whisk together the tahini, lemon juice, and salt in a medium bowl. Gradually add the water, whisking, until the mixture is smooth and blended.

2 Heat the oil in a large skillet. Sauté onions and pine nuts over low heat until the onions are soft and just beginning to color. Add the tahini mixture and the fish and cook, stirring constantly, for 15–20 minutes. The fish should be cooked through and the sauce smooth and homogeneous.

FEYROUZ RESTAURANT AND DELICATESSEN

FEYROUZ CÔTÉ MER
10, rue de Lourmel
75007 Paris
tel: 01 45 79 74 34
métro: Dupleix

Now a fixture on the Lebanese restaurant circuit, Feyrouz restaurant and delicatessen opened in Paris in 1986, and it was one of the first Lebanese establishments to offer take-out delivery and to serve meals in one place. Feyrouz's owners, the Raad family, recently added something innovative to the Parisian landscape. Their fish-only restaurant, Feyrouz Côté Mer, is one of a kind and serves fish the way you might eat it on the beach in Saida or Tyr, in southern Lebanon. Each day Adel Raad goes to Rungis, the enormous Parisian wholesale market at 1:30AM and picks out fish for his restaurant—mullet, pandora fish, sardines, small John Dory, or calamari—which is then baked, fried, or sautéed for customers and served with a small selection of mezzé specially chosen to complement the fish.

MAIN COURSES

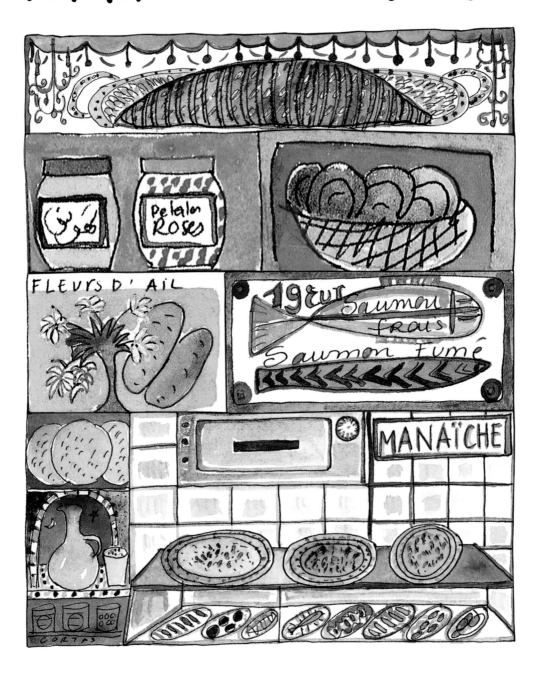

RIMAL GRILLED CHICKEN WITH GARLIC SAUCE
Toum bi Zeit

Meat and chicken are an important part of the menu at Rimal restaurant, and chef Fadi Khoury takes great care in the selection process. Farm-raised chickens are grilled and seasoned simply with thyme. Toum, a garlic sauce similar to the French aïoli but without the eggs, is paired with the grilled chicken. To mix the toum, a blender with multiple speeds works better than a food processor.

SERVES 4

GARLIC SAUCE

1	cup sunflower oil
2	ice cubes, crushed
¼	cup lemon juice
5	cloves garlic
1	medium starchy potato, peeled and cubed
1	tablespoon salt

1	3-pound (1.4 kg) chicken
	olive oil
	salt and white pepper
	fresh thyme

RESTAURANT

RIMAL

94, boulevard Malesherbes
75017 Paris
tel: 01 42 27 61 22
métro: Courcelles

1 Have the sunflower oil, ice cubes, and lemon juice ready near the blender. Place the garlic, (uncooked) potato, and salt in the blender and mix until smooth. With the motor on low, add the oil in a slow, steady stream. Once all the oil is incorporated, increase the speed and add the crushed ice and lemon juice, alternating between the two until the lemon juice is all used. The sauce can be made up to 2 days in advance and kept in the refrigerator.

2 Preheat the broiler or prepare a gas or charcoal grill. Using kitchen shears or a large knife, butterfly the chicken by cutting down one side of the backbone, then turning the chicken around and cutting down the other side to remove the backbone. Place the chicken breast side up on the cutting board, and press firmly on the breastbone to crack it and flatten the chicken. Rinse thoroughly and pat dry. Fold the wings back under the body. Rub lightly with olive oil.

3 Grill the chicken over a medium-high fire or under the broiler, turning occasionally to cook evenly, about 20 minutes per side. Remove the chicken from the grill, place on a cutting board, and sprinkle liberally with salt, pepper, and thyme. Cover with foil and let rest 7–10 minutes.

4 Cut the chicken into 4 serving pieces and serve with a bowlful of the sauce.

LEBANESE FAST FOOD

"Tasty" and "nutritious" are not words ordinarily used to describe fast food, but in Lebanon that is the case: delectable sandwiches are the fast food. As Lorenzo Vacchiotti, a tourist, wrote in a magazine article in 1967, "Wherever you go after Beirut, you will never forget the smell or the taste of *shawarmas,* a large cone of lamb piled up in paper-thin slices that are soaked overnight in juices and spices, then roasted on a revolving spit, sliced vertically into slivers, and served in an envelope of fresh Arab bread stuffed with mint, pickles, and fresh tomatoes." Since then, things have only evolved, with sandwiches reaching new artistic heights.

The Lebanese in Paris have reproduced this vast array of sandwiches in *traiteurs,* or delicatessens. At any time of the day, all segments of the Parisian population, from taxi drivers to well-heeled businessmen, stop in for *shawarma* or falafel, bending over to prevent chunks of tomato, onion, or pickles from sliding down their shirts.

Another place to find *man'ouche* (sandwich) creations in Paris is in the local markets. Fadi Nahra, a restaurant owner and caterer, has been selling his sandwiches and prepared foods in a variety of Paris markets for six years now, in a different neighborhood each day. His clients are mainly French and they love buying the variety of pizza-style specialties he cooks in front of them. Now any Parisian craving Lebanese fast food can easily have a *man'ouches* for breakfast, *shawarma* for lunch, and a falafel sandwich for dinner.

AL DAR TRAITEUR
5, rue Frédéric Sauton 75005 Paris
tel: 01 43 25 17 15
métro: Maubert-Mutualité

PAVILLON NOURA TRAITEUR
27 Ave Marceau 75016 Paris
tel: 01 47 23 02 20
métro: Alma Marceau

AL DIWAN TRAITEUR
30, Ave Georges V 75008 Paris
tel: 01 47 20 84 98
métro: Georges V

KEFTA WITH DATES AND SAGE
Keftas aux Dates et á la Sauge

Kefta is seasoned ground lamb or beef. It can be used in a multitude of ways: made into patties and fried, layered with other ingredients and baked, or, most often, molded onto flat skewers and grilled over charcoal. In restaurants and takeouts in Paris, kefta is generally flavored with chopped onion and parsley and sprinkled with a variety of spices, the same way it is prepared in Lebanon. But Karim Haidar, executive chef at Liza restaurant, has an original approach to kefta: add sage and dates to the minced lamb, then serve the grilled meat with an equally original recipe for m'tabal made with zucchini (see page 230).

MAKES 10 SKEWERS

- - - - - - - - - - - - - - - - - - - -

1   pound (450 g) boneless
    lean lamb, free of fat, gristle,
    and ligaments

2   sprigs fresh sage

17 dates

    salt and freshly ground
    black pepper

1 Working in batches, place the meat in the bowl of a food processor and blend until finely ground. After grinding the last batch, add the dates and sage leaves and blend well.

2 Preheat the oven to 475°F (240°C). Using your hands, knead this last batch into the rest of the meat until it is thoroughly incorporated and a smooth paste forms. Season with salt and pepper.

3 Divide the meat into 10 portions. Mold each portion around a flat metal skewer into a long flat sausage shape, or pat into patties. Grill over a hot fire or cook in the oven for 7–10 minutes.

M'tabal de Courgettes

SERVES 5

3 tablespoons peanut oil
5 medium zucchini, peeled and cut into 3-inch (8 cm) lengths
¼ cup pine nuts
1 cup water
2–3 tablespoons lemon juice
2–3 tablespoons tahini
½ teaspoon 7-spice powder (see Glossary)
salt and freshly ground black pepper

1 Heat 1 tablespoon oil in a large saucepan. Add the zucchini and cook 1–2 minutes, turning to coat with oil. Add the water, cover, and cook over very low heat for 30–40 minutes, or until tender.

2 Using a slotted spoon, remove the zucchini to a colander lined with paper towels and cover with more. Place a weight on top, and press down to squeeze out the excess liquid. Refrigerate for at least several hours, or overnight, to drain completely.

3 In a small skillet, sauté the pine nuts in 2 tablespoons oil until golden brown. Drain.

4 Put the zucchini in a bowl and, using your hands, crush and pull it apart to reach a lumpy texture. Using a fork, mix in enough lemon juice and tahini in alternating spoonfuls to form a thick paste. Season with 7-spice powder, salt and pepper. Transfer to a serving bowl and sprinkle with the pine nuts. Serve as a side dish for the *kefta* (page 229).

MIDDLE EASTERN SHOPS

Paris has a great selection of grocery stores selling Middle Eastern products, many of which are run by Lebanese in the 15th *arrondissement*. These carry a panoply of Lebanese goods, from coffee, bread, pastries, and fig jam to a variety of cheeses, olives, grape leaves, nuts, and ice cream.

Armenians, Syrians, and Turks run other high-quality shops around the city. Heratchian, one of the older stores, is a veritable gold mine for those searching for any kind of ingredient necessary for Near or Far Eastern cuisine. Crates of dried fruit are piled up in the window; open burlap bags of rice, semolina, and dried beans line the walls; and the little metal pots used for making Turkish coffee hang from the rafters. The following is a short list of excellent grocery stores found in different areas of Paris:

L'ORIENTALE (Lebanese)
36, rue du Laos 75015 Paris
tel: 01 43 06 66 00
métro: Cambronne

LES DÉLICES D'ORIENT (Lebanese)
52, avenue Émile Zola 75015 Paris
tel: 01 45 79 10 00
métro: Charles Michels

HERATCHIAN (products from all countries)
6, rue Lamartine 75009 Paris
tel: 01 48 78 43 19
métro: Cadet

SABAH ORIENTAL
(vast array of products from the Middle East and North Africa, including kosher items)
125, boulevard Ménilmontant 75011 Paris
tel: 01 43 55 36 90
métro: Ménilmontant

71, boulevard de Belleville 75011 Paris
tel: 01 43 57 47 49
métro: Ménilmontant

140, rue Faubourg Saint-Antoine 75012 Paris
tel: 01 40 01 01 04
métro: Bastille

VEGETABLES STUFFED WITH RICE
Légumes Farcis sans Viande

This recipe is adapted from the cookbook "Les Secrets d' Alep," written by Florence Ollivry, a Frenchwoman who lived in Aleppo, Syria, and researched its traditional dishes. Aleppo's cuisine is a reflection of the city's ethnic and religious diversity. Persian intonations are evident in the use of pomegranate juice, walnuts, and stewed fresh cherries. Hot peppers and the varieties of kibbeh Aleppo offers are rarely found in southern Syrian and Lebanese cooking. Flavored with hot chili paste and rich, sour pomegranate syrup, these stuffed vegetables can be a filling vegetarian meal or a side dish to meat. The original recipe calls for zucchini and eggplant as long as your index finger and baby bell peppers. If you are unable to find these, use the smallest you can find and reduce the quantity.

SERVES 5

- 5 small eggplants, (3in/8cm) or 3 medium
- 5 small zucchini (3 in/8cm) or 3 medium
- 3 small red bell peppers (or use 3 medium red peppers and omit the green peppers)
- 3 small green bell peppers
- 15 grape leaves, well rinsed and patted dry
- ¼ cup oil
- 2 onions, diced
- 2 tablespoons tomato paste
- 1 tablespoons hot chili paste or harissa
- 2 cups short-grain or round rice
- 2 cups chopped walnuts
- 7 tablespoons pomegranate syrup
- 1 bunch fresh parsley, chopped
- 2 tablespoons sugar
- pinch of salt

1 Hollow out the eggplants and zucchini by removing the stem ends (set aside to use as lids), then cutting out the centers with a knife or apple corer. Use a spoon to scoop out all the pulp, leaving the root end intact. Slice off the tops of the peppers (and set them aside) and remove the cores and seeds.

2 Heat the oil in a large saucepan and sauté the onions until soft. Add the tomato paste, chili paste, and rice, stirring to coat. Pour in 2 cups of water and cook, stirring occasionally until all the water has been absorbed, 5–7 minutes. Remove from heat and add the walnuts, 2 tablespoons of the pomegranate syrup, and parsley. Let cool slightly.

3 Fill the hollowed vegetables, leaving space at the top for the rice to expand. Cover with the "lids."

4 Fill the grape leaves with the remaining stuffing: Lay a leaf smooth side down on your work surface with the stem end toward you. Place a heaping tablespoon of filling in the center, about ½ inch (1cm) from the bottom edge. Pull up the bottom edge of the leaf to enclose the filling, fold in the long sides, and roll up the bundle. Repeat with the rest of the leaves and stuffing.

5 Arrange the stuffed vegetables side by side in a large pot, standing up. Layer the rolled grape leaves on top. Stir the remaining 5 tablespoons pomegranate syrup, the sugar, and salt into 4 cups water and pour over the vegetables. Cover and simmer over low heat for 30 minutes, or until the rice is cooked and the vegetables are tender. Remove the vegetables and serve warm or cold.

KIBBEH NAYYE MADE WITH SALMON
Kibbeh Nayye aux Deux Saumons

Kibbeh nayye, which is served raw, is most often made with lamb, but it's not unusual to use fish. Ask your fishmonger to cut the fillet from the tail end of the fish, where the flesh is firmer. Anis Nacrour gave us this cosmopolitan recipe that he invented, made with both raw and smoked salmon. The salmon must be chopped by hand, since a food processor will turn it into puree!

SERVES 6

- ½ cup plus 2 tablespoons fine or medium bulgar
- 1 teaspoon freshly ground black pepper
- 1 teaspoon ground cardamom
- 1 teaspoon coriander seeds, finely crushed
- grated zest and juice of 1 lime
- juice of 1 lemon

1 Rinse the bulgar in cold water, place in a small bowl, cover with warm water, and soak 10 minutes. Drain and spread out on a kitchen towel to air-dry, then return to the bowl.

2 Combine the pepper, cardamom, coriander, lime zest, lemon and lime juice, and mix well. Pour over the bulgar and mix well with a fork. Refrigerate for 15 minutes.

9   ounces (250 g) smoked salmon

3   tablespoons walnut oil

1   tablespoon sesame seeds, toasted

12 ounces (300 g) fresh salmon fillet

3   tablespoons olive oil

2   heaping tablespoons chopped fresh dill

2   heaping tablespoons chopped fresh chives

VINAIGRETTE

1   tablespoon white wine vinegar

½   teaspoon salt

    freshly ground black pepper

1   teaspoon Asian sesame oil

2   tablespoons olive oil

    lettuce leaves for serving

3 Using a sharp chef's knife finely chop the smoked salmon. Place in a small bowl and stir in the walnut oil and sesame seeds; refrigerate until ready to serve.

4 Remove any skin and bones from the fresh salmon and finely chop. Place in a small bowl, stir in the olive oil and chopped herbs, and refrigerate until ready to serve.

5 To make the vinaigrette, combine the vinegar, salt, and pepper to taste in a small bowl, whisking with a fork until the salt dissolves. Continuing to whisk, add the sesame and olive oils.

6 Just before serving, combine the two salmons with the bulgar mixture and thoroughly mix. Toss the lettuce with the vinaigrette, line the plates with the leaves, and top with the *kibbeh nayye*.

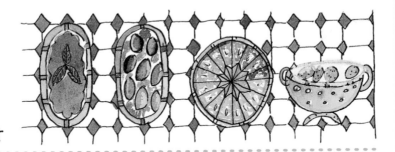

KIBBEH

Kibbeh, made with ground lamb, bulgar (cooked cracked wheat), and grated onions is the preeminent dish in Syria and Lebanon. It is traditionally made by pounding the lamb with a pestle in a stone or metal mortar; the lamb is then kneaded with soaked bulgar and eaten in a variety of ways. *Kibbeh nayye* (considered an aphrodisiac) is akin to steak tartare, although the meat is lamb, or, in some cases, goat. In *kibbeh bil sanniye* (page 236), half the mixture is spread in a baking pan and the other half sandwiched over a filling made with ground lamb, onions, pine nuts, and cinnamon. *Kibbeh rass*, little oval spheres that are served as mezzé in restaurants, contain a filling of cooked meat and pine nuts and are fried. More exotic forms of *kibbeh* can be made with pumpkin or potatoes.

BAKED KIBBEH
Kibbeh bil Sanniye

Kibbeh bil sanniye can be prepared in advance and needs only to be accompanied by a mixed vegetable salad and yogurt to make a complete meal. Lebanese novelist Hoda Barakat makes kibbeh with beef because she finds the lamb in France has too strong a flavor. If you can find lamb with a more delicate taste, use it; or make the kibbeh with two-thirds beef and one-third lamb. Hoda uses rosebuds in her recipe, a nice touch some Lebanese use when cooking kibbeh.

SERVES 5

KIBBEH SHELL

1⅔ cups fine bulgar

1¼ pounds (600 g) ground beef

1 large onion, chopped

1 teaspoon dried marjoram

5–6 dried rosebuds (optional)

¼ bunch fresh mint, leaves only

¼ bunch fresh parsley, leaves only

1½ teaspoons ground cinnamon

1 teaspoon salt

1 teaspoon freshly ground black pepper

ice water

STUFFING

7 tablespoons butter

1 large onion, minced

½ cup pine nuts

1 teaspoon ground cinnamon

1. Rinse the bulgar in cold water, drain well, and spread out on a kitchen towel to air-dry.

2. Working in batches, process the meat to a paste in a food processor. Remove, add the bulgar, and mix well with your hands.

3. Puree the onion in the bowl of the food processor. Add the marjoram, rosebuds, mint, parsley, cinnamon, salt and pepper and process until smooth. Incorporate the processed ingredients into the meat mixture. Working in small amounts, process the meat again, adding 1–2 tablespoons ice water to each batch to keep the ingredients cool, and blend to form a smooth, soft paste.

4. To make the stuffing, sauté the onion in 3 tablespoons butter over medium heat until soft. Add the pine nuts, cinnamon, salt and pepper and cook until the pine nuts are golden, about 3

1 teaspoon salt
1 teaspoon freshly ground
black pepper
12 ounces (350 g) ground beef

yogurt
chopped fresh mint

minutes. Crumble the ground meat into the pan and brown, breaking up any large pieces with the back of a fork. Remove from heat and let cool.

5 Preheat the over to 375°F (190°C). Melt the remaining 4 tablespoons butter and use some to brush the inside of a large casserole (10x14 inches/25x35 cm) or a 15-inch (38 cm) round baking pan. Divide the *kibbeh* mixture in two. Smooth half the *kibbeh* over the bottom of the dish, then spread the stuffing evenly on top. To cover the stuffing with the rest of the *kibbeh* paste, wet your hands with cold water and flatten large handfuls of the *kibbeh* between your palms. Lay them on top of the stuffing, covering it completely and evenly; patch up any holes with more paste as you go.

6 Using a wet sharp knife, score the surface of the kibbeh to form 1-inch (2.5 cm) diamonds, cutting about ¼ inch (5 mm) into the meat. Brush the *kibbeh* with the remaining melted butter. Bake for 35 minutes, or until golden brown. Serve with a bowl of yogurt garnished with chopped mint.

HODA BARAKAT

Hoda Barakat's day job is news director of Paris's Radio Orient, the Arab community's radio station. At night she works on her novels. She has written five. In any spare time, she indulges in her love for cooking. Hoda is from the village of Bsharré, Lebanon, which is nestled 8,250 feet (2,500 m) high in the mountains near the famous Cedars and is the birthplace of Khalil Gibran (*The Prophet*). The area is an apple-growing region known for its goats and lambs. In Bsharré, *kibbeh* is made with tender lamb or goat's meat, and goat's milk is used whenever possible to make *labneh* and *kishk*, a powdery cereal of bulgar fermented with milk and *laban* (yogurt).

In France, where she's been since 1989, Hoda initially went to a lot of trouble to try to reproduce the dishes she made in Lebanon, but she never found "the real taste." In the end, she says, that's what makes you realize you're somewhere else. Now, perhaps out of nostalgia, she is cooking more specialties from the Bsharré region.

BAKED FISH WITH RICE
Sayyadieh

Sayyadieh can be translated as "the fisherman's catch." Fashion designer Gina Diwan's family is from Saida, on the southern coast of Lebanon. The secret of this recipe that she shared with us is to cook the onions until they are almost burnt, giving the broth a deep color and flavor. Using a whole fish results in a more flavorful stock.

SERVES 6

THE FISH

2 pounds (1 kg) skinned fish fillets—cod, halibut, turbot, or bream—or 4 pounds (2 kg) whole sea bass

   vegetable oil

   salt and white pepper

1 teaspoon ground cumin

2 lemons, thinly sliced

THE STOCK

6 onions, thinly sliced

5 tablespoons vegetable oil

3 cinnamon sticks

1 teaspoon cumin seeds

1 To prepare the fish, preheat the oven to 350°F (180°C). Rinse the fish and pat dry. Line a baking dish with aluminum foil large enough to enclose the fish. Place the fish on top of the foil, rub with oil, and season with the cumin and salt and pepper to taste. Spread the sliced lemons over the fish (if using a whole fish, place some of the lemon slices inside) and bring the edges of the foil up to firmly enclose and seal the fish. Bake 15 minutes per pound, or until the fish begins to flake.

2 Meanwhile, place the onions in the bowl of a food processor and blend to a coarse puree. Heat the oil in a heavy saucepan and sauté the onions until they are dark and almost burnt, then reduce the temperature, add the cinnamon sticks,

salt and white pepper

juice of 1 lemon

2 teaspoons ground cumin

2 teaspoons ground cinnamon

2 cups basmati rice, rinsed, soaked in cold water 10 minutes

THE SAUCE

1 cup chopped celery

¼ bunch fresh coriander, leaves chopped

juice of 1 lemon

¾ cup of pine nuts, browned in butter

½ bunch fresh parsley, leaves chopped

cumin seeds, salt and white pepper to taste and cook until the onions are completely soft, about 15-20 minutes. Set aside.

3 Remove the fish from the oven and let rest 10 minutes before opening the foil. Transfer the fish to a platter, reserving the cooking liquid. If using whole fish, remove skin and flake the flesh from the bones. Fillets should be flaked with a fork. Put the fish in a bowl, cover, and keep warm.

4 Pour all but 2 tablespoons (to set aside) of the cooking liquid over the onions. Add 4 cups water, the lemon juice, cinnamon, cumin, salt and white pepper to taste. Bring to a boil, then reduce the heat and simmer, uncovered, until the stock is reduced by half, about 20 minutes. Strain the stock, pressing on the onions with the back of spoon to extract the maximum amount of the liquid.

5 Heat the remaining 2 tablespoons oil in a medium saucepan. Add the rice, stir to coat with oil, and sauté until translucent, about 2 minutes. Pour in 4½ cups stock, adding water if necessary. Bring to a boil, then reduce to the lowest heat, cover, and cook 18 minutes, until the liquid is absorbed.

6 Meanwhile, to make the sauce, combine the celery and coriander with 1 cup water, the reserved 2 tablespoons of cooking liquid, and the lemon juice in a small pot. Gently simmer, until reduced by half.

7 To serve, fluff the rice with a fork, mound onto a large serving dish, scatter the warm fish on top, and sprinkle with the pine nuts and parsley. Pour the sauce into a small bowl to serve alongside.

OUZI
Agneau de Fete

Ouzi is a regional dish, traditionally prepared for large banquets using a whole young lamb, stuffed with rice mixed with almonds and raisins, then slowly roasted until the meat can be pulled off the bone with your fingers. It is seved with a salted yogurt sauce. Some Lebanese in France have ouzi delivered from Beirut via DHL, or order it from Lebanese restaurants in Paris, such as La Reine Zénobie. If you have the time and a large selection of spices, however, it is not difficult to make this adapted version at home.

SERVES 6

1   5-pound (2¼ kg) leg of lamb, trimmed
3   cloves garlic, thinly sliced lengthwise

OUZI SPICE MIXTURE
1   tablespoon freshly ground black pepper
1   tablespoon ground allspice
1   tablespoon ground nutmeg
1   tablespoon ground cinnamon
1   tablespoon crushed rose petal leaves
1   teaspoon ground cumin

1   Rinse the lamb and pat dry. Using a small sharp knife, pierce the leg of lamb all over, making slits about 1 inch deep (2.5 cm). Press the slivers of garlic into the incisions.

2   To make the spice mixture, combine all the ingredients. (Leftover spice mix can be stored in a sealed jar in a cool place for up to 1 year.)

3   To make the marinade, mix all the ingredients except the onion and salt. Place the lamb in a large baking dish and coat with the marinade. Cover with plastic wrap and refrigerate overnight. Return to room temperature before roasting.

1 teaspoon ground coriander
1 teaspoon ground cardamom
1 teaspoon red pepper flakes
1 teaspoon ground ginger
1 teaspoon turmeric

MARINADE
1 tablespoon of *ouzi* spice
   mixture (above)
1 teaspoon ground cumin
1 teaspoon ground coriander
1 teaspoon ground cinnamon
¾ cup yogurt
   grated zest of 1 lemon
   grated zest of 2 oranges
1 teaspoon ground cardamom

1 onion, thinly sliced
   salt
   juice of 1 lemon
   juice of 2 oranges

RICE
3 cups basmati rice, rinsed,
   soaked 10 minutes and drained,
   or long-grain rice (not rinsed
   and soaked)
1 teaspoon salt
¼ cup olive oil
¾ cup slivered almonds
1 cup golden raisins

1 cup yogurt

RESTAURANT

LA REINE ZENOBIE
234, rue Championnet
75018 Paris
tel: 01 42 28 96 31
métro: Guy Moquet

4 Preheat the oven to 450°F (230°C). Spread the onion over the bottom of a large roasting pan. Place the lamb fat side up on top and pour 1 cup water around the meat.

5 Roast the lamb for 15 minutes. Reduce the heat to 350°F (180°C) and cook for another 15 minutes. Pour the lemon and orange juice over the lamb and sprinkle with salt. Cook an additional 15 minutes. (In France, leg of lamb is eaten rare; if you prefer the meat medium or well done, increase the cooking time by 15–25 minutes, after lowering the heat.) Remove the lamb from the oven, cover with aluminum foil, and let rest 10–15 minutes.

6 While the meat is cooking, prepare the rice. Heat 1 tablespoon olive oil in a nonstick skillet. Add the almonds and cook until lightly browned. Remove with a slotted spoon and drain on paper towels. Add an additional 1 tablespoon oil to the pan and cook the raisins until they are plump. Drain on paper towels.

7 Heat the remaining 2 tablespoons oil and add the rice, stirring to coat. Sauté for 1–2 minutes, or until translucent. Dissolve the salt in 4 cups of warm water and pour over the rice. Bring to boil, then cover tightly, reduce the heat to its lowest setting, and cook, without raising the lid, for 18 minutes. Remove from heat, cover the pan with several kitchen towels, and let sit for 10 minutes.

8 To serve, fluff the rice with a fork and toss with the almonds and raisins. Spoon the rice onto a large platter. Slice the lamb and place on top. Stir 3 tablespoons of the juices from the lamb into the yogurt, and serve alongside.

DESSERTS

STUFFED COOKIES
Maa'moul

Maa'moul are soft cookies traditionally filled with dates, pistachios, or walnuts. You can use wooden molds to make patterns on each cookie or create your own by using a fork. Les Délices d'Orient, a Lebanese restaurant, delicatessen, and bakery, uses both fine and coarse semolina for their large maa'moul.

MAKES 24

- 3 sticks butter, melted
- 1½ cups coarse semolina
- 1½ cups fine semolina
- 2 tablespoons orange flower water, to taste
- 2 tablespoons rose water, to taste

FILLING
- ¾ cup pistachios
- 2 tablespoons sugar
- 2 tablespoons butter, melted
  confectioners' sugar for dusting

RESTAURANT
LES DELICES D'ORIENT
14, rue Quatre Frères Peignot
75015 Paris
tel: 01 45 77 82 93
métro: Charles Michels

1. In a medium bowl, combine the semolina flours, melted butter, and orange flower and rose waters. Mix well with your fingers. Cover the bowl with plastic wrap and refrigerate overnight.

2. To make the filling, combine the pistachios and sugar in the bowl of a food processor and pulse until the nuts are coarsely ground. Remove to a bowl and mix in the melted butter. Set aside.

3. Preheat the over to 350°F (180°C). Grease 2 baking sheets. Bring the dough to room temperature. Pinch off large tablespoons and roll into balls. With your index finger, make a small hole in the ball, then push ½ teaspoon of the filling into the opening. Pat the dough back over the hole and place the cookie seam side down on a baking sheet. Repeat with the remaining dough. When all of the cookies have been formed, use a fork to make a decorative pattern on the surface. (The pattern helps the confectioners' sugar stick to the cookies.)

4. Bake the cookies 12–15 minutes, or until lightly browned. Remove to a rack and sprinkle with the confectioners' sugar.

SEMOLINA CAKE WITH ORANGE WATER AND ALMONDS
Namoura

Pâtisserie Azrak is in a former French bakery in Paris, with the original paintings of mills and wheat still on the walls. Robert Azrak manages two separate kitchens in his pâtisserie—one for traditional French bread and pastries, the other for Middle Eastern pastries, which he stacks up in neat geometrical piles on large platters in the window. This semolina cake is moist, fragrant, and elegant, with its scored diamond pattern decorated with whole blanched almonds.

MAKES 24

3 cups coarse semolina
1¾ cups sugar
1 cup whole milk

1 In a large bowl, combine the semolina and sugar. Heat the butter and milk in a small saucepan over medium heat, stirring occasionally, until butter has melted; do not allow the milk to boil. Add to the semolina mixture, along with the orange flower water and lemon zest. Stir well to combine, then let sit at room temperature for 20–30 minutes.

2   sticks butter, melted

1   tablespoon orange flower
     water, or to taste

     grated zest of 1 lemon

3   tablespoons tahini

2   teaspoons baking powder

1   cup blanched whole almonds

ORANGE FLOWER SYRUP

1½ cups sugar

¾   cup water

1   tablespoon lemon juice

1   teaspoon orange flower water

RESTAURANT

PATISSERIE AZRAK

56, rue Vaneau 75007 Paris

tel: 01 45 48 98 16

métro: Vaneau

2 Preheat the oven to 400°F (200°C). Brush the inside of a 13-inch (30 cm) round baking pan or a 9 x 13-inch (23 x 30 cm) tray with the tahini. Add the baking powder to the semolina mixture and stir well, then pour into the baking pan. Place on the middle oven rack and bake for 10 minutes. Remove the cake and score the top in a diamond pattern. Place an almond in the center of each diamond. Lower the temperature to 350°F (170°C) and bake until golden brown, about 40 minutes.

3 Meanwhile, prepare the syrup. Combine the sugar, water, and lemon juice in a saucepan and bring to a boil. Lower the heat and simmer 10 minutes. Remove from heat and stir in the orange flower water.

4 While the cake is still hot, brush the entire surface with syrup, using more or less depending on taste. Let the cake cool before slicing.

ORANGE FLOWER AND ROSE WATERS

Clear, sweet aromatic rose and orange flower waters are essential ingredients for both sweet and savory dishes in Middle Eastern cooking, and have been so since the Middle Ages. Persians are thought to have been the first to use rose water for culinary purposes, but the earliest recipes recording its use were written during the Arab Empire (8th–11th century). Sweet drinks and desserts, as well as certain meat dishes, were flavored with rose water. During the Ottoman Empire, *lokum*, or Turkish delight, was invented and rose water became one of the most popular flavorings for it.

The Moors planted Seville oranges in southern Spain in the 8th century. The fragrant blossoms of these oranges were distilled to make orange flower water, which also quickly became a favorite in Arab and Persian cuisines.

Both Lebanon and Syria still produce rose water and orange flower water for culinary purposes as well as for scents. The French also produce a fair quantity of orange flower water, which has been popular here for hundreds of years—it was introduced during the Crusades. It is distilled and bottled in the South of France.

PANCAKES WITH CLOTTED CREAM AND APRICOTS
Atayef bil Ashta

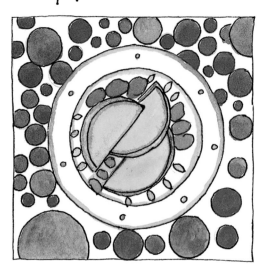

These pancakes are traditionally eaten during festive occasions and especially during the month of Ramadan. The filling, ashta, is a rich clotted cream. In some areas of the Middle East, it is traditionally made with buffalo milk, but more often than not it is made from the thickest part of the cream floating on top of whole cow's milk. In the West, very often ricotta or plain cream are used as substitutes. Karim Haidar, Liza restaurant's alchemist, has created a mixture that mimics ashta not only in taste but also in texture. Served inside light-as-air pancakes topped with cooked fresh apricots, the cream may not be the real thing, but it's delicious all the same.

SERVES 8

APRICOTS AND ALMONDS

2	pounds (1 kg) firm and not overripe apricots
½	cup packed brown sugar
3	tablespoons water
½	cup blanched whole almonds
1	tablespoon Cognac

1 Quarter and pit the unpeeled apricots. Combine the sugar and water in a large sauté pan and heat, stirring, until the sugar has dissolved. Lay the apricot quarters in the pan in a single layer. Sprinkle the almonds on top. Cook over low heat until the apricots are tender but still retain their shape. Remove the cooked fruit and almonds to bowl, and return the pan to high heat. Add the

THE PANCAKES

1¼ cups all-purpose flour

1 tablespoon sugar

1¾ teaspoons baking powder

½ teaspoon salt

¾ cup whole milk

½ cup water

1 large egg, lightly beaten

2 tablespoons butter, melted

vegetable oil for cooking

THE FILLING

¾ cup mozzarella

4 cups mascarpone

1 tablespoon orange flower water

2 tablespoons sugar

Cognac and reduce for 1 minute. Pour the syrup over the apricots and almonds, and cool.

2 To make the pancakes, combine all the ingredients for the batter in a blender and blend well. Wipe a nonstick crepe pan or medium flat skillet with a little oil and place over medium heat. Pour ½ cup of the batter into the hot pan. As the pancake cooks, small bubbles will appear all over the surface. The pancake is done when the underside has turned golden brown and the top has firmed and lost its uncooked appearance; the pancakes are cooked on one side only. Remove the pancake to a plate and repeat with the remaining batter. Let the pancakes cool slightly, then stack, covered with a kitchen towel. The pancakes may be stiff when first cooked, but they will soften as they cool. They can be made 2 hours ahead of time.

3 To make the filling, place the mozzarella in the bowl of a food processor. Process until finely chopped; it will look soft and cottony. Add half the mascarpone, the orange flower water, and sugar and pulse to combine, 5–10 seconds. Remove to a large bowl and whisk in the rest of the mascarpone. The mixture will seem quite liquid at first but will thicken once the rest of the mascarpone is whipped in and will resemble small-curd cottage cheese.

4 To assemble, place 1 pancake on each of the 8 dessert plates, uncooked side up. Put a large dollop of the filling, off center, on each pancake, then bring up the sides to form a cone around the filling. Spoon some apricots and almonds into the open end of each pancake, onto the cream. Drizzle the apricot syrup over the fruit and pancakes. Serve immediately.

PISTACHIO ICE CREAM WITH MASTIC
Glace à la Pistache

Made without egg yolks and perfumed with mastic, this ice cream is exotically different. At the restaurant Rimal, dessert can be a selection of their homemade ice cream with flavors ranging from rose to avocado. This is Fadi Khoury's recipe for pistachio ice cream made with mastic. Middle Eastern ice cream is known for its chewy texture, which is obtained by adding sahlab (see box). Fadi brings his sahlab from Lebanon, but this ingredient is difficult to find. If you are not able to find it, use cornstarch instead, which will make a smooth ice cream without the characteristic elasticity.

MAKES 4 CUPS

- 3 tablespoons *sahlab* (or substitute cornstarch)
- 4 cups whole milk
- 1 cup heavy cream
- 1 cup sugar
- ½ teaspoon mastic, crushed with the side of a heavy knife
- ½ teaspoon sugar
- ½ cup ground pistachios, plus 1 tablespoon chopped

RESTAURANT

RIMAL

94, boulevard Malesherbes
75017 Paris
tel: 01 42 27 61 22
métro: Courcelles

1 Mix the *sahlab* with a little of the milk in a small bowl and set aside. Heat the remaining milk, cream, and sugar in a saucepan to a low boil. Add a ladleful of the hot milk to the *sahlab*, then slowly stir into the pan. Lower the heat to a simmer and stir constantly as the mixture thickens. Continuing to stir, add the crushed mastic and cook for 10–15 minutes. Remove from heat and let cool to room temperature.

2 Add the ground pistachios to the milk mixture. Pour into a mold lined with plastic wrap, cover with plastic wrap, and place in the freezer overnight. Remove and allow to soften slightly, then spoon into the bowl of a food processor and blend until smooth. Pour the mixture back into the mold, cover, and return to the freezer to set for at least 1 hour before serving. (Alternatively, pour into an ice cream maker, and churn according to the instructions.) Serve garnished with the chopped pistachios.

BOUZA—MIDDLE EASTERN ICE CREAM

Anyone who is familiar with Middle Eastern ice cream may remember the first time they tried it—surprise, initially, at the chewy, taffy-like texture, then pure delight on taking in the unusual flavors of rose water, pistachio, or apricot, all sprinkled with chopped pistachios.

Ice cream, or a variation of it, has been made in the Middle East since medieval times. During the Umayyad Dynasty in Iraq, a trade route in snow and ice was established, much of which was imported from Lebanon. The ice was packed in salt and carried by camels to central icehouses. Eventually, sweet iced drinks were invented, called *sharbaat* in Arabic, and the origin of the word "sherbet" in English.

Two ingredients that make Middle Eastern ice cream so different in texture and taste from the ice cream found in the West are mastic gum—a transparent resin collected from small cuts made in the bark of the tree—and *sahlab*, which is made from the starch found in the bulbs of orchids. Mastic is sticky, which adds texture as well as flavor. Natural *sahlab* is hard to find and very expensive, but besides giving your ice cream a delicious flavor, it will add that gummy texture that is unique to Middle Eastern ice cream.

GLOSSARY

This glossary includes suggestions for purchasing as well as substitution recommendations.

ARGAN OIL A rare oil made from the nuts of the knotted and thorny argan tree, which grows exclusively in the southwest corner of Morocco. It can be used to dress salads and vegetables or poured into tagines and stews at the end of cooking. Argan oil can be purchased in gourmet stores and by mail order.

ASIAN BASIL A tropical anise-flavored basil with lush green leaves, purple stems, and flowers. An important flavor note in southeast Asian cuisine, it can be paired with sprouts and other leafy greens to give raw crunch to spring rolls or Vietnamese crepes and is added by the handful to soups and simmered dishes.

BANANA LEAVES Although banana leaves are not eaten, they are used throughout the tropics for serving, cooking, and carrying food. Fresh leaves need to be wiped with a damp cloth to remove dust and dirt. If being used to wrap food, the leaves can be made pliable by passing over a flame. They can be purchased fresh or frozen.

BLACK SESAME PASTE A jet-black paste made from ground black sesame seeds and used in Japanese cooking. It can be purchased in natural or sweetened flavors. Often the oil in the paste will separate and float to the surface; it should be stirred back in. The Japanese also make a white sesame paste, similar in color to Middle Eastern tahini; however, tahini is made from crushed raw seeds and both Japanese black and white sesame pastes are made from toasted seeds, which alters the taste considerably. Available in stores specializing in Japanese products.

BRIK PASTRY A paper-thin pastry from North Africa known as *ouark* in Morocco, *dioul* in Algeria, and *malsouqa* in Tunisia. In France, it is sold under the name brik. The pastry is used to wrap savory or sweet fillings. Substitute sheets of filo if brik is unavailable.

BONITO FLAKES, DRIED Shavings from the rock-hard dried flesh of a tunalike fish. The dried fish is scraped against a sharp blade to produce razor-thin flakes, which are used as a garnish, a condiment, or to flavor stocks. Look for packages of pure bonito flakes since some brands combine bonito flakes with the shavings of other, less-expensive fish. Available in Japanese grocery stores.

BROKEN RICE Literally, grains of broken rice that are culled from the whole grains when rice is processed after cultivation. The Senegalese prefer broken rice or, even better, twice broken rice, for making their national dish, *thie bou dienn*.

CHINESE FIVE-SPICE POWDER An Asian spice mixture composed of star anise, Sichuan pepper, fennel seeds, cloves, and cinnamon. It is said the spices represent the elements—earth, wood, water, fire, and metal—and have medicinal properties.

COCONUT JUICE The clear liquid found inside the hard shell of an immature coconut. It is available canned or frozen and should not be confused with coconut milk. The canned juice has lots of added sugar and is sold as a soft drink. The frozen juice, which often has pieces of floating pulp, can be bought unsweetened and used for braising or to tenderize meats. The juice is available in Asian stores.

COLOMBO A spice preparation used to make a stew by the same name. Brought to the Caribbean by Sri Lankan workers in the 19th century, its flavor was probably similar to an Asian curry powder. Over time indigenous spices replaced the original Asian spices, giving colombo a distinctive Caribbean taste. The ground powder often includes allspice, garlic, coriander, saffron, cinnamon, and generally dried mango or tamarind pulp.

CORIANDER (CILANTRO) A delicate fresh herb also known as Chinese parsley. The entire plant is eaten: the tender leaves and stems, the seeds and the roots. Each component has a slightly different taste. The leaves and stems are often used to garnish dishes, their musky, lemony taste serving as a balance to rich flavors. The seeds have a spicier taste and are used whole or ground in everything from curry powder to cakes. The roots, with an earthier flavor, are crushed and thrown into stews. Fresh cilantro leaves and seeds can be found in most grocery stores but often it is only in Asian markets that you find the plant with roots.

DAIKON A large, tapered, conical root vegetable also known as oriental white radish and used in Asian cuisine. A daikon has smooth white skin and crisp, juicy flesh with a slightly sharp taste. When peeled, this radish can be chopped into soups or stews, grated raw into salads, or pickled. Substitute white turnips.

DASHI Clear stock made from dried bonito flakes and giant kelp (*konbu*). It is one of the major building blocks of Japanese cuisine. Instant dashi (*dashi-no-moto*) is available in powdered and liquid form.

DJANSEN Small, round aromatic seed kernels of the Ndjanssan tree, used in West Africa to flavor fish, meat, and vegetables. The seeds are sold dried and must be soaked in water before being crushed and added to dishes. Djansen is available by mail-order or from shops specializing in products from Cameroon.

GALANGAL ROOT A light pink root with zebralike markings. A member of the ginger family, it has a similar taste but with a note of pepper. Available in Asian markets. Substitute fresh ginger.

HALOUMI A semi-firm Cypriot sheep's milk cheese preserved in salty brine. It is eaten throughout the Middle

East. It has a firm, chewy texture and is valued for its ability to keep its shape even when heated. Halloumi is often grilled or fried.

HARISSA North African chili paste used as a condiment or as an ingredient. It can be purchased ready-made in tubes or cans. Fresh paste is easily made at home.

KAFFIR LIMES (LEAVES) Also known as makrut lime, the flavor of this knobby member of the citrus family is closely associated with the cuisine of southeast Asia. Generally only the bitter rind and dark green leaves are used. Fresh leaves, wrapped in plastic, freeze well and are often sold this way. Dried leaves are not a good substitute.

KONBU Giant kelp gathered from the cold waters off Hokkaido, Japan's northernmost island. The kelp can be several yards long and varies in color and shape depending on the season. This giant seaweed is precut and dried. Its principle use is to make stock, but it can also be reconstituted and chopped into salads or added to brines for pickled vegetables. Often a white chalky residue appears on konbu; don't wipe it off, because it contains natural monosodium glutamate. Unlike the artificially produced MSG, this is not known to cause any side effects and enhances the flavor of the kelp.

LA LOT LEAVES These beautifully shaped, dark green leaves are often sold in Asian shops under their Thai name of *cha plu*. They are used like vine leaves to wrap ingredients. Substitute vine leaves packed in brine or Japanese shiso leaves.

LEMONGRASS This aromatic gray-green grass is used extensively in southeast Asian cuisine to impart a balmy lemon flavor. The tough outer leaves are peeled away, and the bulb and the portion of the stalk up to where the leaves start to branch out are used. If whole lemongrass is called for, the bulb needs to be crushed in order to release its flavor. Fresh lemongrass, wrapped in plastic, freezes very well. Dried lemongrass is not a good substitute.

MANIOC Also commonly known as yucca and cassava, manioc is a big starchy tuber grown throughout the tropics. The root can be eaten in many forms: whole, pounded into a meal, or ground into flour. The leaves are eaten like spinach or thrown into stews. Manioc can be found in Latin American and West Indian stores. The meal and flour are generally sold in Brazilian stores.

MASTIC The resin or hardened sap from the Pistacia tree with a slight flavor of pine. Incisions are made in the stems and branches of the tree and mastic oozes out in the shape of oblong crystals, light yellow or faint green. The brittle crystals must be ground before using but become sticky when crushed. Grinding with sugar reduces this effect. Mastic is used around the Mediterranean to flavor everything from stews to ice creams. It is generally purchased in Greek or Middle Eastern stores in teaspoon amounts sealed in small plastic bags.

MATCHA An expensive green tea powder made from pulverized, first-harvest tea bulbs. Most often the powder is whisked into hot water to make a tea served at traditional Japanese tea ceremonies. However, jade green matcha, which has a sweet, grass-like aroma, is also used to flavor and color Japanese confections. The powder needs to be stored in a cool, dry place. It is often found in the refrigerated section of stores where it is sold. For maximum flavor, use within a month after opening.

MIRIN Often referred to as a wine, it is actually a spirit-based liquid sweetener used exclusively in cooking, especially in marinades, glazes, and simmered dishes. Available in Japanese grocery stores. Substitute sugar syrup.

MISO A thick, creamy, fermented bean paste made from soybeans and a grain, most often wheat, barley, or rice. The Japanese use miso extensively in their cooking, as a base for soup, as a salad dressing, in simmered dishes, and for marinating meats and fish. Miso varies in color owing to the mix of grains used and the fermentation process. White, or *shiro*, miso has a milder taste and darker color; *aka* miso is more mature and has a stronger flavor. Miso is salty, so add judiciously. Prepared miso will keep in the refrigerator for up to one year.

NUOC MAM Also known as fish sauce, this clear brown liquid obtained from salted, fermented fish is a cornerstone of southeast Asian cuisine. It is used much like Chinese soy sauce as the base for dipping sauces or added to dishes to give a rich and fragrant flavor. The strong "fishy smell" disappears when mixed with other ingredients. Vietnamese nuoc mam sauces are considered the best and are more fragrant and less salty than the more commonly found Thai brands. Sauces that are dark, like black tea or cola, are probably oxidized and should be avoided. Store in a cool, dry place.

ORANGE FLOWER WATER An aromatic water distilled from the blossoms of the bitter orange or Seville orange. It is used throughout the Middle East and North Africa to perfume not only sweet syrups, pastries, and desserts, but also salads and meat dishes. In Lebanon it is stirred into boiling water to make white coffee. The flavored water is highly concentrated so a little goes a long way. Orange blossom water is available in gourmet shops and Middle Eastern grocery stores.

PALM SUGAR Sugar obtained from the sap of the sweet palm tree. An important element in southeast Asian cuisine, it is also known as *jaggery*. Palm sugar is light brown in color and has a mild caramel taste. It is sold in pressed cakes or in plastic tubs. The pressed cakes are often grated before being added to recipes.

PANKO BREADCRUMBS Japanese breadcrumbs used to coat food before it is fried. These breadcrumbs are airier, lighter, and less fat-absorbing than regular breadcrumbs and have the remarkable ability to stay crisp even after the fried food is cooled. Available in plastic bags in Asian grocery stores.

PEPE, OR MPEVE Also known as calabash or Jamacian nutmeg. It is the oblong, smooth-skinned, brownish nut of the fruit of the *Monodora myristica* shrub. The soft, marbled flesh is removed from the shell and ground with other ingredients to flavor dishes. Available in stores specializing in products from Cameroon.

POMEGRANATE The pomegranate fruit is consumed throughout the Mediterranean and the Middle East. The fruit is cut in half and the seeds and pulp separated from the bitter membrane. The pink, jewel-like seeds are sprinkled on dishes as a flavorful and colorful garnish or crushed to extract the juice. When reduced, the juice becomes a thick syrup that is stirred into savory dishes. Pomegranates vary in size and color; choose a fruit that is yellow to brick red and the size of a large orange.

POTATO STARCH A white, silky powder extracted from potatoes and used widely in Japanese cooking to thicken sauces or to coat foods before frying. It might be labeled *katakuriko* in Asian markets. Substitute cornstarch.

RAS EL HANOUT A North Africa spice mixture made with the best spices in the shop. There is no definitive list of ingredients. Mixtures usually contain cloves, cinnamon, nutmeg, chilies, cardamom, turmeric, allspice, and rose petals, but sometimes Spanish fly, belladonna, grains of paradise, or monk's pepper can be added. Spices are always better when freshly ground so look for whole-spice versions of Ras el Hanout and roast and grind them yourself. The mix will be more flavorful.

RED PALM OIL The bright red oil produced from the plum-sized fruit of the oil palm. It is the extra-virgin olive oil of the African continent, and its flavor is prized in West African cooking—the distinctive color embellishes any dish. Do not confuse red palm oil with the bronze, palm kernel oil. Available in shops selling African and Brazilian goods.

RICE PAPERS Known as *bang trang* in Vietnam, they are made of rice flour, water, and salt. Air-drying on bamboo mats results in a crosshatch pattern on the surface. Rice papers are white in color and sold in different shapes—circles, triangles, or squares—of various dimensions. Papers that are yellowish in color, or packages that contain lots of broken pieces, are old and should be avoided.

ROASTED RICE POWDER White rice that is dry-roasted until it turns a rich brown color, then ground to a fine powder. It is commonly sprinkled over salads, giving a toasted fragrance and at the same time absorbing juices to keep salads dry. Available in Asian stores in small plastic bags. Will keep for up to one year.

ROSE PETALS AND ROSEBUDS The aromatic flowers of the well-known shrub can be eaten or used to flavor food. Rose petals are often made into jams or sprinkled into stews or drinks. Dried petals and rosebuds, used interchangeably, can be crushed and used as part of a spice mixture. Look for rosebuds or petals that have been grown specifically for consumption—florist roses are often sprayed with toxic pesticides.

ROSE WATER A highly perfumed water distilled from rose petals used in both sweet and savory dishes. Its flavor is powerful so add carefully; just a teaspoon of the liquid will transform a dish. Available in Middle Eastern shops.

SAKE A Japanese rice-based, alcoholic beverage, sake can be sweet or dry. When drinking to accompany a meal, the choice is a matter of personal taste and how it pairs with food. For culinary purposes, dry sake is the most versatile.

SALEP A fine white powder ground from dried orchid tubers and used to thicken ice creams. Salep is expensive and difficult to find. Do not confuse the ground powder with the porridge-like dessert preparation sold in paper cartons with the same name. Available in Middle Eastern shops.

SAW GRASS HERB A long, serrated-leafed herb native to the Caribbean that has made deep inroads into southeast Asian cuisine. It has an aroma very similar to coriander; the leaves of the two plants can be used interchangeably. Saw grass is often torn into pieces and added to soups, noodle dishes, and curries. Available in Asian markets.

SCOTCH BONNET CHILIES Brightly colored, lantern-shaped chilies twice as hot as jalapeños, these are appreciated for their flavor as well as their heat. Added whole to dishes, they will impart their flavor without giving off the full impact of their fire. If you like the heat of chilies, chop and throw them into your dish. Wear gloves or oil your hands when handling chilies, and do not touch your eyes. Available in Caribbean and Latin American markets.

SEMOLINA A word with multiple definitions. Semolina refers to a grade of coarsely ground grain, and it is also a finely ground flour made from durham wheat used for making pasta and a porridge, also known as cream of wheat. The recipes in this book call for the milled grain, specifically durum wheat semolina (there are also corn and rice semolinas). Available in Greek or Middle Eastern shops and natural health food stores.

SEVEN-SPICE POWDER Known also by the Persian name *Baharat*, this harmonious blend can contain anywhere from four to nine different spices. Like Moroccan Ras al hanout there is no one version but most are based on a mixture of cinnamon, cloves, cumin, peppercorns, coriander seeds, cardamom, and nutmeg with a bit of paprika for color. Available in Middle Eastern shops.

SHAOXING RICE WINE A Chinese drinking wine, distilled from rice. Because rice wine for culinary purposes is often of dubious quality, recipes often specify Shaoxing wine. Substitute dry sherry.

SHICHIMI Japanese chili powder, made of a blend of seven different herbs and spices: red chili pepper, white sesame seeds, rape seeds, white poppy seeds, dried yuzu peel, dried algae, and sansho pepper are the most common. It is sprinkled over soups, noodles, or onto grilled meats.

SHISO LEAVES Also known as Perilla or Beefsteak plant and used in Japanese cooking. Both red and green shiso leaves are available. The red leaves have a stronger flavor, similar to anise, and are used most often as a coloring agent for preserves. The green leaves taste mildly of cinnamon and are chopped into dishes to add flavor like an herb. The leaves can also be used to wrap food, such as sushi and rice. Available fresh from Japanese stores.

SHRIMP, DRIED Small peeled shrimp dried in the sun with a strong, pungent flavor, which diminishes with cooking. Look for shrimp that are bright pink in color indicating freshness; gray or dark shrimp should be avoided. Generally sold in small plastic bags, they keep indefinitely in a sealed jar in the fridge or can be frozen.

SHRIMP PASTE Fermented, pulverized salted shrimp with a distinct pungent odor that diminishes with cooking. The grayish pink paste is packaged in glass jars and will continue to mature over time, darkening in color and taking on a stronger aroma. Used to flavor soups, salads, dipping sauces, and dishes containing beef or pork. Substitute with anchovy paste.

SOBA NOODLES Brownish gray Japanese noodles made from a mixture of buckwheat and wheat flour. They are similar in size to spaghetti.

STAR ANISE A small star-shaped seed pod from a tree native to southern China, it is an essential element in five-spice powder and commonly used in braising liquids. It is a prerequisite for making the Vietnamese soup, pho.

STICKY RICE Also known as glutinous rice, although rice contains no gluten. Its most pronounced characteristic is its stickiness: the grains adhere, making it easier to pick up with fingers or chopsticks. In Laos, it is a savory staple, steamed and eaten at almost every meal. Elsewhere in southeast Asia it is used principally in sweet dishes.

SUMAC A granular spice made from the crushed and ground berries of the sumac bush. Sumac has a sour, astringent taste reminiscent of lemons. The reddish brown spice is sprinkled over salads, fresh vegetables, and meats. It is also an important flavor element in zaatar, a popular Lebanese spice mixture. Sumac is ground with salt, with quantities varying from brand to brand, so always check seasoning before adding.

TAHINI PASTE A thick, creamy paste made from ground, raw sesame seeds used in Middle Eastern cooking. Tahini is stirred into sauces and vegetable dips and also used to make sweet confections. The paste can vary in quality; lighter colored paste is preferred over a darker color; less expensive brands are generally more bitter. Because tahini contains no emulsifiers, the oil in the natural product separates out and floats to the top of the jar, and it should be stirred back in before using.

TAMARIND PASTE A sour, thick paste made from the pod fruit of the tamarind tree and eaten throughout the Pacific Rim and the tropics. Tamarind is used like lemon juice to deliver a tangy flavor to dishes. Tamarind paste is sometimes labeled tamarind concentrate and available in Indian or Asian shops.

TONKATSU SAUCE A thick, fruity Japanese condiment similar in taste to Worcestershire sauce. It is used like ketchup to accompany breaded and fried foods. It was originally created as a sauce for the fried, breaded pork cutlets by the same name. Available in Japanese grocery stores.

UDON NOODLES These thick, white wheat noodles are similar to Italian pasta but with a softer texture and neutral taste. Available in Japanese stores.

WAKAME The most highly consumed seaweed in Japan, it is found fresh in spring but available year round in semi-dried or dried form. Used predominantly in soups, but also sprinkled into salads.

WASABI A nose-tingling, eye-watering Japanese condiment made from the gnarled root of the *Wasabia japonica* plant, it has a taste similar to horseradish and a vivid green color. The Japanese finely grate the fresh root into a smooth paste, which is used to flavor food. It is rare to find the fresh wasabi outside of Japan. Cans of powdered wasabi or tubes of the bright green paste are available in Japanese grocery stores and are an accepted substitute.

WONTON WRAPPERS Chinese wonton wrappers are square sheets of thinly rolled wheat dough resembling fresh uncooked pasta. They are available fresh or frozen in Chinese supermarkets and often in ordinary supermarkets. When buying wrappers, choose thinner over thicker.

YET A dried, smoked mollusk used to flavor West African dishes, particularly *tie bou dien*. Substitute any strong-flavored, smoked fish.

ZAATAR A strong aromatic herb and also the name of a popular Lebanese spice mixture. The fresh herb has flavor notes of marjoram, oregano, and thyme and can be eaten raw in salads. Dried, it generally becomes part of the spice blend also know as zaatar, which consists of the herb mixed with sesame seeds and sumac in varying proportions. It is very rare to find the fresh herb outside of the Middle East, but the spice blend is available in Middle Eastern grocery stores.

INDEX

ACKNOWLEDGMENTS

We'd like to dedicate this book to our children, Clara, Hugo, Elliott, Mischa, and Lucas who good-naturedly ate tagines and lamb mafe when they might have just wanted a plate of pasta. To Bassem Snaije who suddenly remembered at the end of the Lebanese and Syrian chapter, that he had eaten Ouzi as a child when visiting his grandparents in Damascus.

Immeasurable thanks to Sue Young for her expertise and help with all aspects of the cooking. Bashar Azzouz provided much constructive criticism during tastings. Many thanks to Jacqueline Kiang and Beatrix de Koster for translations and suggestions for titles, and to Christine and Philippe Wojazer for general support and photographs. Thanks to Nada Fuleihan for help with Arabic on the Lebanese chapter. Countless thanks to Rosemary Stimola for "seeing" the project and making it happen. And last but not least "mille mercis" to Anja Schmidt, our editor at DK, and the rest of the DK team.

This book could not have been written without the generous participation of new and old friends—special thanks to Therese Fischer Djimbong, Alexandre Bela Ola, Ngai Liu, Ghenima Agaoua, Farouk Mardam Bey, Karim Haidar, Anis Nacrour, Gina Diwan and the many others who contributed to this project. Thanks also to Mort Rosenblum who encouraged us at the very beginning, and to Pui Lai for teaching us about Southeast Asian herbs.

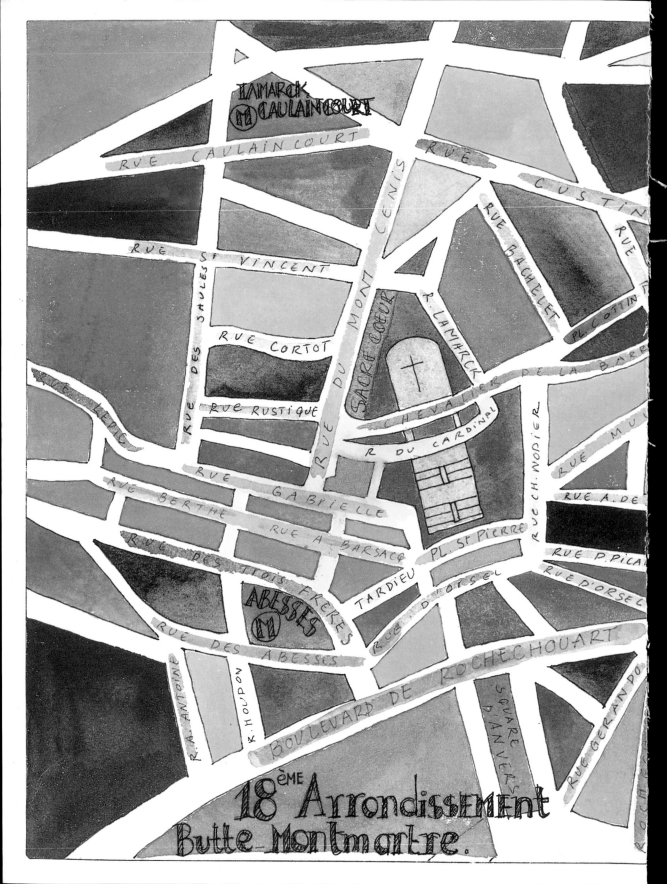